P9-CKE-516

PENGUIN BOOKS

THEY CALLED IT PASSCHENDAELE

Over the past twenty years Lyn Macdonald has established a popular reputation as an author and historian of the First World War. Her books are *They Called It Passchendaele*, an account of the Passchendaele campaign in 1917; *The Roses of No Man's Land*, a chronicle of the war from the neglected viewpoint of the casualties and the medical teams who struggled to save them; *Somme*, a history of the legendary and horrifying battle that has haunted the minds of succeeding generations; *1914*, a vivid account of the first months of the war and winner of the 1987 *Yorkshire Post* Book of the Year Award; *1914–1918: Voices and Images of the Great War*, an illuminating account of the many different aspects of the war; and *1915: The Death of Innocence*, a brilliant evocation of the year that saw the terrible losses of Aubers Ridge, Loos, Neuve Chapelle, Ypres and Gallipoli. Her most recent book, *To the Last Man: Spring 1918*, has just been published by Viking. All are based on the accounts of eyewitnesses and survivors, told in their own words, and cast a unique light on the First World War. Most are published in Penguin.

Lyn Macdonald is married and lives in London.

LYN MACDONALD

THEY CALLED IT PASSCHENDAELE

THE STORY OF
THE BATTLE OF YPRES AND OF
THE MEN WHO FOUGHT IN IT

PENGUIN BOOKS

To all the soldiers who served in the
Ypres Salient and, in particular, to the boys
of the 13th (Service) Battalion, The Rifle Brigade,
this book is dedicated in admiration and with love.

PENGUIN BOOKS

Published by the Penguin Group
Penguin Books Ltd, 27 Wrights Lane, London w8 5tz, England
Penguin Putnam Inc., 375 Hudson Street, New York, New York 10014, USA
Penguin Books Australia Ltd, Ringwood, Victoria, Australia
Penguin Books Canada Ltd, 10 Alcorn Avenue, Toronto, Ontario, Canada m4v 3b2
Penguin Books (NZ) Ltd, Private Bag 102902, NSMC, Auckland, New Zealand

Penguin Books Ltd, Registered Offices: Harmondsworth, Middlesex, England

First published by Michael Joseph Ltd 1978
Published in Penguin Books 1993
7 9 10 8

Copyright © Lyn Macdonald, 1978
All rights reserved

Set in 9.5/11pt Monotype Bembo
Typeset by Datix International Limited, Bungay, Suffolk
Printed in England by Clays Ltd, St Ives plc

Except in the United States of America, this book is sold subject
to the condition that it shall not, by way of trade or otherwise, be lent,
re-sold, hired out, or otherwise circulated without the publisher's
prior consent in any form of binding or cover other than that in
which it is published and without a similar condition including this
condition being imposed on the subsequent purchaser

Contents

List of Illustrations

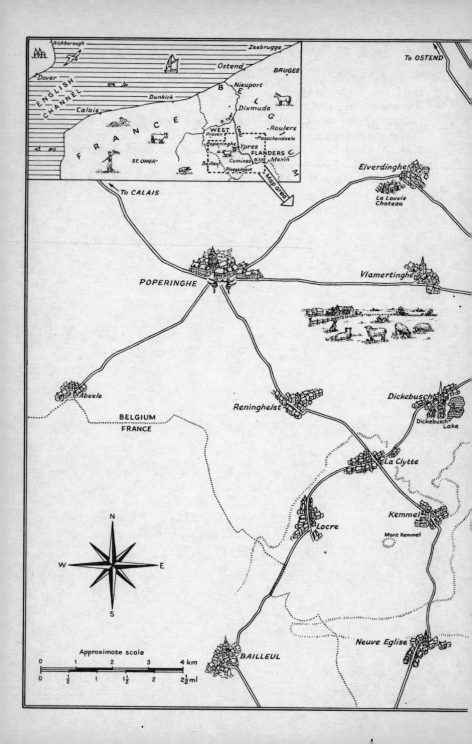

Richborough

Dover

ENGLISH CHANNEL

Calais

Zeebrugge

Ostend

To OSTEND

BRUGES

B   Nieuport
  E
    L   Dixmude
  G
Dunkirk   Roulers

FRANCE

WEST
Proven   Passchendaele
Poperinghe
St. Omer   Ypres   FLANDERS
              Comines   Menin
Bailleul
            Ploegsteert

Map area

To CALAIS

Elverdinghe

La Louvie
Chateau

POPERINGHE

Vlamertinghe

L'Abeele

BELGIUM
FRANCE

Reninghelst

Dickebusch

Dickebusch
Lake

La Clytte

N
W   E
S

Locre

Kemmel

Mont Kemmel

Approximate scale

0   1   2   3   4 km
0   ½   1   1½   2   2½ ml

BAILLEUL

Neuve Eglise

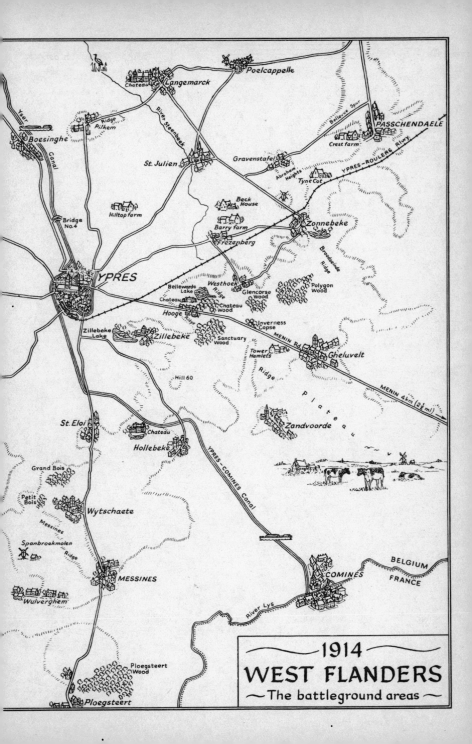

1914
WEST FLANDERS
~ The battleground areas ~

The Salient

The aspect of a salient upon a map is familiar to most of us. It is a piece of ground projecting into the enemy lines and offering, therefore, peculiar disadvantages and dangers to the defenders. The Hun can shoot right across it. A salient is an awkward place. But how awkward none can realise fully unless he has tried the following experiment.

The top of the Ypres Salient is somewhere about the trenches in front of 'Y' Wood. Place yourself at night in one of these ditches, moving with care so that the mud and water does not sluice over the top of your gum- or thigh-boots (assuming that you are fortunate enough to possess a pair), and turn your back, for a moment, upon the diligent Boche who is no doubt busily engaged in draining a lake behind his line into your temporary abode. Look at the salient. You will never get a better idea of its extent for it is outlined with the Very lights of which the enemy has so inexhaustible a store. To right and left of you the lights stretch far into the distance. But it is not the distance which impresses you, it is the lack of distance, the short space between that light which has just gone up, far away on the right, and that light which has just fallen far away on the left. That little space – one might think it merely a few hundred yards – is the neck of the salient, and if the Boche gets through there, from either side, or from both sides at once, what hope have you and your pals and the thousands of men round Ypres? Now you know what a salient is.

Author's Foreword and Acknowledgments

If this book reads like a novel, or even at times like a horror story, please do not blame me. It is all true, or rather it is compiled from more than 600 true stories and eyewitness accounts of men and women who were there in the blood-bath of Ypres. Some of their experiences are reproduced in their own words as they were recorded. Many more are incorporated in the text, and the tiniest details have contributed to building up a picture of life as it was for the Tommies and Anzacs and Canucks who were at Ypres in that terrible summer and autumn of 1917. Writing this book was a straightforward task of compiling and interpreting their experiences in the light of the events which took place as the campaign unrolled. The facts were all there. There was no need for imagination to be brought to bear on them, for the events were beyond imagining.

Although it has of necessity been compiled from the recollections of old people, this is a story about boys and young men and women, many still in their teens, who were snatched from a safe and circumscribed world, still basking in the afterglow of those Edwardian summers when God was still in his Heaven and a third of the atlas was firmly shaded in the pink of the British Empire. This is their story, faithfully recorded as they remember their experiences, their thoughts, feelings and conversations – and they remember them vividly. The experience of that 'Great' war could never be forgotten. Perhaps Bill Fowler, who was a stretcher-bearer with the 13th (Service) Battalion, The Rifle Brigade, summed it all up when he said, 'In a way I lived my whole life between the ages of nineteen and twenty-three. Everything that happened after that was almost an anti-climax.'

Mere words cannot sufficiently express my gratitude to all the people who have taken the time and trouble to cast their minds back and talk and write about their experiences. Nor can I set one above another by selecting particular names for particular thanks. I can only hope that they will feel that this book does them justice. Their names are listed at the back and I should like every one of them to know how grateful I am for his or her co-operation and assistance.

This book has been a team effort. It would have been impossible for one person to have tackled the magnitude of work and research involved, or to have accomplished such a task within ten years without assistance. John Woodroff deserves my special thanks, not only for indirectly sparking off the idea in the first place, but for his meticulous checking of all the military facts and for his unabating willingness to meet and talk to old soldiers. Tony Spagnoly also ranged far and wide in his search for old soldiers and, throughout the three years during which this book has been in preparation, he has never flagged in his enthusiasm and has sacrificed much of his time to the task of checking personal stories against the bald facts recorded in regimental records and histories. Above all, his wide knowledge of military tactics and history and his personal feeling for the period have made a contribution of incalculable value to this book.

Of my BBC colleagues I should like to thank Alan Rogers, Head of Current Affairs Magazine Programmes, for his unflagging interest and encouragement; and Ritchie Cogan, not only for his enthusiasm and interest, but for devoting innumerable evenings and weekends of his spare time to assisting with the interviewing.

I am also deeply grateful to Tony Spagnoly, John Woodroff and Ritchie Cogan for accompanying me on many trips to Ypres and tramping in all weathers and seasons almost every inch of the ground that formed the salient. I particularly remember a freezing November dawn, five o'clock in the morning on the Bellewarde Ridge. We had the consolation of knowing that it must have been worse for the soldiers in 1917 – but there were times when we felt that it couldn't have been *much* worse.

I must specially thank Mr A. E. Thorne, MBE (now deceased), Honorary Secretary of the 13th (Service) Battalion, The Rifle Brigade, Old Comrades Association, for his constant interest, advice and help and many introductions.

Baron Yves de Vinck, proprietor of Hooge Château, was unfailingly courteous and helpful and my thanks are due to him, as well as to Dr Canapeele in Ypres, who spent valuable time talking to us about the campaign, and showing us his collection of maps and books.

Mr P. D. Parminter, now resident in Ostend, has a unique knowledge of the salient, for he not only served there during the war but stayed on afterwards during the period in which the battlefields were cleared and the land reconstructed, as an officer of the Army Graves Service. His knowledge, advice and interest have been of the utmost help and he has most generously showered me with contemporary printed material which was absolutely unavailable elsewhere. He also provided the key to unravelling the diary of the Dickebusch priest, Pastor van Walleghem, which had been privately published in Flemish by a historical society, and 'volunteered' his nephew and niece, John and Nenette Parminter, to undertake the monumental task of translating it. They did so with the utmost good humour and interest and, with unfailing patience, resolved the many queries that arose. It is largely due to their efforts that I have been able to present a complete picture of the salient as it was when the Army was there.

The Ypres Tourist Office was exceedingly helpful on our many visits and I should like to thank Jan Breyne for his patience and kindness, which was only equalled by that of Pierre Claus in the Belgian Tourist Office in London, who cleared up many points for us and put us in touch with valuable contacts in the Belgian Army.

I am greatly in the debt of various members of the Commonwealth War Graves Commission. In Ypres, Bob Wall and J. Priestley-Dunne, whose knowledge of the area was invaluable and, in Britain, to Clem Stephens and Mike Shepherd, who were always able to answer queries in five minutes flat and did so with unfailing interest and courtesy.

Alma Woodroff not only transcribed some 300 hours of recorded interviews but typed the draft and the final manuscript with the sort of meticulous efficiency and interest that goes far beyond the call of duty. For this I am greatly in her debt.

I should like to thank David Higham Associates for permission to quote from *The Supreme Command 1914–1918* by Lord Hankey; *The Times* for permission to quote from their contemporary newspapers; the Ypres League for permission to quote from *The Ypres Times*; Genootschap voor Geschiedenis, Société d'émulation, for permission to quote from *De Oorlog Te Dickebusch En Omstreken 1914–1918* by Pastor van Walleghem; and Francis, Day and Hunter for permission to quote the words of 'A Bachelor Gay Am I' and 'The Laddies Who Fought and Won'.

Lastly, and most importantly, I have to thank my able assistant, Vivien Bilbow, who has not only done the lion's share of the monumental amount of work involved in organising and following up the contributions of some 600 or so people, but has masterminded the whole operation and, by some mental feat which I, at least, consider to be miraculous, has always been able to produce the right information at the right moment. Without her hard work and constant support, this book would certainly never have been written. That may be a cliché, but, with my hand on my heart, it is true.

LYN MACDONALD
LONDON, 1978

Part 1

The Big Bang

Chapter 1

Before 1914 the ancient city of Ypres had been one of the gems of
Flanders. Not that many people outside Belgium had ever heard of it, for, in
tumbling from its pinnacle as one of the great cloth towns of the middle
ages, Ypres had also tumbled into obscurity. A sleepy backwater of less than
20,000 inhabitants, whose prosperity largely depended on the harvest of
hops and corn and beets growing on the plains beyond the ramparts that
enclosed its medieval towers and high-gabled houses.

Four years of war turned Ypres into a ghost town. Not a leaf grew on a
tree. Scarcely one stone stood upon another. From the battered ramparts the
eye swept clean across a field of rubble to the swamp-lands beyond. The
jagged ruins of the Cloth Hall tower, still pointing an angry skeleton's finger
at the sky, were the only evidence that a town had ever stood there.

By 1920 it was the booming mecca of the first mass-explosion of tourism
in history. The single third-class fare from London to Ypres was a mere £1
12s 6d – a little less than the average weekly wage of the lowest-paid
workers. A package-deal was even better value, for a four-day excursion,
including travel, hotel accommodation and meals, could be arranged for as
little as £3 17s 6d. In the Twenties, tens of thousands of people travelled to
Ypres, packing the cross-channel steamers to the gunwales, pouring into
trains at Ostend and pouring out again at the shabby wooden sheds that
served as a temporary station.

In the face of such an influx, accommodation was a problem. The
construction of hotels was naturally not at the top of the list of priorities in a
city whose returning inhabitants were still living in cellars and huts; but
there were inns in the surrounding villages and organisations like the
YMCA; and the Church Army, which had put up temporary wartime
buildings in the area as canteens for the troops, turned them into hostels to
provide for the needs of the post-war visitors. Their needs were simple, for
they regarded themselves less as visitors than as pilgrims.

They were mostly women, these pilgrims. Some of them were accompanied by a husband, or a father, or a son. More often by a sister or a daughter
because their husbands and fathers and sons were already here. A whole
generation of young men lay buried beneath the Flanders mud.

Of the million men who had been killed in the Great War, a quarter of a million lay in the few square miles around Ypres. Their graves marked the perimeter of the dreaded salient which, at all costs and for no reason that in hindsight seems good enough, had to be held. It would be more correct to say that the *cemeteries* marked the perimeter of the salient, for the salient itself is a graveyard. Under its farms and woods and villages lie the unrecovered bodies of more than 40,000 soldiers who died or drowned, wounded in the mud. In spring and autumn their bones are still turned up by ploughs and ditching machines. The salient was a slaughterhouse. Around Ypres the fighting never really stopped, but, from time to time, it intensified. After the war, the Battle Nomenclature Committee, in its wisdom, saw fit to entitle those periods of intense fighting the First, Second and Third Battles of Ypres. In the popular mind all the agony and suffering of the salient became associated with one word. Passchendaele. For 'Passchendaele' stood for all that was dismal, all that was futile and, by a strange quirk, all that was glorious in the history of warfare. In all the history of warfare, no campaign was more catastrophic, no 'victory' more empty. Passchendaele stands on the summit of the slopes that surround the city of Ypres. The troops called them hills.

Of course, they weren't really hills at all. They were folds in the ground sloping gently up from the flat plain of Flanders. In peacetime it is strollers' countryside, patchworked with fields and copses, farms and hamlets separated by such leisurely gradients that it is hardly worth stopping to admire the view. Hill 60, sixty metres high. Hill 40, forty metres. Hill 35, an insignificant pimple on the landscape. But the ridges surrounded the salient, and it seemed as impossible for the British armies to break out of it as it would be for a canyon to burst free of the Rockies.

The salient was formed by accident, forged by retreat and held by iron determination. After the opening mêlées of the autumn of 1914, the weakened remnants of the Allied forces found themselves occupying a line that straggled inland from the coastal town of Nieuport along the southern bank of the River Yser. It bulged out to follow the rough semi-circle of low ridges to the east which seems to hold the city of Ypres in cupped hands, snaked back along the high ground to the west and, where it billowed down to merge with the plain, swung south past Armentières and Arras, deep into France and east again to the Swiss border.

Sitting astride the ridges above Ypres, the army was able to take an interesting view of its situation. In front of it was occupied Belgium, a land invaded but still unscarred by war, and across it at a safe distance was the ace in the German hand – the great railway junction of Roulers. It scarcely mattered that the line to Ypres and the coast had been effectively cut. The soldiers could see for themselves, as the steam engines puffed busily back and forth across the plain, that a network of communications ran back from Roulers into Germany itself, to the very gates of the Ruhr armament factories, to the very doors of the depots where troops gathered for the front.

Behind them the land rippled gently down to the moated ramparts of Ypres. On a clear day, beyond its spires they could just see glinting in the distance the waters of the English Channel, disturbingly close to their backs. Ypres was the key to the channel ports – and the Germans knew it. It was obvious to them that the line of troops was thin and the sporadic gunfire told all too clearly of a shortage of ammunition (a quarter of the guns had been taken back from the firing-zone because they had no shells to fire). It would be a pushover.

To a certain extent it was. In the autumn of 1914, in twenty-two days of bitter fighting the ragged British army was pushed over the rim of the ridges, down the slopes of the shallow saucer, downwards and inwards, closer and closer to Ypres at its back. And then, almost within hailing distance of the Menin Gate, it stopped.

The place was Nonne Bosschen – Nun's Wood, a wedge of thicket on the breast of one of those deceptively gentle rises halfway between Passchendaele and Ypres. The German commanders drew in their breath for one final crushing attack. Streams of guns poured up to stiffen the bombardment; the troop trains steamed into Roulers with reinforcements of crack Prussian Guards, fresh and untried, but trained to razor-sharp precision. As far as the depleted British Expeditionary Force was concerned, the only thing which could be remotely described as 'reinforcements' was the embryo Kitchener's Army of volunteers, which – between vigorous bouts of button polishing – was still learning to form fours and shoulder arms on village greens and playing fields on the other side of the Channel.

But reinforcements of a kind nevertheless arrived, hurrying up the road from Ypres in hastily formed platoons of cooks and spud-bashers, dish-washers and orderly-room clerks, sanitary orderlies and plump waiters from the officers' mess, storemen and quartermasters, wagon drivers and messengers – a raggle-taggle bunch of non-combatants who had never seriously expected to find themselves at the business end of a rifle. This was a point of minimal importance in view of the fact that there were barely enough rifles to go round.

Into the line they went to fight with picks, with shovels, with entrenching tools; but ready to snatch up firearms as they fell from the hands of the killed and wounded and to use them at point-blank range to drive off the enemy swarming across their trenches. The attackers were thrown back.

The line held. The honours of the day, in that first battle of Ypres, belonged indisputably to Fred Karno.

The remnant of the British army stood its ground, and gradually it began to grow. On walls and buildings all over Britain, the Empire and the Colonies, recruiting posters erupted in a rash of patriotic fervour. Boys newly grown-up and only just weaned from a schoolboy diet of G. A. Henty's adventure yarns, flocked to join up in numbers that, in the first months, were embarrassingly large for the military authorities to cope with. In France the recruits were desperately needed. But at home sergeant-majors approaching retirement looked in despair at the motley hordes they were expected to transform into battalions of disciplined soldiers, while quartermaster sergeants tore their hair and despaired of being able to clothe, billet and feed them. Nineteen was the official minimum age for enlistment, but recruiting sergeants could be helpful.

'How old are yer?'
'Seventeen and a half, sir.'
'Run along, sonny, and come back when you're nineteen ... tomorrer.'

The recruiting offices were besieged by boys desperate to get a sniff of the fighting before the war ended, as it surely must, by Christmas. And not only in Britain but throughout the British Empire, from Calgary to Cape Town, from Bombay to Brisbane. Soon on every tide the troopships were arriving, their decks lined with waving, cheering soldiers in stiff new-smelling khaki. By April 1915 the weary troops who had held the precious salient around Ypres throughout that first cold and soggy winter had been reinforced by a cheeringly strong contingent of Canadians and a reputedly tough-fighting regiment of the Indian Army. The French sector was being strengthened by troops from their colonies of Algeria and Morocco and gradually the first newly-trained battalions of Kitchener's volunteers trickled across the Channel. Armaments and ammunition were still in short supply and guns were restricted to firing a certain number of rounds a day, but the salient had what it had previously so woefully lacked – men. And manpower, at that stage in the war, was all-important in the eyes of military commanders, schooled and nurtured in the tradition of cavalry campaigning. Caught up in the detail of the task of actually getting something which approximated to an army on to the field, the commanders could hardly be blamed for failing to realise that this war would be fought under different rules, under different circumstances and under conditions of undreamt-of hardship.

The harbinger of all the horrors to come arrived late in the afternoon of a perfect spring day. And it arrived at Ypres. The first heavy shells began to crash into the town late in the morning, sending the Saturday-market crowds flying to the shelter of the cellars, and at midday the guns began to pound the outlying villages and the roads leading from them into Ypres. So far the civilians had done their best to ignore the war, but when the gunfire tailed off early in the afternoon the population was in turmoil, and soon a procession of refugees was on the move. With whatever belongings they had been able to salvage piled on to wheelbarrows and handcarts, they poured westwards out of the town, swarming along the roads that led to Elverdinghe, Poperinghe and Dickebusch. They passed farms and meadows where green peacetime grass had long since disappeared under regiments of bell-tents; and field kitchens where steaming cauldrons of stew bubbled and simmered, ready to be ladled into canisters and transported to the troops in the forward areas beyond the canal.

Some horse-drawn limbers were already clattering on their way, loaded with ration canisters. Seated on them, taking their ease while they could, were the men of the carrying parties on whose broad backs they would travel the last lap into the line. That is, if they ever got there, for in spite of the MPs who were doing their best to control the chaos, the sweating horses were making heavy weather of getting the wagons through against a determined tide of refugees, who were less frightened by the threats of the cursing drivers than by the threat of the big guns behind.

At five o'clock the guns started up again. Walls crumbled and crashed in the dying town, as if to encourage the last stragglers on their way. On the extreme northern edge of the salient, far to the left, there was the distant popping of light field artillery. But it was disregarded by those who happened to notice it between the roars of the heavy shells that were hammering Ypres into dust and debris. It was common knowledge that Algerian troops had just taken over the French line on the Canadians' left, and no doubt they were quite properly firing on enemy objectives as an exercise in order to register the accuracy of their guns. It was known as 'shooting yourself in', a preliminary which was as necessary for the efficiency of the gunners as it was unpleasant for the enemy, who were naturally provoked into replying with retaliatory gunfire. In reality the situation was somewhat different. So different that no soldier on earth had ever experienced anything like it before.

It came on the breath of the light evening breeze as it sprang up in the north, a thick yellow-grey cloud that rose from the enemy lines and drifted gently across to the Algerian positions, enveloping the terrified men in a retching, throat-catching suffocating fog. Behind it came the German infantry, fixed bayonets at the ready, seen terrifyingly through streaming eyes as they loomed out of the trailing vapour, helmeted and gargoyle-masked. As they advanced, the Algerians broke and ran, staggered or crawled away from them and from the deadly gas, but the sanctuary they sought was down-wind. The gas travelled on their heels.

The chaos behind the lines became uncontrollable. On the Poperinghe Road, bedlam broke loose as teams of half-crazed horses and riders plunged on to it from the road leading to the Yser Canal, closely followed by mobs of infantry streaming back across the fields. Ambulances, hastily summoned, added to the traffic of confusion, and the demoralised troops, some wounded, lay blind and choking along the roadside. By eight o'clock the situation was all too clear. Fifty guns had been abandoned and there was an undefended gap in the line four miles long.

It was the Canadians who saved the day. They were in the most desperate situation of all, for the collapse of the French lines meant that they now had four miles of absolutely nothing on their left. Not being able to use their infantry in the dark, the Germans switched their tactics to heavy shelling. All night the bombardment continued but somehow, in spite of it, the Canadians managed to deploy to the left to cover the gap, somehow they managed to mount a counter-attack, somehow the casualties were evacuated, somehow reserves were brought up and spread in pitifully small numbers along the gap to try to establish a new line. They had little chance of succeeding.

The Germans rushed in no less than forty-two fresh battalions, and against them, devastated by heavy bombardment, the effort of twelve Canadian and six weak British battalions was unavailing.

The sensible thing would have been to withdraw from the salient, abandoning Ypres, and to establish a stronger line in the rear beyond the canal bank, a tactical possibility which had indeed been earlier considered. But emotion was riding high, at least in Britain, where the flags waved and the drums beat and the newspapers trumpeted forth glory in every edition. Public opinion, like Queen Victoria during the Crimean War, was not interested in the possibility of defeat. Public opinion, however, was not trying to hold the salient. Public opinion was not manning a line of trenches bombarded by six times as many German guns as there were guns to retaliate. Public opinion was not required, for want of gas-masks, to urinate on its sock and clap it over its nose as more noxious gas-clouds rolled inexorably towards it.

The appalling casualty-lists were read with horror, but in the spirit of the times they only served to stiffen the resolve of a nation in mourning. For these were not casualties of the regular army of professional risk-takers which, in any event, now hardly existed. They were the volunteers, 'Our Boys' who such a few short months ago had marched off, wreathed in beams of enthusiasm, to do their bit, and 'Our Boys' must not be said to have done their bit in vain. If they had died to protect Ypres, then Ypres must not be given up.

For somewhat different reasons, the French commander, General Foch, was of the same opinion, which in no uncertain terms he brought to bear on the perplexed Commander of the British Force, Sir John French. The Germans must be kept occupied in the salient so that too much pressure might not build up on the line further south. The Commanders of the Army on the spot saw things differently. General Sir Horace Smith-Dorrien, heading the Second Army, proposed to draw back and reduce the salient to Ypres and its outskirts. French refused to consider any such thing, promptly removed him from his command, and appointed General Sir Herbert Plumer in his place. Plumer's first action as Commander was to order an only slightly less drastic strategic withdrawal. By then French had no alternative but to agree, and at the end of May 1915, five weeks after the first gas attack, the withdrawal took place. In those five weeks 60,000 men had been killed, wounded or were missing. The grim and dreadful salient was consolidated. One day people would call it immortal.

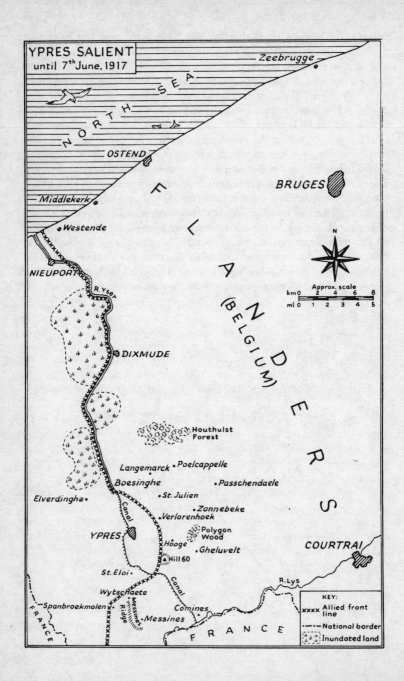

YPRES SALIENT
until 7th June, 1917

NORTH SEA

Zeebrugge

OSTEND

BRUGES

Middlekerk

F L A N D E R S (BELGIUM)

Westende

NIEUPORT

R. Yser

DIXMUDE

N

Approx. scale
km 0   2   4   6   8
ml 0 1   2   3   4   5

Houthulst
Forest

Langemarck   Poelcappelle

Boesinghe   Passchendaele

Elverdinghe   St. Julien

Zonnebeke

Verlorenhoek

YPRES   Polygon
Wood

Hooge

Gheluvelt

Hill 60

COURTRAI

St. Eloi

Canal

R. Lys

Wytschaete

Comines

KEY:

Spanbroekmolen

Messines Ridge

Messines

FRANCE

F R A N C E

xxxx Allied front
     line
─ ∙ ─ National border
     Inundated land

Chapter 2

The salient was tiny. In the north it had been pushed back right to the bank of the canal, leaving the Second Army the merest precarious toehold on the other side. Then the line crept gradually forward to enclose Ypres in a loop that reached a scant two miles up the Menin Road, swung round to Zillebeke, and bulged back again to run below the high ground of the Wytschaete–Messines Ridge. The Germans, now occupying not only the high ground but the nearer villages of St Julien, Pilkem, Verlorenhoek and Hooge were like schoolboys standing round the edge of a pond, plopping stones into the water. But the 'stones' were shells fired by batteries of heavy guns which, clustered as thick as flies on a pool of treacle, radiated out from the rim of the salient.

At some point in history the Flanders plain lay under the sea. It is reclaimed bogland, which it was only possible to inhabit and cultivate by constructing a complicated network of drainage ditches that farmers, under penalty of a heavy fine, are still obliged to maintain. In spite of the ditches, when there is heavy rain the land quickly becomes waterlogged, for there is no gravelly topsoil to filter away the moisture, nothing but a yard or so of heavy clay, which in all but the driest weather gives soggily beneath the feet. Beneath its covering of meadows and hopfields Flanders is a natural bog. When the guns started up and the shells plunged down, shattering the drainage and tearing the earth apart, it rapidly turned into a quagmire.

To the hard-pressed troops holding the salient, the guns never seemed to stop. It was a unique military situation. Two armies, one virtually surrounding the other, and both on the defensive. The Allies were sitting tight in defence of the salient, while the Germans sat tight around it in defence of the high ground. For more than two years, apart from some fierce localised skirmishing, it was stalemate. The British were there to stay, and so were the Germans who had the advantage of men, materials and abundant supplies in a wide back area, which unlike the narrow strip of land between Ypres and the sea was relatively unharassed. They used this advantage to dig themselves in as no army had ever dug in before, with ferro-concrete reinforced with a forest of iron rods, each one

five-eighths of an inch thick. As soon as the new Allied line was established around the truncated salient the Germans started to build.

It was useless to try to construct a conventional trench system with
deep dug-outs such as the Germans had on the Somme: in the northern
swamp, trenches simply filled up with water as fast as they were dug. The
answer was the concrete pillbox, with walls and roofs three feet thick,
over which mud and sandbags could be stacked for camouflage and further protection. The idea originally was simply to shield the support and
reserve troops from the ever-increasing fire from British howitzers and
field guns, but they withstood bombardment so successfully – the shells
merely bounced off them – that it was soon realised that as strongpoints
they would be well-nigh impregnable. So, taking advantage of the cover
afforded by the folds in the shallow slopes, the construction work went
on, tier upon tier, until the saucer of the shallow valley was an amphitheatre of concrete strongholds with narrow slits through which observers had a grandstand view of everything that moved on the stage-like
salient below.

Except for the dug-outs which had been burrowed into the thick
ramparts around Ypres and some parts of the back areas well behind the
town, the Allied troops had no such comforts. For one thing (and it was
the old, old story) there was a shortage of concrete and a feeling that such
shelters would not be worth the trouble and expense. More important, the
Allies were, at least in theory, an army on the attack and the provision of
such sturdy bastions might have been detrimental to the offensive spirit of
the troops. So the British and Colonial forces had to throw up breastworks of mud as best they could and crouch behind their barbed wire in a
series of stinking ditches half-sunk in the morass. For more than two years
this was the British front line.

Keep your head down. That was the rule in the salient if you intended
to survive. Even the Germans had picked it up. Where the two lines were
close together and things were quiet, there was a daredevil excitement in
making contact with the enemy, just to remind yourself that there was
someone out there in the dank blackness beyond the line.

'I want to go home to my wife!'

The wail would come from some soaked and fed-up Tommy shivering
away the long hours between the issue of the rum ration and the dawn
stand-to; and if within earshot there happened to be one of the many
Germans who, before the war, had worked in a barber's shop in Hackney
or in a West End restaurant, a shout would return.

'Keep your head down, Tommee, or she'll be a bloody widow!' And, as
his companions in the trench cursed him for an idiot for attracting the
unwelcome attentions of the enemy, a machine-gun would rattle and

spatter across the mud, sweeping the length of the trench, searching and probing for the unwary in the sudden eerie light of a flare.

The big guns, too, searched and probed. All day the reconnaissance aircraft, both British and German, were buzzing the skies across the salient. Almost as high the great whales wallowed, each carrying a sharp-eyed observer in the basket below. The grey balloons were British, the black ones German. But the Germans also held the ridges, and from them artillery officers, through binoculars engineered to high-powered magnification by Messrs Zeiss, could delineate almost to the centimetre not only the roads but the duckboard tracks along which the troops would have to travel when darkness fell. With Teutonic precision the guns were trained along their length.

At dusk it was time to shoulder your load and be on the move. The relieving troops went out through the Menin Gate, marched for a mile over the broken shell-pocked *pavé*, then struck out north-east to Hooge Ridge, or south-east towards Zillebeke. They slipped and slithered along the wooden tracks that wound across the swamp, heads hunched like turtles between their shoulders as if the weight of rifle, bandolier and knapsack would shield them from flying shrapnel and the fountains of mud and slush thrown up by the explosions. The lucky ones got a 'Blighty' – a neat, sharp blow that fractured the shin-bone and stamped your ticket for home. The unlucky few were hit and slipped unnoticed into the mud. Most struggled on until they arrived sodden, filth-encrusted and weary at the dubious shelter of the watery ditch where, come what may, they must stick it out as best they could until the next company of mud-soaked men struggled up the broken track to relieve them. Nerves were taut. Tempers were frayed. But even displays of temper could lead to a nervous laugh.

Corporal T. Newell, No. 102096, 171 Tunnelling Coy., Royal Engineers

It was the rule for the man in the lead to pass back to the man behind him word of any obstruction, like a hole in the duckboard. Word was passed back, 'Mind the hole', and everybody muttered it over his shoulder to the man behind. And then the man behind Corporal Leake stepped slap into a hole in the duckboard into a foot of watery clay. Leaky turned round to help him out with the bloke cussing and swearing. Leaky, in his broad Yorkshire, whispered, 'I *said* mind t'ole.' The bloke said, 't'ole be buggered. It was a bloody *great* 'ole'.

For men like these of the Royal Engineers, the ordeal of the night was, at the same time, better and worse, for they made up the working parties.

Their night would be spent in gruelling sweating labour, often out in front of the line strengthening the trench, replacing barbed wire in front of it; and should a nervous hand inadvertently let go one end of the taut metal it rushed back to spring on to the roll with a *ping* that seemed to reverberate for miles. Then the heartstopping flares would go up from Jerry across the way, and resisting the fatal temptation to fling yourself to the ground you froze like a statue in its unearthly glare, hoping to be mistaken for the indeterminate outline of a shattered tree.

Private W. G. Bell, No. 4640, 9th Btn., Army Cyclist Corps

If Jerry got the idea that there was a working party out in front – and it didn't take him long to get the idea because he could hear the shovels hitting stones, you know, and fellows swearing and when the Very lights go up you see silhouettes of fellows moving about on the surface – he'd put down a creeping barrage of shells, coming nearer and nearer all the time. It was a wonder anything lived. I was only in one, but, my God, when you heard them coming nearer and nearer you thought the next one was coming to drop right on you. Oh! It was frightening, though. Very frightening! And then he'd traverse the field with machine-gun fire. He'd start at one corner and come right across the field from side to side. Searching.

You'd be lying on the surface. Any dent in the ground you'd stick your head down as far as you could ram it. There might be a shell-hole, there might not, but you had to lay flat on the ground when these creeping barrages came and they were terrible things. You don't think you're coming out of it. There's the blast of them, you know, and you can hear the steel, awful sound, piece of steel as it goes by you. It would cut you in half, a piece of that shell. He'd search out a working party out in the front. He'd know. You couldn't disguise the fact that the men were out there working. Some of them would even take to smoking. Now that was a stupid thing to do. I've known fellows get down in the shell-hole for a spit and a drag as they used to term it – right out there in the advance position, right out in No Man's Land, you know. Tried to light a match and have a smoke. Some fellows would do that – anything for a smoke. You can't imagine it – every night, every night, every night. You wonder whether you'll ever see the next day. You could hear the guns go *boomph* and then *sssssssboomph. Sssssssboomph.* They were getting nearer. They'd swamp the sky with Very lights and you'd see the white smoke from the blast – explosions going up. It was all haze like a London fog, only white, under the light of Very lights, and these shells coming over and the bloomin' guns keep on going *boomph*, *boomph*, and over came the shell. You're petrified. You couldn't get up and run – what's the good of running? You might run into it. You've only got to lay there and hope that the next one's going over further back.

I'll never forget the experience of a creeping barrage. We were out night after night in different fields, different positions. We wouldn't know where it was. We had no instructions. You'd find yourself somewhere just getting dusk and you didn't know *where* you were. No Man's Land. There was no buildings, there was open country, a few hedges, perhaps a few stumps of trees. That was it. You didn't know where on earth you were. You didn't care, anyway.

A salient, says the dictionary, is a piece of land pushed forward into hostile territory so that the enemy is ranged around it on three sides. Few of the soldiers carried dictionaries. They merely knew that a salient was a place where you got shot. In the front. From either side. And also in the back.

The enemy guns had a perfect field of fire from their concealed positions on the shoulder of high ground which ran south of Ypres – from Hill 60 at Zillebeke through Wytschaete to Messines. Turned inwards towards the salient they could shoot right across it; more unnervingly, they could shoot up it from the rear so that you never knew from which direction a shell would come. There was no escape. Not even for the armourers and orderlies, the cooks, the quartermasters, the clerks and telephonists, whose jobs seldom took them far from the supporting base camps in the back areas of the salient. From Messines Ridge the guns could just as easily drop shells into Poperinghe, ten miles to the rear of Ypres, as they could drop them into Potijze a thousand yards in front of it.

Unless the Germans could be removed from that Ridge, there was no possibility of the Allies ever being able to advance. To withdraw was out of the question. So, decided General Plumer, if the Germans could not be thrown off the Ridge by conventional methods of attack, then the Ridge itself must be blown sky-high – and the enemy with it.

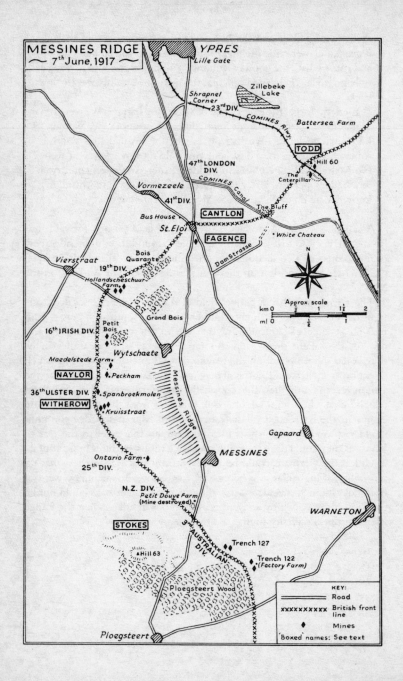

MESSINES RIDGE
~ 7th June, 1917 ~

YPRES
Lille Gate

Shrapnel Corner
23rd DIV.
COMINES Rlwy
Battersea Farm
Zillebeke Lake

TODD
Hill 60
The Caterpillar

47th LONDON DIV.
COMINES Canal

Vormezeele
41st DIV.
The Bluff

Bus House
CANTLON
St. Eloi
xxxxxxxxxxx
FAGENCE
White Chateau

Bois Quarante
DamStrasse

Vierstraat
19th DIV.
Hollandscheschuur Farm

Grand Bois

N

Approx. scale
km 0 ½ 1 1½ 2
ml 0 ½ 1

16th IRISH DIV.
Petit Bois

Wytschaete

Maedelstede Farm
NAYLOR
Peckham

36th ULSTER DIV.
Spanbroekmolen
WITHEROW
Kruisstraat

Gapaard

Ontario Farm
25th DIV.
MESSINES

N.Z. DIV.
Petit Douve Farm
(Mine destroyed)

WARNETON

STOKES
Hill 63
3rd AUSTRALIAN DIV.
Trench 127
Trench 122
(Factory Farm)

Ploegsteert Wood

KEY:
——— Road
xxxxxxxxxx British front line
♦ Mines
Boxed names: See text

Ploegsteert

Chapter 3

The plans were laid meticulously and far in advance. Early in the new year of 1916, in full view of the enemy a few hundred yards away on the high ground, the engineers started to dig. They sunk mineshafts behind such camouflage as there was – in the yard of a shattered farm in front of Messines; under the hummock of bricks that marked a ruined cottage in front of Spanbroekmolen; but in most places, as at Hill 60, the tunnel descended at an angle from a sandbagged emplacement inside a well-dug and reinforced trench, a little way behind the front line. The men of the Durhams who worked in the trench, homesick for the streets of Gateshead, christened it Bensham Avenue.

At twenty-four, Martin Greener was a veteran. In the middle of 1915, as a subaltern with the 9th Battalion, Durham Light Infantry, he had been given the responsibility of forming a mining section.

Captain M. Greener, 175 Tunnelling Coy., Royal Engineers

I was chosen because I came from a mining family. We picked a lot of Durham pitmen out of the infantry and that was how we began. The Germans were blowing our trenches with very shallow mines and the powers-that-be said, 'Now look, we must stop this and you must start to countermine.' Which we did. In the Ypres salient we were certainly the first to do it and that went on for quite a long time. Then the tunnelling companies were formed and I was seconded from the Durhams to the Royal Engineers, to 175 Tunnelling Company, and put in charge of number 4 section. That's when we started on the deep mining. The big stuff.

The big stuff required the help of real experts to carry it out, and Tom Newell was certainly an expert. In the midst of his infantry training with the Worcestershire Regiment he was surprised to be given a travel warrant from Wareham in Dorset, orders to report to the Royal Engineers' depot at Chatham, and no other instructions whatever.

Corporal T. Newell, No. 12096, 171 Tunnelling Coy., Royal Engineers

When I got to the depot I was told to go to a certain barrack room
and await orders. Gradually, twenty or so other men from various
regiments drifted in, everyone wondering why we were there. It
wasn't until a pal of mine arrived, a chap who'd been in the same
Rescue Brigade as myself before the war, that it turned out that we
were all miners and members of Mine Rescue Brigades from pits all
over the country.

   The next day we were kitted out for overseas duty and officially
transferred to the Royal Engineers. We at least were already in the
army, but we were sent to join a group of eighty men who'd come
straight out of the mines. They were all kinds, lads of twenty, men of
sixty with no army training at all, but they were issued with rifles and
ammunition, whether or not they knew how to fire them, and two
days later we were in France. It must have been hard on some of the
old boys, for we had to march all the way from Steenwerck, through
Bailleul, on through Neuve Eglise to Vlamertinghe Farm. When we
did get there, we were handed strips of green canvas and stakes and
told to make our own bivouacs in the fields – this, mind you, just
about three miles from the front line and shells whizzing around a lot
too close for comfort. There we joined up with some Welsh miners
who'd been transferred from the Monmouthshire Regiment, and
together we formed the 171 Tunnelling Company, Royal Engineers.

   The tunnelling companies were the élite. The civilians, who had been
hurriedly drafted in from the coal-mines or from construction work in
the sewers, were paid the princely sum of six shillings a day – a sore point
with their workmates who, having been already in the army, continued to
draw the standard Tommy's pay of one humble shilling. The risks and the
danger were the same for all.

   First the shafts had to be dug through the heavy brown clay, lower still
through a stratum of water and sand, and deep into the blue clay which
was the core of the salient. These shafts were to be deeper, the tunnels
longer and the mines bigger than ever before.

   The sections were divided into shifts of eight men, four to work at the
face digging cut the clay with broad-bladed picks, stopping every foot or
so to shore the mud walls and roof with timber supports – four foot six
inches high, two foot nine inches wide. Behind them in this confined
space, other men filled sandbags with the hard blue clay, toting them to
the shaft bottom to be winched up to the surface.

Captain M. Greener, 175 Tunnelling Coy., Royal Engineers

You'd shift thirty or forty sandbags in a shift, or more, and you couldn't dispose of the dirt during the daytime. It had to come out at night. You had to be very careful about the disposal of the dirt if you were mining in blue clay, because the stratum of blue clay was deep down, far below the level of the ordinary trenches. If you collected a pile of sandbags with blue clay you had to get rid of it quickly, because the Germans would shell it just to see what was in it. You had to take it out and distribute it as best you could at night, behind the trenches, well away from the line, so that the trenches didn't look any different. That was the great thing. And that was the big problem, the disposal of the dirt from the mine. But we had carrying parties from the infantry. We were always using the infantry.... It was no wonder they called them the PBI!

Lance-Corporal John Wilson wasn't a miner but he *was* in the Durhams, and for a long time in 1916 the Durhams were holding the line at Hill 60.

Lance-Corporal J. Wilson, No. 52764, 12th Btn., Durham Light Infantry

In and out. In and out. It was a hot spot all right. Jerry knew there was something going on there and he never left us alone. We got a lot of Minenwerfers around there. 'Minnies' we called them. They made a great bang and they turned over and over as they came. We feared those more than we feared heavy artillery shells. I was in D company. We'd do forty-eight hours in the line and then we went into the billets, into support. The billets were in tunnels too. Larchwood saps, they called them. It was an overgrown dump of earth that had been lying there since they'd excavated the railway cutting that ran straight up through our trenches to the German line, and the REs had made these dug-outs in it for the miners and the troops in the line. It was only yards behind, but you felt a bit safer in there. There were two rows of beds – just timber frames with wire-netting across them, but you could lie down on them and put your overcoat on top of you and your haversack for a pillow. There was a passage in between with duckboards laid along it, for it was always swimming in water. They weren't exactly billets. Just sleeping bases for the people who were in support immediately behind the front line ready to be called upon. That's when we'd be put on these working parties to help the REs. We carried the sandbags in empty and we carried them out full. And we had to carry them some distance! You had to get them well away, far back from the line. Sweating like pigs, working all night in among the shelling and then back to the tunnel before daylight or, if you were unlucky, into the trenches, with the bullets flying all round you.

Below and beyond the trenches, deep under the earth, twenty-one tunnels were being slowly driven forward towards the Germans on the ridge. Down there it was quiet in the dripping gloom. The men worked silently and spoke in whispers. As the tunnels gradually lengthened, they piled the sandbags of excavated clay on to bogies with rubber wheels, which could be silently slid back to the shaft along wooden rails. Only the breath of a murmured remark, the dull scraping away at the clay, the drip of water, the faint hum of the dynamo that powered the pumps, the fans and the dim electric lamps, disturbed the silence. All the time the men were listening. For the Germans were tunnelling too, honeycombing the earth with passages that splayed out from a central gallery in a dozen directions, searching for the British tunnels they knew full well must be there. When suspicious noises were heard, if the officer in charge of the section did not happen to be in the tunnel, it was the sergeant's job to go and fetch him. The sergeant in charge of Captain Greener's No. 4 section was a miner called Deeming.

Captain M. Greener, 175 Tunnelling Coy., Royal Engineers

He came from Backworth in Northumberland and he was a splendid man. Always on the go. Nothing seemed to worry him and you could always depend on him. He came to me and said, 'I think you'd better come in and listen.' So we went down the shaft. By that time we had some decent listening apparatus. We had what they called geophones. It was a little round ball about three inches across and you put that against the clay, and you had a tube coming from that with two earpieces, and you listened. If you heard anything, especially at night, you could be pretty sure that there was someone coming from the other direction, countermining. That time we did have a bit of trouble; it was just after we started it, early in 1916. We were down to seventy feet and it was unusual for the Germans to mine as deep as that, but we were certain they were there. It was a very anxious job, because you never knew what was going to happen. Quite a few of our tunnels had been blown in by the Germans and, of course, if you happened to be out in the tunnel beyond that blow, you'd had it. No way of getting out.

When we heard them tunnelling towards us the only thing to do was to get in first and blow them up. We did this with a small mine we called a camouflet. It would be about five hundredweight of explosive and we set it and tamped it with sandbags so that it would explode in the direction where we guessed the Germans were, hoping to blow their tunnel up. We cleared the men out of our own tunnel and set it off. Perhaps we got the Germans. It was hard to tell. But the trouble was it made a terrible mess of our own workings. We had to clean the whole thing out and almost start again.

It was nerve-racking, and exceedingly hard too, for the work went on twenty-four hours a day. We split the sections into groups and worked eight hours on, sixteen hours off. When the men came off a shift they were given a rum ration, and it was the officer's job to see that the man drank his rum and didn't hoard it, because the pitmen had a habit of doing that. Well, one particular man had evidently been able to do it and he got blind-drunk. Running through our positions and on through the German positions a hundred yards further on was the old railway line. We called it The Cut and the bottom of it was just a mass of mud, corpses, everything you could think of. Heaven knows how he managed it but this chap fell right down into The Cut. He was making a frantic noise, roaring like a bull and staggering all over the place, but the odd thing was that not a shot was fired, even though it was daylight and in full view of the Germans. We had to get ropes and haul him up, and not a soul was shot at. The Germans didn't bother. I think they were enjoying the fun. We were rather less amused. But there was no fuss made. The man wasn't charged or anything. For one thing he was a really good worker and in that sort of situation, doing that sort of ghastly job, you had a much closer contact between the men and the officers. You got to know them well. You were all concerned with getting the job done. You turned a blind eye to a lot of things. They were all characters these Durham pitmen.

Four days in the tunnels. Four days out at rest. But going out to rest was a doubtful privilege, and the journey back to camp at Vlamertinghe often cost more in casualties than the four-day stint in the front line. The crouching hours of toil, newly completed, often seemed preferable to the weary men to the long slog back across the duckboards through the hail of screaming shells. If you made it to Hellfire Corner there was transport to take you to rest billets at Vlamertinghe. Transport of a kind!

Captain M. Greener, 175 Tunnelling Coy., Royal Engineers

They were horrible lorries and you felt totally exposed in them because the road was always under shellfire, and you couldn't just rattle through it since the wretched lorries would only do six or seven miles an hour. The men were always playing hell about having to go up and down in these lorries. We'd far rather have walked, but of course we had to take material up and down. When we got to the rest-billets, that was just as bad. What with the Germans shelling it practically every night, we had no 'rest' there at all. Still, we took advantage of that situation. At least, our quartermaster sergeant did. He made up his mind we were going to get rid of these appalling lorries, so he waited until the camp was being shelled, belted out of his dug-out and chucked a few Mills bombs at them until they were nicely ablaze. 'Lost by enemy action.' Very neat. We got Packard lorries after that.

The transport went faster, but to the men clawing inch by inch through the clay deep beneath the salient, the work went painfully slowly. Then someone had a bright idea. A boring-machine, carefully designed for the purpose, would do the job faster than men. Six boring-machines would complete the job in no time. The order was given for one experimental prototype. It was built by the Stanley Heading Machine Company of Nuneaton at the then considerable cost of £6,000, a vast monster with a cutting head specially designed to make short work of tunnelling through the hard strata of clay that lay beneath the salient. It weighed seven and a half tons and it took twenty-four enormous crates to contain its components on the journey to Folkestone, and three General Service lorries to transport it from Boulogne. It arrived there on 17 February 1917, but it was not until 4 March that it was switched on.

The chosen site was the tunnel at Petit Bois, but the task of getting the machine there, within yards of the German front line, was fraught with difficulty. Light railways intersected the front but they were meant for the transport of small wagons containing ammunition and essential supplies. The 7½-ton monster was quite beyond its capacity. Again and again, night after night, the wagons were derailed by the weight of the top-heavy crates, and the cursing, sweating engineers were faced with righting them and manhandling the huge crates back on board. It was hardly miraculous that the Germans began to get wind of a 'secret weapon'. They did not know exactly what it was but they did know that something was up, and the guns on the ridges above gave Petit Bois their undivided attention. Somehow, in that storm of shells and explosions the monster escaped unscathed. Under cover of darkness it was painstakingly uncrated and assembled, inched down the sloping shaft to the tunnel and switched on.

The delighted engineers charted its progress; one hour, two feet forwards – two hours, four feet forwards – three hours, six feet forwards. The designers were right, the machine could work at three times the speed of men. They marvelled at the perfection of the tunnel that it carved, a smooth six feet in diameter. All the tunnellers needed to do now was follow its course to shore up the smooth walls with timber, and carry back the clay which had been so effortlessly removed. At the end of their shift, seven hours after the machine had started, they switched it off. It refused to start again. When they crawled over to inspect the cutting head the tunnellers found that it was inextricably caught in the mud. It took a whole day of digging to free it and set it boring again.

Now the engineers were in a dilemma, for the machine had to be switched off at intervals if it were not to overheat, but there was no retroactive mechanism to pull the bore back out of the earth when it came to a stop; and the weight of the clay which pressed in upon the drill was greater than the momentum of the engine designed to drive it forward. Again and again the great bore was dug out. Again and again it jammed. There were also problems with the electricity supply from the small generators, which could not produce enough consistent power to feed the monster. The fuses blew so often that the weary men who were nursing the machine along its checkered way ran out of heavy fuse-wire. When one of them, rather more weary and exasperated than his companions, also ran out of patience and mended one of the big fuses with the only wire he had to hand – which happened to be heavy barbed wire – the secret weapon gave up the ghost altogether. It had excavated just 200 feet of tunnel. The experts who had designed the machine and accompanied it so enthusiastically to Flanders set off back to London with their tails between their legs, abandoning the tunnel and leaving the wonder-weapon to sit there to eternity held fast beneath eighty feet of Flanders clay.

There were more hazardous set-backs, as German countermining increased in intensity. Blows and counterblows. Tunnels lost and restarted, and the mine at St Eloi lost altogether when the line was forced to fall back during fierce attacks as the Germans searched for the workings. Sometimes the fighting took place far below in the tunnels themselves. It often happened in the early days that in the shallower systems one side or the other accidentally broke into the enemy galleries.

One day we broke into the top of an enemy gallery, and as the enemy were heard close by, an emergency charge of fifteen pounds of gun cotton was tamped and fired near the hole. Actually, while the charge was being lit, the enemy were heard trying to enlarge the hole which they had discovered in their gallery. After the charge had gone up and the mine was reported free from gas, an exploration party was organised and an advance was made into the enemy gallery. This gallery was lit by electric light and when the Germans heard our party advancing they turned on the light. But our officer had foreseen this danger. He had run ahead and had cut the leads of the lamps well forward of the party, with the result that only the part of the gallery occupied by the enemy was illuminated. Two Germans were seen advancing, one of whom was shot. Both sides then retired, and after two attempts to destroy the gallery with small charges we eventually placed a charge of 200 pounds in position and exploded it, with the result that the German gallery was entirely closed up and the column of smoke and gas of the explosion which arose from the shaft gave our gunners accurate information of its position, and very effective firing practice on the German trenches interrupted the German mining activity for some time. Our miners had been working for five days within twelve feet of the German gallery and had not been heard.*

Such hair-raising escapades were usually in shallower saps; and shallower saps there had to be, well-sprinkled with listening-posts, so that the German countermining could be detected. But what the Germans did *not* know was that other, deeper systems of tunnels were being driven far below the tunnels they had detected. Work was going faster now, for the clay-kickers had arrived, the cockney navvies who had kicked their way through remarkably similar clay to drive the tunnels of the London Underground. Miners like Tom Newell, who worked in eleven of the Messines tunnels, were quick to pick up the technique.

Corporal T. Newell, No. 12096, 171 Tunnelling Coy., Royal Engineers

To be a good clay-kicker you had to be long-legged, young and strong. At the age of twenty-one I was all three. You lay on a wooden cross made out of a plank with the cross-strut just behind your shoulders. The cross was wedged into the tunnel so that you were lying at an angle of forty-five degrees with your feet towards the face. You worked with a sharp-pointed spade with a foot-rest on either side above the blade, and you drove the blade into the clay, kicked the clay out, and on to another section, moving forward all the time. With the old broad-bladed pick we could only get forward at best six feet on every shift, but when the clay-kicking method was introduced we were advancing as much as twelve feet, or even fourteen, on a shift.

Early in 1917 almost five miles of tunnels had been excavated, and nineteen of them were complete. The carrying parties came up by night through the firing-zone, each man staggering under the weight of a fifty-pound bag of ammonal, knowing that it would need no more than a single bullet or a red-hot scrap of shrapnel to pierce the bag and blow him to kingdom come. '*Fifty yards between each man and don't bunch up anywhere.*' The order came out of bitter experience. Captain Greener was not the only tunnelling officer who remembered the ghastly night when half a dozen men of a party of the Kensingtons, all with ammonal on their backs, had clustered round the top of the shaft at the moment a rifle grenade came across. The consequences were difficult to forget.

But now the big chambers had been excavated at the end of the tunnels, deep under the German positions; the ammonal was packed tightly into them; the wire of the firing mechanism had been led back along the tunnels; and the tunnels themselves were packed back for many yards with sandbags, so that the full force of the explosion would fly upwards to the objectives. The Germans were sitting on a time-bomb. But, except at Hill 60, their suspicions were allayed. Their listening parties heard nothing. Their counter-galleries were untapped. Beneath the screaming shells and explosions far above, the tunnels lay silent as tombs.

Every day the completed tunnels were tested with electrical charges to make sure that the mines were still operational, for there was always the chance that the explosive could have been affected by damp. Nothing happened. Up until May it was the best-kept secret of the war, and at this stage in the war the Allies badly needed a success. General Plumer was determined that they should have one.

For two years General Plumer and his Second Army had held the salient, or what remained of it. For all that time he had ground his teeth at the Germans glaring down from above like some baleful evil eye; had groaned over the mounting casualty-lists; had stood by impotently, defending his miserable mudpatch.

In almost three years of raging warfare the Allies had lost 2,000,000 men, killed, wounded or captured, and gained all too little ground. In places the line had been advanced a mile or so, but, in the main, nothing had changed except for the growing numbers of dead lying thick on the narrow strip of land that separated the trenches. The mingled stench of cordite and putrefaction lay like a cloud over the Western Front.

It had lain thickest of all over Verdun and above the Somme. Now, across the front from Arras to the Aisne – where British, Canadians and French had been wiped out by the thousand in the push designed to bring the French, in one spectacular leap, within an arm's length of victory – the stench of slaughter was so intense that even the Supreme Command, far away in London, gagged on it. Added to that there were reports that the French Army was in a state of mutiny. The eyes of the politicians and the commanders swivelled towards the north. There was nowhere else they could turn, for in spite of Lloyd George's itching to divert guns and troops to Italy to deal a final deathblow to the soft underbelly of the Germans on the Austrian front, it was obvious, as the summer of 1917 approached, that a Flanders campaign was the only practical possibility. If, indeed, there ought to be a summer campaign at all. Lloyd George was inclined to think that the armies should continue a defensive holding-operation for the rest of the year and husband their resources for an all-out effort in 1918. Sir Douglas Haig (who had succeeded General French as Commander-in-Chief) thought otherwise. The Battle of Messines, long planned to gain the comparatively limited objective of breaking out of the salient, if successful could become part of a greater design. The charge was already set. It only remained to light the fuse.

General Sir Herbert Plumer was equally enthusiastic, for above all, Messines was his baby. After two years of standing still with his feet held fast in the clay of Ypres, he was absolutely determined that his baby was going to be a bouncer. In the still incomplete tunnels at Hill 60 and St Eloi the shifts were doubled, and the effort redoubled. The maps and plans, long drawn up, were dusted off and meticulously gone over point by point. The roads from the south and from the ports rumbled night and day under the wheels of convoys of supply wagons and ammunition trucks. In the vanguard a thousand horses pulled the carriages of field guns that would soon take up position to reinforce the batteries due to fire the opening bombardment. The rails of the line to Poperinghe burned hot under the wheels of trains groaning with heavy artillery, and a million sparks rang off the cobbled roads beneath the boots of the men marching towards the salient to fight the battle.

Chapter 4

They marched in easy stages of ten or twelve miles a day. They were seasoned soldiers these, who had survived the Somme and Arras and Vimy, and most had already had bitter experience of the Ypres salient. Plumer was taking no chances with raw troops. These men had come out of the line, and the drafts fresh from Blighty had been sent in to take their place. Fighting battalions had been rested, reformed and stiffened with returning wounded, now pronounced fit after gruelling retraining in the notorious camp at Etaples which the troops called 'the bullring'. Most of them were glad to be out of it and back with comrades on the march.

Behind the grumble of the distant guns it was spring in France. Farm-workers in the fields waved as the endless khaki columns went by. Village children ran excitedly alongside the marching soldiers until their legs could keep up no more. And every girl from Armentières to Poperinghe who had the slightest pretension to youth and beauty (and the soldiers assessed these qualities with the utmost generosity) blushed beneath a barrage of whistles, roars of bawdy compliments, and an interminable serenade which although incomprehensible became through repetition increasingly familiar:

> *Landlord have you any good wine?*
> *PARLEYVOO*
> *Landlord have you any good wine?*
> *PARLEYVOO*
> *Landlord have you any good wine*
> *Fit for a soldier up the line?*
> *INKY PINKY PARLEYVOO.*
> *Farmer have you a daughter fine?*
> *PARLEYVOO*
> *Farmer have you a daughter fine?*
> *PARLEYVOO*
> *Farmer have you a daughter fine?*
> *Fit for a soldier up the line?*
> *INKY PINKY PARLEYVOO.*

Then up the stairs and into bed
PARLEYVOO
Then up the stairs and into bed
PARLEYVOO
Then up the stairs and into bed
Da-da-da-da da-da-da-da . . .
INKY PINKY PARLEYVOO!

And so on, in a thousand ever-bawdier variations. If Mademoiselle from Armentières hadn't been kissed for forty years, there wasn't a Tommy in the British Army who was not ready, willing and able to rectify her forlorn situation immediately.

The strains of 'Tipperary' and 'Keep the Home Fires Burning' might very well be bringing a lump to the throats of audiences at concerts and music-halls at home, but the troops on the march preferred more exclusive ditties. In that respect the 11th Battalion of the Prince of Wales' Own West Yorkshire Regiment was more fortunate than most, for it had the distinction of counting a genuine songwriter among its officers. He was 2nd Lieutenant Levey, who came from a musical family and, having been named after a well-known violinist of the day, sported with pride his given names of Sivori Antonio Joachim. The ditties which he had composed for the delectation of the junior officers of his mess had permeated downwards (which, in the light of their frequent and lusty renderings, was not remarkable). The 11th POWs had adopted as their marching anthem a song which celebrated the comparative delights of a training camp in Blighty:

Rugeley, Rugeley,
We're all enjoying it hugely.
To and fro we gaily go,
We're always on the tramp,
But if you think that Cannock Chase
Is a lively and attractive pla-a-a-ce,
You'll be rugeley awakened
When you come to Rugeley Camp!

So sang the 11th as they foot-slogged towards the salient, and their indulgent officers joined in – Hobday and Knowles, Todd and Ostler, Miller, Wood and Porter and, of course, Levey himself, his huge frame towering above them all as he marched in front of his company on legs like tree-trunks. Of them all, Jim Todd was the only one who would still have two legs to carry him out again.

In the back areas of the salient the troops trained and trained again. Life was pleasant enough for the newly arrived troops, manoeuvring in the May sunshine over untouched fields and meadows which were marked and taped out to represent the areas of attack. *Advance with your company. Stick with your platoon. Stop and consolidate at your objective while the next wave passes through you to the next line of attack.* In one of those pleasantly unopposed practice attacks 2nd Lieutenant Jim Todd of the 11th Prince of Wales, waiting at the tape that represented his company's objective on the crest of Hill 60 for the 12th Durhams to pass through, was astounded to recognise a corporal of the Durhams as John Wilson. When the two young men had last met they'd been kicking a football around the park in their native Sunderland. But in this more serious game there was only time for an exclamation of surprise, a hasty greeting, a clap on the shoulder and the Durhams were past and on their way to the next innocuous objective.

In addition to the field practice, the officers attended briefings. Convoys of them were brought from training camps all over the area to study the ground they would attack, on a vast-scale ground model of the Messines-Wytschaete Ridge which had been laid out on the slopes of the Scherpenberg. It had been painstakingly constructed by the sculptor Cecil Thomas, now an officer in the 23rd Battalion of the Middlesex Regiment, and it was not unusual to see General Plumer himself on one of the wooden observation stands gazing down on it intently. In those weeks before Messines, Plumer seemed to be everywhere. Often close to the front line (too close, thought his staff), inspecting the arrangements for himself, or touring the gun lines as more and more batteries pulled into their positions. Next morning he would be in Bailleul, taking the salute in the main square, for whenever it was possible he made a point of greeting – albeit in such a formal way – the troops coming into the salient and into his command. He even popped up at St Omer in the south and visited the Second Army School of Instruction – a training school for officers. Six weeks before, as the smartest soldier in his platoon, Bill Morgan had been picked to go there.

Private W. Morgan, No. 24819, 10/11th Btn., Highland Light Infantry

I wasn't an officer, of course, but they needed soldiers to practise on, so to speak, and to show the young officers how things should be done. They picked a certain number of soldiers from each regiment and sent them there. We were a demonstration squad for bayonet fighting and hand-to-hand combat. It was a kind of commando course, jumping trenches and jumping over walls and all that sort of thing. You had to be tough. We had some really tough sergeant-majors and they certainly put us through it. They made us a really smart squad, and then we had to demonstrate in front of the officers. We were all picked troops. I'd got the stick, you see. I got it twice. That's an award for the smartest soldier in the guard – well turned out with a good rolled coat. It had to be neatly rolled up at the back and then tied to your belt. And I was also pretty good at shouldering arms and fixing bayonets and that sort of thing. All of us who were picked to go to St Omer were pretty good, although I'm saying it myself.

General Plumer came down to inspect us. This was just before the Battle of Messines. A lot of the young officers were going to be in it, and General Plumer was the sort of man who wanted to see for himself that everything was going well. He was a great man. Just a little fellow and he looked a bit like Lloyd George, but he was a fine man to speak to. He wasn't a bit standoffish. He spoke to all the ranks. We had a concert that night and he stayed over to see it. I was to sing a song and I was so excited when I saw him sitting there in the front row with all the high-ups that I completely forgot the second verse. The hall was packed with people and there was I up on the stage in a kilt. Well, there was only one song I could sing, wasn't there?

> I'll never forget the day I joined the 93rd,
> The chums I used to run with said
> They thought I looked absurd,
> They saluted me and ran around me in a ring,
> And when I wagged my tartan kilt
> They all began to sing:
> Chorus: He's a braw, braw Hielan' laddie,
> Private Jock McDade,
> There's no' another like him
> In the Scots Brigade.
> Reared amang the heather,
> Ye' can tell he's Scottish built
> By the wig wig wiggle wiggle waggle
> O' his kilt. . . .

Bill Morgan was well into his stride now. It hardly mattered that he had forgotten the second verse. In his excitement, he simply launched into the first verse all over again, strutting round the stage swinging his kilt in the approved manner, and the whole audience joined in. He sang it twice more and when he ran out of breath they raised the roof with applause and whistles. Beaming in the front row, General Plumer clapped harder than anyone else.

It was a welcome moment of relaxation because Plumer, at that moment, was carrying more strain and responsibility than any other commander on the Western Front. Only a day or so previously, on 15 May, the Supreme Commander, Sir Douglas Haig, in the course of a heated altercation, had made it all too clear that the success or failure of the Messines enterprise would be on Plumer's shoulders and on his shoulders alone.

The Germans were well aware that something big was going on at Hill 60. On 4 April they had blown two shallow mines in an effort to destroy the tunnels. A few days later on 9 April they had sent over a strong raiding-party to try to discover the workings. There was bitter fighting but the Australians, who were then holding the line, had managed to beat them off at the cost of heavy casualties; but it was doubtful if they could protect the mines much longer.

The Germans switched their attention below-ground and tunnelled furiously in an effort to find the mine. On 15 May the listeners in the galleries below heard them working very close to the charge – so close that they could actually hear the windlass only yards away as the spoil from the German workings was winched back to the head of the shaft. Haig lost his nerve. He proposed to Plumer that the Hill 60 charge should be exploded ahead of time. General Plumer refused. Haig raged. Plumer remained implacable. Unless all the mines went up together the Messines campaign would go off at half-cock, and in the conduct of the war so far there had been too many half-successes. In Plumer's view a half-success was a half-failure. The engineers had calculated the rate at which the Germans were tunnelling and Plumer was convinced that they would just beat them to zero hour. Perhaps he would beat them only by inches but it was a risk he was prepared to gamble on. But all the time he watched the preparations for the battle, doubt gnawed at the back of his mind.

The German High Command was also beset by doubt. The Germans knew very well that an attack was bound to take place soon, and from their positions on the high ground observers had been able to see the movement of troops, guns and transport. Furthermore, security was not what it might have been, for the Belgian civilians seemed to know an inordinate amount about the preparations for the battle. Certainly there was plenty to see. In the village of Dickebusch, for example – far enough away from the battle zone to be occupied still by its civilian population, but right in the middle of one of the main arteries of communication – Pastor van Walleghem, the priest of Dickebusch Church, kept a revealing daily diary throughout the war. On 15 May he wrote:

Together with the Dean of la Clytte and three other friends went to Scherpenberg to look at a model of present-day Wytschaete. Behind Café DeZonne on the slope of the hill a scale model of the whole of Wytschaete has been made. All in relief as seen by air reconnaissance. Bricks to show the ruins; cement-strips to simulate the trenches; barbed wire, sticks and twigs represent the woods; numerous name-plates giving the names of farms, trenches or woods. Mostly the English names adopted by the English themselves. Those who know the area say that everything is very accurate; however, when one sees this it must be acknowledged that Wytschaete is strongly defended and will be difficult to take. Officers and soldiers come here to study the area. The walk is prohibited and we have to be satisfied with a look from the outside. All the same we're still able to have a reason-ably good look.

If five civilians were able to stroll casually near enough to the actual plan of the forthcoming battle to take 'a reasonably good look' at it, it is not surpris-ing that the Germans were suspicious. It is only surprising, in the light of the Intelligence reports which they undoubtedly received, that they did not act on their suspicions. But they were notoriously overcautious. The German Command had received full information about the mutinies in the French Army, but although they registered the fact that morale was low they did not fully believe them. Had they done so, a concerted effort against the French forces further south might virtually have brought the war to a close and this, of course, was what the offensive in Flanders was designed to prevent.

Haig and Plumer would have given a year of their lives to know what was going on in the minds of the commanders of the German Army holding the salient. It was Haig's fear that if the Germans had more than an inkling about the mines laid deep beneath their most heavily guarded strongpoints on the Messines–Wytschaete Ridge, they would simply with-draw to prepared positions further back – in which case the great ex-plosion would simply go down in history as no more than the most expensive fireworks display of all time. Had he been in the place of the German Army Commander, Crown Prince Rupprecht, that is precisely what Haig himself would have done, and indeed the Germans were consid-ering a tactical withdrawal along these lines. But the decision was made to stand fast and, when the inevitable attack came, to defend the ridge to the last man. After all, the German forces had won every round in the salient so far, and in spite of the fact that their forces were now overstretched and there was beginning to be a shortage of trained men and munitions, they presumably saw no reason why, with their geographical advantages, they should not win this round too.

★

With 80,000 troops going over the top after the mines went up, jumping-off and assembly trenches had to be dug. They were dug by night and camouflaged so that, by day, they would be invisible to the observation balloons and reconnaissance aircraft of the enemy.

Private W. G. Bell, No. 4640, 9th Btn., Army Cyclist Corps

You say, 'What did you do in the Cyclist Corps?' 'We dug up half of France!', I always say. We used to cycle up as near to the front line as we could and dump our bikes, 300 of us there was. We stacked our bikes in the field and then we went to where there was a dump of pick-axes and shovels, and we'd follow the officer, single file, and we found that there was a white tape lying right across the fields. Mind you, this is pitch-dark now. There's Very lights going up all over the place. You could only just see the bloke in front of you. No rifles. Nothing. We only had tin helmets on and a water bottle. You could see the fellow in front of you and you followed him – falling down holes and cursing and swearing. The officer would stop where the white tape ended, then he'd say, 'You 'ere. Step out, one, two. You 'ere. Stick your spade in. Now, go on. Get down. Six feet deep.' And you wouldn't half dig! You'd dig like fury. And, of course, if your spade hit a stone out in the fields at night, it didn't half sound. Directly old Jerry heard it, up go the Very lights and it was like daylight, and round would come his machine-guns, raking along the line. When he passed over, you were up again, digging like fury. Of course, directly you got a bit of a parapet up you felt safe.

Well, we got artful. It was supposed to be six feet down. What we did, we got about four feet down and then we'd dig one big hole – a bit deeper than the trench we'd dug, you see. Then we used to sit down at the bottom of the trench and the artillery officer used to come along the top of the trench, you see, and he'd say, 'Are you down there?' 'Yes, we're down here.' But we were only down about four feet. In the end, we were rumbled. Our officer used to come along the trench himself on the bottom there, and another officer used to walk along the top with a six-foot rod, and they used to guide it along with him at the top. Made sure it was six feet.

I think we had about three months of that. Every night, every night, every night – three months. Up at night, back in the morning when it was just breaking dawn, and then the rest of the day was for ourselves but up again at night. Out in the front. You hadn't got anything, only these picks and shovels. You couldn't have your rifle.

You couldn't see anybody to fire at, anyway. No. You simply had to take what was coming to you, and when we got back and jumped in that front-line trench and back through the communication trenches and out on the fields at the back, and got our bikes, I don't mind telling you, we heaved a sigh of relief. Night after night. We lost a lot of fellows though, like it.

On 30 May the preliminary bombardment began. It was the most powerful of the war and this time there was no shortage of shells. They lay dumped near the guns by the hundred thousand, and there was a gun for every seven yards of front. At the southern end of the ridge near Ploeg-steert Wood, which the troops called Plug Street, the New Zealand gun-ners were on Hill 63. It was a traditional 'hot spot' because it was the first line of fire. Even if the flashes of the guns were not seen from their positions just over the brow of the hill, there was no mistaking where the fire was coming from, and the German guns habitually gave it their full attention. In the slit trenches behind the gun pits, and in the dug-outs burrowed and tunnelled into the hillside beside them, casualties were high and life was uncomfortable. Now that the batteries had been reinforced and the bombardment had started in earnest it was more of a hot spot than ever. Nevertheless, between hauling up ammunition, diving into the trench to escape the flying shells or trying to snatch a little off-duty peace, if not quiet, in a dug-out, Gunner Bert Stokes of Wellington, New Zea-land, somehow or other managed to scribble a few words in his diary every day.

Gunner B. O. Stokes, No. 25038, New Zealand Field Artillery, 13th Battery, 3rd Brigade

Friday, 1 June. Into another month – how time flies. Twenty-four hours now since the bombardment started and today has been a Hun day out. All last night and today he has been strafing our batteries and roads hot and strong. During the night he put over shell-gas and our men had to sit up at the guns for a couple of hours with gas helmets on. Our battery had two casualties today. We were unloading ammuni-tion until about 6 pm. I was one of the ration party. We have to go and draw our rations from the dump up the road. We waited until 11 pm. There was no sign of the ration cart so we came back again.

The roads, as Bert pointed out, had been getting it hot and strong, and the 13th Battery of the New Zealand Field Artillery was not the only contingent of soldiers to go hungry to bed that night. But next day Bert

Stokes, who went down early for the rations and had a hearty breakfast, had a piece of news which set him agog.

> Today I was informed that I am one of the battery forward runners. This means that when the battle gets under way we hop the parapet with the infantry, so crack hearty, Bert. There are nine of us with Lt. Jones and we go over with the third wave. I expect I'll be just as well off there as anywhere. It will be a great experience for me and I think I'd rather this job than that of a driver bringing up ammunition. This evening the battery moved to another position on Hill 63. It was about 11 pm before all the guns were in, but I did not get to bed until after midnight.
> Sunday, 3 June. This afternoon Fritz started shelling this hell. It doesn't take the Hun long to find out when the battery has pulled in. The majority of us got well down the tunnel out of the way. Fritz got one of our dumps of about 200 rounds. Bombardier Wallace was wounded in the leg. We had a stunt arranged for 3 pm, but Fritz got in five minutes before us and pasted the hill and all around heavily. Then all our guns started. What a din there was. Each day sees this front getting more active. We are all the time wondering when we are going to get word to kick off. I suppose the heads know best. But there seems to be a lot of delay.

However, the padre at Dickebusch was soon able to make a pertinent entry in *his* diary.

> 6 June. At midday was told by an officer that offensive will take place at 3 am tomorrow. We were advised to keep it quiet, which did not prevent me from hearing the same information from several other people during the course of the afternoon.

The only thing he got wrong was the time. The mines were due to go up at 3.10 am. But not everyone was as well informed as Pastor van Walleghem.

2nd Lieutenant Naylor of the Royal Field Artillery had been in the salient since the end of October 1915, and the first he heard of the existence of the mammoth mines was at a briefing of senior officers just two days before they went up. In ordinary circumstances a mere subaltern in charge of a gun position would not have been present on such an occasion, but Colonel Simpson, who commanded the brigade, had lost his adjutant, and Jimmy Naylor was appointed in his place to act as orderly officer and assistant adjutant. Like Bert Stokes he was to 'hop the parapet' with the infantry. In the heat of an attack the job of an infantry officer was to look after his troops and, if he could, to gain his objective. He could hardly be expected to send back more than the most basic information about his own situation, but, in order to direct the course of the battle, headquarters needed information, and needed it badly. It was the custom to send over officers and runners from the artillery to observe as much as possible and get the news back as best they could.

The prospect of this job suited Jimmy Naylor very well, for he was a lad with a taste for adventure. Taking advantage of the fact that their parents were in India, where their father was serving as an officer in the Royal Horse Artillery, both Jimmy and his brother had run away from school and joined up in May 1912. At first Jimmy had been a trumpeter, and as he grew not only in experience but in stature he was promoted to NCO; a few months previously, he had been commissioned. On the eve of the battle he attended the final briefing; listened to the final pronouncements of the senior officers in the respectful silence that was expected of a junior subaltern, even if one did happen to be acting adjutant; synchronised his watch with theirs; shook hands; and left with Colonel Simpson for the front line. He was just nineteen years old.

The 11th Battalion of the Prince of Wales' Own West Yorkshire Regiment had spent the day at Battersea Farm, just off the road from Zillebeke to Hill 60, and a lot too close to the line for comfort. 'Farm' was something of a misnomer, although it might have been one when a London regiment had given it its homely name in the early days of the war. Now it was nothing but a heap of ruins, with a few dug-outs huddled around it. In the cellars of this salubrious spot, the officers had done their best to make themselves at home. You couldn't have called it an officers' mess exactly, but by some devious miracle Levey had managed to bring up his portable gramophone. In the tension of the approaching battle no one felt much like singing, but the music helped to while away the hours of waiting, between writing letters, smoking and snoozing; and the need to keep winding up the wretched machine gave them all something to do. Levey hadn't been able to bring many records, but among the few he *had* brought was a well-worn favourite:

> At seventeen he falls in love quite madly
> With eyes of tender blue.
> At twenty-four he gets it rather badly
> With eyes of a different hue.
> At thirty-five you'll see him flirting sadly
> With two or three, or more.

When he fancies he is past love,
It is then he meets his last love,
And he loves her as he's never loved before.

They played it over and over and over again. Outside, in the warm evening air, the soldiers stretched on the ground or leaning on their packs in assorted attitudes of repose, heard it too. It seemed like a touch of home. When you went on leave, even if you only spent a few hours in London, it was almost obligatory to go to Daly's Theatre to see the hit musical *The Maid of the Mountains*. That song was the show-stopper. Hearing it now brought it all back. The music. The applause. The warm cocoon of the theatre. The warm handclasp of your girl. Home.

The rations came up. There were canisters of stew, good and hot, and good strong tea, well-laced with rum, to wash it down.

Dusk fell. It was time to go.

Tom Cantlon was keeping a wary eye on the whereabouts of his officer as he marched with C Company of the 21st Battalion of the King's Royal Rifle Corps towards the front. It was not an easy thing to do because it was dark now, and since the KRRs were to form part of the first wave of infantry to attack they had the longest distance to go to the front line.

The KRRs were fed up. They'd been on the move, more or less, for thirty-six hours now. In an hour or so they would be going over the top, and they'd be going over without so much as a drop of rum. The rations had caught up with them all right, an hour or so earlier, but Jerry had seen fit to put over a salvo of whizz-bangs as soon as they had been dumped, and the precious rum jars had been smashed to smithereens. It was not an unusual occurrence. The jars were stamped with the initials of the Special Ration Department. The soldiers preferred to believe that the letters actually stood for the prognosis 'Seldom Reaches Destination'. Tom had broken the gloomy news to Lieutenant Harrison, who was thereby saved the trouble of dishing out the rum ration.

'Never mind, Cantlon,' said Harrison, patting the water bottle slung on his hip, 'you'll get a drop before we go over. Remember, if anything happens to me, there's a drink in this bottle.'

Like many other infantry officers, Harrison carried two water bottles in an engagement, one containing whisky for the comfort of shocked or wounded men. Harrison was a good sort all right, and he was particularly good to his servant, Rifleman Cantlon. Every time he sent him off for a message, for a packet of cigarettes or a pad of writing paper, he would give him ten or twenty francs, and he never failed to say, 'Keep the change.' As a result, Tom always had plenty of money. This was just as well because

Alf Bicknell, his mucking-in chum in No. 3 Platoon, never had any at all.
Alf was a good-humoured cockney from Poplar who was always broke,
and not only broke but mortgaged to the hilt. On pay parade days, back in
camp at la Clytte, Alf managed to stay solvent for approximately thirty
seconds after receiving his money. *Hold out your hand. Receive five francs.
Salute. One step back. Another salute. About turn* – and Alf was broke again!
But he was a good pal and Tom had no objection to sharing the proceeds
of Mr Harrison's generosity with him. What he *did* object to was Alf's
irritating habit of imitating the noise of approaching shells, a bellicose
parlour trick which he had perfected to a fine art. He was doing it now as
they trudged towards the line – as if there weren't enough shells coming
over and noise going on without Alf joining in. 'Why don't you shut it,
just for a change?' said Tom wearily. 'Whizz–z–z–z–z–z BANG!' replied
Alf. Rumless, No. 3 Platoon plodded glumly on.

With all the noise going on, it seemed ridiculous that the lads of B
Battery had spent a couple of hours earlier in the day wrapping sandbags
round the wheels of the gun carriages, to muffle their sound. Just before
departure, they had even swathed the hooves of the patient horses who
were pulling the guns. Ridiculous! Or so, in a moment of comparative
silence, one of the bombardiers observed ironically to Sergeant John
Miller. Sergeant Miller merely grunted in return. His job was to get the
forward guns up as close as possible to the front line to cover the infantry
as they went across. And with Jerry, monarch of all that he surveyed from
the ridge that now loomed up faintly in front of them in the darkness,
that was a task which could not have been achieved in daylight.

Now there was only an hour or so of darkness left before the kick-off.
It was little enough time to get even these light guns into position and
ready to fire. They had to get them right up almost to the front line with,
for once, no thought of finding any cover that would conceal the flashes
as the shells streaked from the muzzles. Luckily, the carrying parties had
already made many journeys to dump a plentiful supply of eighteen-
pounder shells, so there was just one ammunition wagon at the back to
worry about, but still it would be touch and go. There was no possibility
of deploying as they moved up. The gun carriages had to stick to the road
and the road was a mess. What with the Germans replying to the artillery
bombardment for days past, and the shells still flying across, the road was
littered with debris, broken wagons, dead mules, and even the bodies of
dead soldiers scattered all over it. Some attempt had been made to push
them towards the side of the road, but so thick was the movement of men
and transport in these hours before the battle that it was impossible not to
run over them. The men on the limbers knew that those forward guns

just had to get there, but dark as it was as they bumped and jolted along, they were careful not to look down.

The heavy section, Machine Gun Corps, was also on the move. They had little, if anything, to do with machine-guns. To be precise, they were the tanks. The men who manned them as they lumbered up behind the troops, waiting to jump off, were the young buccaneers – at least in their own eyes. For they were the dashers. Adventurous lads, whose comfortably-off families had been able to indulge their sense of adventure by endowing them with that exciting mechanical toy of the pre-war years – a motor cycle. And a motor cycle, in those days before the war, was adventure indeed.

The lucky few were a band of brothers bound together by subscription to a periodical – *The Motor Cycle*. Its pages they had eagerly studied week by week, turning them with fingers from which no amount of scrubbing would entirely remove the grease-stains. Nick Lee was one of this exclusive coterie, and one of the first to have answered an appeal in its columns for recruits who were able to drive and had a sound knowledge of the internal combustion engine. They were needed for a new unit to be called the Motor Machine Section of the Machine Gun Corps. The original idea, back in 1915, was to form teams of two men, one to ride the motor cycle and the other to man a machine-gun mounted on a side-car. Such teams, it was imagined, would be able to range far, wide and fast over battle-zones, wreaking havoc on the enemy as they went. In theory it was a good idea. In practice, as the armies settled down to trench warfare, it was useless. So the army was left with a nucleus of young men of high calibre who, by now, were all crack shots. What was it to do with them?

The answer was to train them to use the new secret weapon. It was Winston Churchill's idea and, as First Lord of the Admiralty, Churchill had had a finger in the pie of the development of the revolutionary 'land ships'. They looked like nothing on earth, but by stretching the imagination no more than a little the huge lumbering monsters might just pass for travelling water tanks; and so, for security reasons, 'tanks' was chosen as a cover name. The crews had other names for them and each crew christened its own tank. One was called *Autogophaster*, another *Otasel*. The tanks in Nick Lee's section were named after shows then running in London: *Oh I Say, Look Who's Here, Watch Your Step, We're All In It, So Search Me*. Nick's crew christened their first tank *Keep Smiling*.

The tank and its crew had managed to keep smiling, more or less, through a number of more-or-less disastrous attacks over terrain which was totally unsuitable for tank movement. Then *Keep Smiling* was

knocked out by shell-fire in November 1916. Her crew thought it appropriate that her successor should be christened *Revenge*.

Now, as *Revenge* and the sister tank *Iron Rations* sat with the other tanks
of A Battalion close to the jumping-off point, her crew felt particularly
pleased with themselves. It had taken them three days to make the journey from their base, travelling by night and parking by day in a wood or
ruined farmhouse in order to escape aircraft observation, and two days
before departure it had been decided that the name of every tank should
start with 'A', the identifying letter of the battalion. No problem, the boys
agreed. They would change the name to *Avenger*. The suggestion was
turned down and authority decreed that *Revenge* and *Iron Rations* should
become respectively *Apple* and *Apricot*. But, in the midst of the battle
preparations, no one had time to supervise the rechristening ceremony
closely. It was Jock Duncan's idea to blot out the original name by smear-
ing a temporary coating of mud and water over it, and it was therefore a
simple matter, at the first stop, to rub the mixture off again. So *Revenge* and
Iron Rations were going into battle under their own cock-snooking 'colours'.

It was quiet in the tank with the engine switched off, and the crew
talked among themselves as they waited – the driver, Jock Duncan; the
corporal-in-charge, Nick Lee; Fillingham; Preece; Chapman; Bolton; and
Banner, who was universally known as 'Connie' because of his incessant
talking about his sweetheart who bore that name. Suddenly it became
quieter still. An hour before the battle the big guns stopped and the
German batteries, doubtless thankful for the respite, stopped too.

The area around Wytschaete is renowned for nightingales. Apparently
undeterred by the pulverising shell-fire of the last few days, as silence fell
over the front they began to sing. The night was warm and starry. The full
moon sailed high in the sky. Forty minutes before zero hour everyone was
in position. Everyone except C Company of the 21st KRRs. They were
lost. Or at least Tom Cantlon's platoon was lost, for the trenches were
crammed with men encumbered with equipment, and in the communication trenches it was impossible to make your way except in single file.
Tom had long ago lost sight of Lieutenant Harrison, or any other officer
for that matter. The jumping-off positions had been taped and marked
'first wave', 'second wave' and so on, with assembly trenches numbered
right up to '32' at the rear. But the infantry of the 41st Division were
spread right across their sector of the front, at the bottom of the ridge
between Messines and Wytschaete, and the 21st KRRs could have been
anywhere on the first-wave tapes. As the guns fell silent, No. 3 Platoon
began to get really worried.

★

Some of the 36th Ulster Division had also had trouble in finding their exact position. Lieutenant Witherow of the 8th Battalion, Royal Irish Rifles, had at last succeeded in rounding up his men. He was relieved and excited too because he knew that they were about to make history. They were positioned at Kruisstraat, just to the right of where the great Spanbroekmolen mine would go up, and they were to be the very first troops across in the vanguard of the first wave of infantry. On their left was the 16th (Irish) Division, and for the first time in history Ulster and southern Irish regiments would be fighting side by side. There was a certain advantage in being the first troops across, for the enemy would have no time to set up a retaliatory bombardment, but nevertheless casualties were bound to be heavy. Lieutenant Witherow looked around at the impassive faces of the soldiers near him. Happy is the man, he thought to himself, who has not got a vivid imagination. But still, who was to know what another man might be feeling? Doubtless his own expression was equally impassive.

In his advanced headquarters some miles away in a railway carriage on a siding near Godwaersveldt, Sir Douglas Haig was sound asleep in bed. At his headquarters, rather nearer the front, General Sir Herbert Plumer began to pace the floor.

All along the front the plungers that would fire the mines were brought out from the dug-outs, and the engineers waited in a ferment of anxious excitement. It was General Plumer's plan but it was also their work which was about to be proved. In a matter of minutes all the planning, the toil, the preparation would culminate in the greatest man-made explosion the world had ever seen – or felt. No one quite knew what the effect would be. It was not entirely impossible that it would set off an earthquake or, at the very least, a shock wave which would bury the troops alive, German and Allied alike. At three o'clock along the length of the front from Ploegsteert to Hill 60, after checking the time on the illuminated dial of his watch, each officer gave a quiet order. Right along the front the troops, as quietly as their heavy equipment would allow, scrambled out of the assembly trenches to lie flat behind the rear parados. All except No. 3 Platoon of the 21st KRRs.

'Well, every other blighter in this platoon's had a go at finding the battalion,' announced Tom Cantlon in a hoarse whisper, 'I might as well have a go too.' He pushed his way to the front and the platoon pressed on. They knew that they were very near the front line, but unless they found the battalion in the next five minutes they would be left behind and lost in the confusion as the troops advanced. Five minutes later, by a happy fluke, Tom stumbled on the right trench and scuttled into it with the platoon at his heels. Suddenly they were challenged in a whisper: 'Halt. Who goes there?'

Tom found himself staring down the barrel of Lieutenant Harrison's revolver. 'It's only me, sir.'

'Where the devil have you scurvy lot been? There's only seconds to go now, before the mines go up.'

Mines? It was the first No. 3 Platoon had ever heard of them.

'Quick, up behind the rear parados or you'll be buried alive.' Lieutenant Harrison scrambled up behind them and the men lay flat and waited. The silence of suspense pressed down on 80,000 men lying prone on the earth. Some of the troops were astounded to hear a nightingale sing as they waited.

The tension was worst of all at Hill 60, where the Germans were known to have been tunnelling within inches of the charge. It was by no means certain that they had not reached it, for the listening galleries and tunnels had been cleared many hours before. Lieutenant Todd, lying out behind the jumping-off trench with his men, mentally went over his instructions. If the mine did *not* go up the infantry were not to wait for it. They were to go ahead as soon as the barrage opened. But what would happen if the explosion were merely late? Todd tried to push the thought from his mind and glanced at his watch. Ten seconds to zero.

In front of Spanbroekmolen, Captain Greener was standing upright in a trench. Immediately behind him a dark shape flapped slightly in the breeze that preceded the dawn, and somewhere in the back of his mind he marvelled that an observation balloon could have been brought so close to the front line. Its crew lay flat around it beside the piled-up gas cylinders, ready to start the job of inflating and hoisting the balloon as soon as the troops went over.

Five seconds to go. The officer beside him bent over the plunger. Four – three – two. Far to the rear, as if in signal, a single gun fired.

ZERO

Lieutenant J. Todd, 11th Btn., Prince of Wales' Own Yorkshire Regiment

It was an appalling moment. We all had the feeling, 'It's not going!' And then a most remarkable thing happened. The ground on which I was lying started to go up and down just like an earthquake. It lasted for seconds and then, suddenly in front of us, the Hill 60 mine went up.

2nd Lieutenant J. W. Naylor, Royal Field Artillery

Our plunger was in a dug-out, and the colonel and I were actually standing outside the dug-out because we both knew what was going to happen and we wanted to see as much as we could. The earth seemed to tear apart, and there was this enormous explosion right in front of us. It was an extraordinary sight. The whole ground went up and came back down again. It was like a huge mushroom.

Captain M. Greener, 175 Tunnelling Coy., Royal Engineers

The earth seemed to open and rise up to the sky. It was all shot with flame. The dust and smoke was terrific. And all this debris falling back.

Rifleman T. Cantlon, No. 33419, 21st Btn., King's Royal Rifles

We could hardly believe it. We couldn't take our eyes off it. We'd only known about it a minute or so before and we could hardly believe our eyes. None of us had seen anything like it ever. It was just one mass of flames. The whole world seemed to go up in the air.

2nd Lieutenant J. W. Naylor, Royal Field Artillery

I can see it now! It was tremendous. One almost felt 'Good old England.' You wanted to wave a little Union Jack. Thank God we've done something. It had a tremendous moral effect. To sit there day after day in these ghastly trenches with nothing of any importance happening and suddenly you get a major thing like that. It goes home. It's good!

Corporal T. Newell, 171 Tunnelling Coy., Royal Engineers

We all just stood looking. And then the officer beside me, the one who'd pushed the plunger, I heard him say, 'There! That's avenged my brother.'

And then the barrage started. The infantry went over.

Chapter 5

MESSINES RIDGE
CAPTURED

ATTACK ON NINE-MILE
FRONT

BRILLIANT BRITISH
SUCCESS

OVER 5,000 PRISONERS

*The following
telegraphic dispatches
were received from
General Headquarters
in France yesterday:*

11.05 am — *We attacked at 3.10 am this morning the German positions
on the Messines–Wytschaete Ridge on a front of over nine miles.*

*We have everywhere captured our first objectives and further progress is
reported to be satisfactory along the whole front of the attack. Numbers of
prisoners are reported already to be reaching collecting stations.*

The Times, Friday, 8 June 1917

Tom Cantlon, who had seen service on the bloody battlefields of the
Somme and Arras, had never seen anything like it.

Rifleman T. Cantlon, No. 33419, 21st Btn., King's Royal Rifles

They didn't seem to have any wits about them. We didn't even have
to bother to take them prisoner. We didn't have to trouble about
sending anyone to escort them back. We just saw them coming at us
through the smoke, running towards us like jellies. They didn't know

where they were. You just jerked your thumb backwards and they ran off towards our lines – and on we went.

Waiting in an assembly trench to go over in the second wave, the 10th Worcesters could see nothing of the battle but smoke and flame from exploding shells. As dawn spread across the sky the dust thrown up by the erupting mines still hung thick in the air. Through the fog the first wounded started to appear, but the first inkling that Henry Russell and his companions had that the battle was going well was when the Germans started stumbling towards them.

Acting Lance-Corporal Henry Russell, No. 39891, 10th Btn., Worcestershire Regiment

They were white, haggard and half crazy with fright. One big German, naked to the waist and with horrible wounds on his face, chest and back, staggered in our direction. Shorty bawled to him to cross the trench by the bridge which had been placed near us overnight. The wounded man misunderstood, and thinking that some fresh horror was overtaking him, suddenly gathered strength and took a flying leap into the midst of us. This was rather startling, but with the help of a certain amount of dumb show we directed him to the nearest dressing-station, and after we had helped him out of the trench he went on his way. The second line was taken and more wounded and prisoners came into view. Carrying parties with bombs and ammunition set out for the new lines, and then came the order to advance.

We jumped out of the trench relieved that the long wait was over, and after getting into some sort of order we marched in artillery formation across the open ground. I felt curiously helpless. The din of the guns behind and the shells in front prevented us from hearing whether the enemy artillery was in action, but no shells appeared to be bursting anywhere near. I fully expected to hear the sudden roar of high explosives, or the crash of shrapnel, but it was singularly absent and we gained confidence with every step. We crossed the enemy front line, which was but the wreckage of a trench system, and when nearing the second line we opened into extended order, just as we had done in the rehearsals of a few days before.★

And over on Hill 60, just as they had done in the rehearsals a few days

★ Extract from his book *Slaves of the War Lords* (Hutchinson, 1928).

before in the sunny fields behind the line, Corporal John Wilson of the
12th Durhams went past the shoulder of Lieutenant Todd of the West
Yorkshires. It was an unbelievable coincidence. In the heat of the battle
there was no time for chat, just a hasty clap on the shoulder as before.
'Good luck, John lad.'
  'Good luck, Jim.'

*Lieutenant J. Todd, 11th Btn., Prince of Wales' Own West Yorkshire
Regiment*

The Durhams were going forward. Our job was to stay where we
were and consolidate the new line. We'd skirted the craters and got
up to what had been the German front line and taken it over, but the
trouble was that it was facing the wrong way round – the line of fire
was facing the direction where our positions had been, and now that
we'd chased the Germans out of it that was no use to us. And, of
course, we found a lot of German pillboxes up there and had to clear
them out. There were quite a few Germans in them and we'd shout
in to them to come out; if they didn't, then we chucked a bomb in.
They came out fast enough then! It was eight or nine in the morning
before we got properly dug in and by then the Germans had started a
counter-barrage, so we were having some casualties. Corporal Scott
came up to me during the counter-attack and said, 'Mr Porter's been
killed, sir.' I said, 'All right, Corporal! I'll come down in a few
minutes.' He said, 'I beg your pardon, sir, I was made a sergeant
before we went in.' I said, 'Well, keep your ruddy head down or
you'll be a blooming angel before you go out!'

The Times, Friday, 8 June 1917.
*In the capture of the ridge, both north and south Irishmen have their share.
Northerners and Southerners, Protestant and Catholic troops, fought along-
side of one another and, whatever may be party feeling at home, it is as well to
know that the feeling between the two bodies here is most cordial. The
Southern Irishmen recently presented a cup for competition between the
various companies of the Northern force, and of late there has been swearing of
the utmost rivalry as to which would get to the top of the Messines Ridge first.
I do not yet know which did, but I have no doubt that both were first in good
Irish fashion.*

Some of the Irish never got there at all. Just to the right of the great
Spanbroekmolen mine, in front of Kruisstraat, Lieutenant Witherow – in
obedience to his orders – had set off with his Company as soon as the

protective barrage opened. But the Spanbroekmolen mine was late in going up. It exploded fifteen seconds behind the rest, and in that fifteen seconds Witherow's Company had got well out into No Man's Land.

Lieutenant T. Witherow, 8th Btn., Royal Irish Rifles

We'd made it through the machine-gun fire and had almost got to the German positions, when a terrible thing happened that nearly put an end to my fighting days. All of a sudden the earth seemed to open and belch forth a great mass of flame. There was a deafening noise and the whole thing went up in the air, a huge mass of earth and stone. We were all thrown violently to the ground and debris began to rain down on us. Luckily only soft earth fell on me, but the Lance-Corporal, one of my best Section Commanders, was killed by a brick. It struck him square on the head as he lay at my side. A few more seconds and we would have gone up with the mine.★

The Times, Friday, 8 June 1917.
From our Special
Correspondent
Our Artillery was magnificent. No praise can be too high for the work of our airmen. The 'Tanks' rendered useful help. Indeed, beside the attacking infantry, who behaved everywhere with perfect gallantry, all branches of the Army collaborated splendidly in attaining the great result.

Rifleman T. Cantlon, No. 33419, 21st Btn., King's Royal Rifle Corps

It was the first time I'd ever seen a tank close to. I just kept beside it, I couldn't see my officer, and by this time the Germans were firing a counter-barrage back at us, and the last I'd seen of Mr Harrison he was caught in between our shells and theirs, so I thought *he* was gone. I couldn't see any of my other mates either, so I just kept on going with the bunch that was around me, near to this tank.

The odds are four to one that the tank round which Tom Cantlon and his fellow troops were clustering, like so many chickens round a hen, was *Revenge* or the sister tank *Iron Rations*. Both were attacking in the same

---

★ Many of the Irishmen, both Southerners and Northerners, who were killed by the fall-out from the Spanbroekmolen mine lie where they fell in tiny Lone Tree cemetery, just down the hill from the Spanbroekmolen mine crater. Of the twenty-one mines laid, two failed to fire. In 1955 one exploded in a field, set off by lightning during a thunderstorm. The other is still lying somewhere in the area. Its exact location is unknown.

sector, ranging, like the other tanks, in pairs – the male tank (*Revenge*) equipped with cannon, and the female tank (*Iron Rations*) equipped with machine-guns.

Corporal A. E. Lee MM, No. 32198, A Btn., Tank Corps

There were eight tanks altogether in our sector, coming from various points. We each took our own route and we really felt that we were coming into our own at last, being used properly at the right time on good ground. Our job was simply to help the infantry. A runner came up and shouted, 'We're held up by machine-guns, just over on the right.' We went over, found that quite a lot of infantry were taking cover, and a hundred or so yards ahead we could see where the bullets were coming from. So we just drove straight at it, firing as we went, and of course that was the end of that. Once we got near they just put their hands up. We stopped firing if they surrendered. But if they hadn't surrendered we'd just have kept on going, right over the top of them. When we got further on to what had been the German support line, there were still a lot of them firing from these concrete pill-boxes and the infantry couldn't get past. *Iron Rations* kept them busy while we went round the back, and we just simply blew the doors off with our cannon. It took about three shells to take the door off.

The only problem we had was when our sister tank got ditched. That often happened with the tanks. The track would cut through soft earth, wet earth, and sink in until the ground was tight up under the belly of the tank. Then the track just spun round without gripping anything and the tank was 'ditched'. It was absolutely against orders to stop, in fact it was a court-martial offence. But we weren't going to leave *Iron Rations* there. At that time we had two heavy cables – one heavy cable for each tank and this was hooked over the top, shackled to the front and the rear. Well, we'd practised towing out, and we could see that *Iron Rations* was ditched, so we went across to her and two of her men got out. One of them unshackled the cable at the rear of *Iron Rations* and the other pulled it over to the front, and as we came by he pulled our shackle-pin out and put his cable in. We didn't even stop. We just carried on until we took the strain and then pulled *Iron Rations* out. But we knew that we were disobeying orders in going close together. Apparently they would rather have had the two tanks ditched, unable to do anything, than orders being disobeyed. Later in the day, *we* got ditched and *Iron Rations* did the same service for us.

The boys of the tank crews were a law unto themselves. Having mown down anything that moved in front of the advancing infantry and lumbered through to their rallying-point at the second objective, they waited to see what was going to happen and meantime had their lunch. It was all very well for the Tommies, thankful enough to hack open the tins of bully beef they carried in their packs, but the crew of *Revenge* turned up their noses at such simple fare.

Corporal A. E. Lee MM, No. 32198, A Btn., Tank Corps

In the tanks we were very epicurious, and we'd bought supplies at the local canteens and the shops in the towns before coming into the battle. This time we had tinned sausages. They were cold, of course, but they were still quite a treat for us, because we hadn't had any for a long time. Before we went into action we always had a whip-round, and everyone contributed as much as they could to the pool. Most of us had a bit more than our pay, sent by our folks at home, so we always had a few pounds to spend. We had a couple of bottles of whisky on that occasion as well, so we were very well equipped in the way of food and drink. Of course, we weren't supposed to take whisky and rum in the tank with us but who was to know! There wasn't a lot of room, but if you were careful you could find places for it, even if it meant dropping a few shells out.

So we got to our rallying-point and we got out of the tank, because by that time the battle had gone on, and we were eating our sausages and discreetly drinking our whisky when an infantry runner came across and asked for the senior officer. The senior tank officer went over to the telephone, for the signallers had managed to lay a line and get it going. He came back saying that things had gone so well that day that they were running a fresh division up in motor lorries and cars, all the transport they could get, and we were going to start on what had been intended to be the *second* day's battle at two o'clock. Of course, they couldn't get fresh tanks up, so we had to carry on. We were rather enjoying ourselves so we didn't mind carrying on.

Tom Cantlon, waiting on the same line, would have sold his soul for a swig of Nick Lee's whisky, or even for a drop of water. For the infantry, the heat, the dust and the discomfort of mouths parched dry with excitement was almost the worst part of the battle. By twelve o'clock most water bottles were empty, and although the rations were already on their way it would be some time before they got there. All along the consolidated line, flares were burning. The Allied aircraft, which on that day almost had the sky to themselves, were taking back reports of the positions the troops had reached. The guns were already on the move. Looking back from the crest of the ridge Lieutenant Witherow could see them moving forward with the transport wagons close behind. Seeing the exposed positions which the Allies had so triumphantly vacated just a few hours before, he could hardly believe that they had existed for so long under the nose of the enemy.

The infantrymen who in the confusion had become detached from their own particular units took advantage of the respite to try to rejoin them. Tom Cantlon, meeting up with a group of KRRs, was amazed when one said to him, 'Your officer's looking for you, Tommy-boy.' He was also delighted to discover that Lieutenant Harrison was still alive, for he remembered that water bottle full of blessed whisky. When he eventually found him taking possession of a German pillbox to set up Company Headquarters, Tom was too desperate even to salute. 'Got a drop in the bottle, sir?' he croaked, 'I'm gasping for a drink.'

'Not a drop, Cantlon. It's all gone, hours ago.'

Tom turned away gloomily and looked out through the now-silent gun slit of the captured pillbox, down to where the transport wagons could be seen making their way – oh so slowly – to the foot of the ridge, where the carrying parties waited to bring up the precious water.

In a shell-hole further along the ridge John Wilson and his platoon of the Durhams – now well beyond Hill 60 consolidating the second line of advance – looked up at an innocent cloud in the blue June sky, like thirsty men imagining a mirage in the desert, and hopefully spread a groundsheet to catch any raindrops it might condescend to bestow. The cloud sailed innocuously past. The platoon swore. 'By God', said Lance-Corporal Wilson, 'wherever I am, after this lot's over, if I want a smoke or a drink I'm going to make ruddy sure I'll have one.' Between them they had plenty of cigarettes, but with a parched tongue cleaving to the dry roof of your mouth, there was no comfort to be found even in a fag.

During the lull at about two o'clock Captain Greener was making his way back, for the job of the tunnelling companies had not finished when the mines exploded. They were specialists in dug-outs and fortifications, and it was their job to see that the German dug-outs were safe after the infantry had taken them. All morning he and his men had been following the troops of the Irish Division, checking the captured dug-outs for bombs and the booby-traps at which the Germans were so expert.

Captain M. Greener, 175 Tunnelling Coy., Royal Engineers

The Germans had a habit of booby-trapping anything. There might be a dug-out with a fireplace in it and a chimney, and in the chimney there would be a bomb. Or perhaps a revolver left on the table, and you'd pick that up and you would pull a pin out of a bomb. Some of the dug-outs had steps leading down into them, and you never went down without rolling something down those steps first because there could be a mine or a bomb under one of them, and if you trod on that step, up it went. They booby-trapped their dug-outs as a matter of course and kept everything disconnected while they were in them; but when they saw that something was happening and that there was a chance of their losing that position, they would connect them up again.

On that day at Messines we did find a few things, especially in the support lines further back, but they hadn't really had time to do much. However, it was our job to check them all, to neutralise anything that had been left in the way of bombs, and then to let the infantry know what dug-outs they could use and where was a good place for headquarters and that sort of thing. We went across with the Irish Division and we could have practically gone anywhere that day. The support line was no bother and the final objective was no bother, so by about two o'clock I was on my way back. It was my first chance to look at the crater that the mine had made, because we'd been told not to go near it on the way across. Even later in the day we weren't allowed to go right into it because of the gas – the poisonous fumes from the explosive. But we had a very good look at it. The damage of a mine of that size on the surrounding trenches has to be seen to be believed. It was terrific. Everything had gone, certainly within a hundred yards of the lip of the crater. It was an absolute shambles. Some of these concrete pillboxes had been turned right over. Scores of tons they weighed and they'd been tossed up in the air, foundations and all, and turned upside down.

The Times, *Monday, 11 June 1917.*
The attack was so successful everywhere and the resistance was so smothered by the weight of our assault that the experiences of really hard fighting were very few. The New Zealanders seem to have had, perhaps, as formidable a part of the line as any, with the village of Messines itself as the chief objective.

The German guns against them were apparently quicker in getting to work and less helpless than on some parts of the front of attack, and the New Zealanders had to go through heavy shelling.

Detached from the guns to go forward as a signaller-observer with the infantry, it was Bert Stokes' first experience of an infantry battle. And he was in this hottest sector of all.

Gunner B. O. Stokes, No. 25038, 13th Battery, 3rd Brigade, New Zealand Field Artillery

We went over with the second line of the first wave of infantry, up and over the sandbags from the trenches in front of Ploegsteert Wood. I was so stunned by the spectacle of the explosions, and the tremendous din that was going on from the guns and machine-guns as we ran across No Man's Land – from shell-hole to shell-hole, through barbed wire and ditches – that we'd gone possibly a hundred yards before I realised what was happening. Soon we came to a concrete dug-out, and I was just about to walk on past it when one of the infantry boys waved me back. He disappeared for a moment and then, while we were all standing there trying to get our breath, we saw him dragging out a German machine-gun, all by himself. At the same moment a dozen Germans appeared, as meek as you like, all with their hands up crying '*Kamerad*'. All except two of them. They rushed at our officer, Mr Jones, both of them with rifles. He raised his revolver and shot them, one after the other, quite calmly.

In spite of his months on Hill 63 feeding the guns with the shells that hammered into the German positions a few hundred yards away, these were the first Germans that Bert Stokes had seen. But there was no time to stand and stare. As the infantry advanced, on went the signallers with them, rolling out the heavy yards of telephone cable as they went.

Now the German dead lay thick on the ground, and right at Bert's feet there was a feeble movement. A German boy lay face-downwards with a great red stain spreading across the back of his grey tunic. His frightened face turned and looked up as the big New Zealander approached. Bert stopped and knelt down beside him. As he turned him and propped him up with an arm round his shoulders, looking into the boy's grey dirt-streaked face, Bert was shocked out of his excitement. He had noted with almost clinical detachment the limp bodies of the German dead flung all around like rag dolls; now, looking down at this boy, for the first time in years he felt like crying. All he could do was to give him a drink. The German soldier drank thirstily from the water bottle but as Bert tried to lower him back to the ground the boy clutched at his legs, crying and pleading.

'I can't stay with you, matey, I *can't*. I've got to get on, see? They'll come and get you, honest they will.'

He turned to pick up the heavy roll of cable and the boy tried to crawl after him. 'The ambulance men will see to you, they're coming up behind us.'

Bert Stokes plunged on into the heat and the dust, hoping that he was right.

Gunner B. O. Stokes, No. 25038, 13th Battery, 3rd Brigade, New Zealand Field Artillery,

Our artillery barrage was about 500 yards in front of us and hung like a curtain. We pushed on towards Messines and before long were on the right of it. The country we had passed over was ploughed up terribly. Nothing but shell-holes and it was very warm and dusty. Now the Hun dead were lying in every direction and this makes you realise what war really means, especially when one also sees our own dead lying there. But so far our casualties seemed to be fairly light with not a great many killed in the initial stage, mostly wounded. We could see our lads pushing on in front of us and we kept following up, but we were now finding it much harder. It was a case of shell-hole to shell-hole as the enemy shells were beginning to stream over. Many times shells lobbed a little too near and you could feel the blast of the explosions rippling over you.

We reached our destination and ran a wire to a shell-hole where we decided to stop. It was as good a place as any. The 'Dinks' (New Zealand Rifle Brigade) were holding our front line in Unbearable Trench about a hundred yards ahead of us. This trench had been our first objective and the boys were digging in for all they knew. We were now about 800 yards past Messines to the right. We established a communication with our group and began to send through messages.

At the other end of the front, the old drive which had led up to the White Château in the days before the war was called the Damstrasse. It was known to be strongly fortified by the Germans and it had received particular attention from the long-range artillery before the battle. This was the second objective of the 41st Division, which included Cantlon of the King's Royal Rifle Corps, Lee of the Tanks, and Fagence of the Queen's Royal West Surrey Regiment. Tom Cantlon had stopped with his battalion at the first objective and now, having captured it, they became the support-line troops as the fresher forces of the second wave passed through them to take the next objective.

On top of the ridge the KRRs dug in furiously, while the Engineers hauled materials up the slope and started digging communication trenches. The shelling was heavy, so they wore their tin hats. But the June sun was hot. The REs drove the bayonets of their rifles into the ground, hung their tunics on to the butts, and worked in shirtsleeves.

Far ahead Victor Fagence was advancing with his battalion.

Private V. E. Fagence, No. 10081, 11th Btn., Queen's Royal West Surrey Regiment

I remember crossing the Damstrasse, which had been considerably smashed up by our shell-fire. There were scores of dead Germans strewn around; some of the bodies were in grotesque positions but we had no time to stop and look. We were ordered to dig in about a hundred yards beyond, so we hurried on and reached the position in which we were to dig our front-line trench. It didn't matter how tired you were. You dug as fast as you could, because it was a matter of life or death to get some protection against the enemy shell-fire. We soon had a trench about three or four feet deep and that gave us a certain amount of shelter. By now we were all absolutely parched, not just with the long advance and the warmth of the day, but with the smell of cordite and the dust. But we knew that there would be some sort of a dump in the rear, so one of our officers ordered me to go back and fetch a couple of two-gallon petrol tins filled with water. I ran back, found the dump, picked up a tin in each hand and started to go back to our new trench. On my way back and over to my right I saw one of our men sitting on the parapet of a trench with his back towards the enemy. The German shells were falling and exploding all about, everyone who was on the move was dodging hither and thither to try to avoid the explosions, and I couldn't keep my eyes off this chap. He just sat there as calm and composed as anything in the middle of all this. It seemed so bizarre and so odd that he should be sitting back there instead of being up forward with the others that I dodged my way across, through the shell-holes, to see what it was all about. As I got nearer I saw that his face was very pale, and as I got up to the trench I could see why. The poor fellow was stone dead. His right leg had been completely severed between the knee and the thigh by a large shell splinter. It was lying there, all jagged, in the bottom of the trench and all his blood had poured out from the stump of his leg over it. There was nothing I could do for him. I hurried back with my two tins of water and reported it to the officer. He sent an NCO and a stretcher-bearer back. It was too late to help him, of course, but they were able to get his identity discs and paybook and anything else he had on him to send home.

Having accompanied the troops beyond the Damstrasse, the early after-noon had passed as successfully, and for the crews of *Iron Rations* and *Revenge* as enjoyably, as the morning. They were high on excitement.

Corporal A. E. Lee MM, No. 32198, A Co., Tank Corps

At the Green Line, the infantry started digging in and we patrolled in front until they were reasonably well consolidated, and then we had a consultation. We got out of the tanks, the two whole crews, *Iron Rations'* and ourselves. What shall we do now? We did have the choice. Our job was done, so we could have gone back, but we felt we hadn't had enough excitement; so off we went into what was still German territory, shooting at everything we could see.

About five o'clock we came up to a field. There was a farmhouse in the middle of it and behind that a wood, and all of a sudden machine-gun fire started spurting from this farmhouse. We hadn't realised until then that it was a strongpoint, but we'd practised manoeuvres of this kind so often that we knew exactly what to do. We went left and *Iron Rations* went right and we started attacking the farmhouse from both sides. Well, after about half a dozen shells we must have hit something inflammable in the farmhouse, perhaps some petrol cans or some small-arms ammunition. Flames started belching out of one of the windows and to our absolute amazement we suddenly saw all these Jerries streaming out of the back door. There must have been two or three hundred of them, and they just bolted and ran and made for this wood about a hundred yards away. We both swung half-right, both tanks, and started firing at them in crossfire. Very few of them made it to the wood.

When the resistance had finished we turned away. We were get-ting pretty low on ammunition and low on petrol too. We'd pene-trated about five miles into enemy territory, so we decided we'd better make for home.

At just about this time, 2nd Lieutenant Jimmy Naylor had almost given up hope of getting 'home'. He'd been on the go all day long (and most of the night before) but he didn't have the faintest idea whether or not his efforts had been of the slightest use. He'd been sent up with the infantry to observe the situation and he had certainly done his best to make sense of what was going on – noting the positions of the infantry, so far as that was possible in the confusion of the fighting, and reconnoitring suitable places to which the guns could move up.

The trouble was that he hadn't been able to find any means of getting messages back to Battalion Headquarters. Five of them had started off at daylight – Jim Naylor, a Canadian subaltern, two telephonists and a runner. The job of the telephonists was to run wires out to certain points on the ridge and establish communication with Battalion Head-quarters. The runner would then go ahead with the officers, and when necessary would run back to the telephones with their messages. In case the system broke down, the Canadian officer, McKenzie (on loan to the 36th Ulster Division), also carried a basket containing two homing pigeons.

The system did break down. Very early on, McKenzie's telephonist was killed outright by a shell splinter. Then the runner was struck by a machine-gun bullet. The remaining telephonist simply disappeared. One moment he was there, the next he was nowhere to be seen. Naylor and McKenzie split up.

2nd Lieutenant J. W. Naylor, Royal Field Artillery

I got precious little information, I'm afraid. All I got was just enough to justify my going forward. I was able to report that there were short battles going on, hand-to-hand fighting. I did what I'd been asked to do, which was not very much, and that was the end of that. Then I tried to get back to the HQ dug-out in the line. The German artillery had pulled itself together by then and had opened up on our lines, so I was travelling through fire, with shells coming down all over the place. I heard it coming, the one that got me. I remember I threw my arms over my head. I felt a thump as a great clod of earth hit me, and that was the last I knew.

All day, Jimmy Naylor lay unconscious at the foot of the ridge. At dusk, as the reliefs were making their way up to the new line to relieve the battle-weary troops, he came round. To his delight, he found that he was able to move, to stand, even to walk, though it was a painful journey, that last half-mile over rough country to the HQ dug-out.

He reported to Colonel Simpson, gave his somewhat out-of-date infor-mation and struggled down to the advanced dressing-station, to face an-other excruciating hour while an RAMC Colonel dug and probed about in his head and neck and extracted eighteen small pieces of shrapnel, each the size of half a pea. The stinging antiseptic was dabbed on and the wounds dressed.

'That's the best I can do,' said the Colonel. 'But I think you'd better get on down to the casualty clearing station.'

Naylor wouldn't hear of it. 'I'd rather not, sir. I'll be all right when I've had a bit of a sleep.'

'Well, you'd better lie down here for a while.' The Colonel was a kind-hearted man of an age to have sons not much younger than Jimmy. 'I'll tell you what, my lad, there's a thing here called a medical comforts chest, and a colonel is allowed to open this chest and give a chap anything that he asks for, so what would you like?'

'Anything, sir?'

'Anything, old chap!'

'I'd love a bottle of Guinness, sir.'

'Then you shall have it.' Sitting in the field dressing-station – his head still spinning with the noise of the battle, his ears filled with the low moans of the badly wounded as they lay waiting to be carried out of the line – pale and dirty, feeling distinctly the worse for wear, Jimmy Naylor sat drinking his Guinness and enjoyed it as he'd never enjoyed a drink before.*

That evening, far to the south, soldiers from miles around had poured into the camp at Limencourt to attend a concert. It was a rather special concert, for Harry Lauder was the guest star. The majority of his audience had not yet heard the news of the victory in Flanders, for it would not be officially reported until the next day. But Harry Lauder had heard about it unofficially, for he had dined in the officers' mess. He made a last-minute addition to his programme and provided the troops with an appropriately rousing Grand Finale.

> When the fighting is over, and the war is won,
> And the flags are waving free,
> When the bells are ringing,
> And the boys are singing
> Songs of victory,
> When we all gather round the old fireside,
> And the old mother kisses her son,
> A' the lassies will be loving a' the laddies,
> The laddies who fought and won.

---

* McKenzie returned four days later after he had been reported 'missing'. He was completely unscathed and brought back valuable information. When he was asked why he had not sent it back by carrier-pigeon, he replied, 'Pigeons? I ate 'em!'

The troops liked it. Lauder's own son, Captain John Lauder of the Ist Battalion Argyll and Sutherland Highlanders, had been killed at the front six months before.*

In the Ypres sector the long day of battle was drawing to a close, but the guns still rumbled and the shells still roared overhead. Tomorrow the enemy would have rallied his depleted forces and would be certain to launch a counter-attack. Where the fighting had been hardest, fresh troops marched up to take over the new front lines, now well beyond the ridge.

The 11th Battalion of the Prince of Wales' Own West Yorkshire Regiment marched wearily out. It was a long plod in the dark, back to Battersea Farm. They were too exhausted, they had left too many mates behind on Hill 60 to feel like rejoicing. They only wanted to sleep. Jim Todd was ravenous. Back in the cellar dug-out at Battersea Farm someone had left a jar of jam and a half-empty tin of condensed milk on the box that served as a table. Jim attacked them with a dirty spoon and scraped and scraped until there wasn't a morsel left. It wasn't the ideal menu, but it would do. For years he was to remember the uncanny quiet of the cellar, lit by one flickering candle. Levey's gramophone still stood open, just as he had left it twenty-four hours ago. Jim wound it up and lifted the needle on to the record that still lay on the turntable.

> *At seventeen he falls in love quite madly*
> *With eyes of tender blue,*
> *At twenty-four he gets it rather badly*
> *With eyes of a different hue,*
> *At thirty-five . . .*

They were all gone. Porter, dead. Wood, dead. Hobday, dead. Miller, dead. Knowles, dead. Ostler, dead. Seven other officers wounded. Levey's right leg blown off.†

> *. . . you'll see him flirting sadly*
> *With two or three or more.*
> *When he fancies he is past love*
> *It is then he meets his last love*
> *And he loves her as he's never loved before.*

* Captain J. Lauder is buried in Ovillers Military Cemetery near Albert.
† Levey at first appeared to be recovering but later had to have his other leg removed and died of complications. The officers who died are buried in one grave, Plot 7, Row N, Grave 5, in Railway Dugouts Cemetery, Zillebeke.

In London the cast of *The Maid of the Mountains* took curtain after curtain at the end of its 200th performance. Chattering and laughing, the audience filed out of the theatre bound for home or for supper at the Criterion. In the darkened streets newsboys were already crying the early editions of the morning newspapers. 'Great victory at Messines! Read all about it! Great victory at Messines!'

Part 2

The Interlude

Chapter 6

To Field-Marshal Sir Douglas Haig from His Majesty the King:

> I rejoice that, thanks to thorough preparation and splendid cooperation of all arms, the important Messines Ridge, which has been the scene of so many memorable struggles, is again in our hands. Tell General Plumer and the Second Army how proud we are of this achievement, by which in a few hours the enemy was driven out of strongly entrenched positions held by him for two and a half years.

King George V had wisely waited until the expected German counter-attacks had been launched and had failed before sending his congratulatory telegram to his Commander-in-Chief in the field. On Saturday, 9 June the message was despatched, and on the same day the King had another pleasant duty to perform. The Yanks had at last arrived, or at least a contingent of the vanguard had arrived, and their chief, Lieutenant-General Pershing, went with his staff to Buckingham Palace to receive the royal welcome. These Americans of the vanguard were regular soldiers, and it would, of course, be impossible for America to mobilise, train and despatch a large, effective army to the battlefields of Europe for many months to come. But by next year the Americans would be in Europe adding the full force of their manpower and materials to the war effort.

If David Lloyd George could have called a moratorium on the war until that happy day arrived, he would gladly have done so. But he had Haig to contend with and Haig had other ideas. A campaign in Flanders had been part of the strategic plan which had been drawn up early in the war, and now, flushed with the success of Messines, Haig was more than ever convinced that it was the right course of action to take. His motives seemed to himself to be beyond dispute. A part of the French army in the south was in a state of mutiny, and a campaign which would concentrate the German effort in Flanders would take the heat off the French and give them time to recuperate. It would also take the heat off the Russians, far away to the east, for revolution had broken out, the old military structure was gone and, faced with the might of the German assault, the

Russian armies under the weak provisional government were teetering towards collapse.

But most of all, Haig wanted to make a resounding breakthrough out of the salient and beyond, and then swing his armies northwards in a circular movement towards the coastline. There they would bombard the ports of Ostend and Zeebrugge in an operation which would coincide with a simultaneous attack from the sea. Once the ports had been captured the Germans would no longer be able to use them as U-boat bases, the disturbing shipping losses would drop dramatically and the enemy would be so worn down and demoralised that collapse might swiftly follow. It seemed to Haig that, as surely as day must follow night, the second stage of his long-planned Flanders offensive must follow the triumph of Messines.

On 17 June, Haig travelled to London to attend a meeting of the War Cabinet in the confident expectation of receiving its blessing.

The salient had appeared on the maps as roughly the shape of the letter S in reverse – the bulging top sector running from Boesinghe round Ypres to Hill 60, and the bottom bulge running from Hill 60 round to Messines. Now that the Germans had been shrugged from the shoulder of high ground south of Ypres, the lower bulge had been straightened out. Had any members of the War Policy Committee noticed that the salient had now assumed the form of a question mark, they might have been struck by the symbolism, for in their view a question mark hung over the whole future of the campaign in Flanders. The first meeting with the Cabinet took place on the morning of 19 June and from Haig's point of view it was a disaster, for it was not so much a meeting as a grilling. They bombarded him with questions – Prime Minister Lloyd George, Bonar Law, Lord Curzon, Lord Milner, General Smuts and General Robertson. Even the Secretary to the War Cabinet, Colonel Hankey, had made some pertinent points. It would be difficult to decide which of them was the most pessimistic. Haig put his case with all the force he could muster, but he got nowhere and at one o'clock he departed, disgruntled and upset.

The mood of the country had changed. It was the 312th day of the third year of the war, and there was precious little left of the spirit of flag-waving enthusiasm that had swept through the country in 1914. There had been too many tales of the blood-bath at the front, too many men returning shattered in mind and body, too much scrutinising of the long closely-printed casualty-lists published daily in the press, too many blinds drawn in homes throughout the land, too little progress, too few victories, and too little hope of a speedy end to the war and all its horrors.

And in London, at least, the war had arrived on the doorstep. There were frequent Zeppelin raids, and public fury had been aroused when children were killed by a bomb dropped in the East End of London earlier in the week. On 20 June they were given a mass funeral at Poplar Parish Church and it was followed by a public meeting to demand reprisals.

While it was going on, Haig was again confronting the War Cabinet at Downing Street. Lloyd George, correctly gauging the public mood, had drawn up a memorandum which he had presented to Haig setting out his considered objections to the plan of attack. They ranged from the foolhardiness of proceeding without the whole-hearted support of the French (which they were obviously, at that moment, incapable of giving), to his doubts that the army could break out of the salient and make the advance of thirteen miles that would bring Ostend within range of its guns. He reminded Haig that in four months of bitter fighting on the Somme, the scene of the last 'summer campaign', it had only been possible to advance *seven* miles, and that those seven miles had been soaked with the blood of the largest number of casualties ever recorded by any army anywhere. Too many battles had already been fought for limited objectives which, putting it bluntly, were of little strategical importance. The Somme, Vimy Ridge, and even, he added courageously, Messines. But, first and foremost, Lloyd George feared that more heavy losses of men in yet another inconclusive battle would have 'disastrous effects on public opinion'. How could the War Cabinet gamble with lives 'merely because those who are directing the war can think of nothing better to do with the men under their command'? Surely it would be better by far to mark time until the Americans were ready and the French had recovered.

Although Haig had marshalled his arguments and had convinced himself of their worth, he might well have had to bow to the War Cabinet, against his own better judgement, had it not been for a dramatic development. The First Sea Lord, Admiral Jellicoe, dropped what Haig himself described as a bombshell. He stated categorically that shipping losses, due to enemy submarines, had been so enormous that unless the ports of Ostend and Zeebrugge could be captured the war could not continue. His exact words were, 'There is no good discussing plans for next spring – we cannot go on.' ★

The Cabinet was shaken. Most of its members, including Lloyd George, secretly believed that the First Sea Lord was exaggerating the situation. But nevertheless he had put a doubt into their minds. They all went off to

★It was an unfounded argument for two reasons. Firstly, the shipping losses, which had indeed reached worrying proportions, were, thanks to the convoy system, showing signs of diminishing. Secondly, the submarines were mainly operating from German ports. There were only a few submarine bases on the Belgian coastline.

think it over. The following day, 21 June, there was another meeting and another clash between Haig and Lloyd George, about which Haig later huffily wrote:

> Lloyd George made a long oration, minimising the successes gained and exaggerating the strength of the enemy. His object was to induce Robertson and myself to agree to an expedition being sent to support the Italians. It was a regular lawyer's effort to make black appear white! He referred with a sneer to my optimistic views.

But Lloyd George was wavering. Finally, it was agreed that the French government should be sounded out as to what, if any, support they would be able to give to the proposed offensive. In the meantime Haig was authorised to carry on with his preparations.

On 27 June, Haig returned to France well pleased with himself. His preparations, he was happily aware, were already well in hand. In his big staff-car, speeding inland from Boulogne to his headquarters at Montreuil, he passed convoy after convoy of lorries, and mile after mile of soldiers plodding northwards to Flanders.

A few days later another staff-car containing a still more illustrious occupant was travelling along the same road. King George V was on his way to visit his troops in the north and to see for himself the scene of their victory at Messines. They put on quite a show for him. Several battalions of men had spent several days rehearsing it. After a thorough inspection of the grisly hard-won ridge, which was still under intermittent shell-fire, the King returned to the back area where, for his edification, the battle was to be re-enacted. It was 6 July, exactly a month since some of these same men had been going up the line to take part in the battle. Now they were to do it all over again. But this time the gunfire was represented by harmless rolls of drums. The creeping barrage which had protected them as they advanced was represented by men on horseback holding flags, who went in front of the mock-attackers, just as the curtain of shells had gone in front of the real ones. Slowly the troops advanced behind it, across the sunny meadow, and dashed into the 'German' trench, where they naturally met with no opposition. On the contrary 'Germans' by the score tumbled out of the trench with their hands high above their heads. It was a singularly bloodless victory, and so gratified were the spectators that the troops gave a repeat performance.

In Flanders unprecedented numbers of men and weapons were pouring continuously into the back areas of the salient in preparation for the coming offensive, and beyond the salient itself the Germans too were busy. If the British War Cabinet still had doubts about where the blow should be struck, the Germans had none. Their observations and Intelligence reports told them all too clearly that it would be struck in Flanders.

Had Haig's plan for the next step of the offensive followed swiftly upon the victory of Messines, when the German forces were demoralised and shaken, then with the fine summer weather on their side the Allies might have had a very good chance of breaking out of the salient and pushing on to capture the Channel ports. Tactically Haig's plan was sound. Whether such a theoretical victory at the extreme northern tip of the extended Western Front would have had any effect on the outcome of the war is debatable. But while the politicians argued in London and the armies basked in the afterglow of victory, and while the commanders played at soldiers with their monarch, the fine summer weather was slipping by. Already a month had passed since the capture of the Messines Ridge and almost another month was to elapse before the second stage of the offensive was launched. Through the long summer days, battalions of German engineers toiled and sweated in the sun, building more and more strongpoints and concrete pillboxes, until they stood like tombstones in a graveyard all over the slopes that surrounded the salient. They believed that they were working against time. In fact, they had time and time to spare.

Around the salient and on the newly captured territory beyond the Messines Ridge, the troops were still holding the line. There the shelling and fighting had hardly diminished. But in the back areas, where hundreds of thousands of men had been gathered in preparation for the coming offensive, the soldiers of Great Britain, her Empire and her Allies were virtually on holiday.

Chapter 7

For most of June and July the sun burned high and hot. The fine weather was broken only by occasional thunder storms that rolled and crashed across the plain and temporarily turned the trenches into streaming torrents. But most of the troops thronging the back areas between Ypres and the coast in the hot midsummer of 1917 suffered no more inconvenience than that of having a football match rained off.

In fact, there were football matches galore. There were field days and horse shows. There were sports; and battalion, regimental and divisional sports days where the honours were hotly contested. As more and more battalions poured into the sector, as farmlands almost disappeared under acres of burgeoning canvas, and pigs made room for men in unsavoury requisitioned barns from Bailleul to Brielen, the fever of sporting competition was whipped up by officers who realised that training could not be carried on for much more than half the day and that the troops had to be kept occupied for the other half.

There was leave, too, for as many men as could be spared, and half a dozen trains a day left Poperinghe, bearing thousands of delighted Tommies cheering and yelling from the windows. The nurses, from the tented hospitals along the line, laughed and waved as the trains went by, before turning back to their wards and the grim duties of every day. For those who couldn't go on leave there was 'rest'.

Gunner B. O. Stokes, No. 25038, 13th Battery, 3rd Brigade, New Zealand Field Artillery

We've moved to Westhoff Farm for a rest. The whole 3rd Brigade was there. We made ourselves comfortable, but as to rest, well, I can hardly say it was that. Certainly it is a rest from the line, but Westhoff is neither out of the line or in it. It's just far enough back to say you are behind the lines and yet not out of reach of the Hun shells. Then again, when you are resting like this all the officers are here too. When the guns are in action nearly half the officers are with them. Now we have them here, all very efficient and busy trying to find

plenty to keep us occupied, so there's plenty of red tape and regimental activity. During our stay at Westhoff a chap is continually polishing boots, buttons, bandoliers, and then there's the never-ending job
of caring for the harness. What a job! Just as if we were back in camp
in New Zealand or England. I prefer it to be a bit rafferty, such as it is
when we are at the guns. At Westhoff we are not left alone for two
minutes. That's the objection to these rests. Otherwise it's a good
spell away from action.

The New Zealanders grumbled but put up with the discipline. With
the Australians, it was quite a different matter. They didn't have the least
intention of being pushed around and they did their best to make sure
that nobody else was pushed around either.

On the march north to the salient the 10th Royal Fusiliers were given a
few days rest at Strazeele. Their quarters were not particularly attractive:
some of the men were under canvas in a field, the officers had set up
headquarters in a farmhouse and the rest of the men were put up in barns
and outbuildings. Charlie Miles, with his fellow runners and the Battalion
Signals Section under Sergeant William Read, was allocated a lodging in
the upper storey of a barn. To be more precise it was a shelf, reached by a
ladder, which was normally used for storing hay. These humble quarters
were something of a comedown for the 10th Royal Fusiliers, for it was
the Stock Exchange Battalion.

In the early days of recruiting, fired by collective enthusiasm and the
War Office recruiting gambit that pals who joined up together would not
be separated, large groups of men had joined up *en bloc*. They came from
every level of society. In the north the men of whole streets, or even small
towns, had joined up together in one glorious and exciting gesture that
had turned bitterly sour during the slaughter on the Somme the year
before. The terrible telegrams were frequently delivered to almost every
house in a particular district, and in the course of an hour whole towns
were plunged into mourning. There were battalions composed of neigh-
bours, of workmates and also of more exclusive brotherhoods. By some
administrative mystery, when Charlie Miles and two of his mates had
gone along to enlist at the recruiting office in Gray's Inn Road in London,
they were enrolled in the Public Schools Battalion. This was a matter
which only came to light when Charlie had his first interview with his
Commanding Officer, who made a point of greeting each new recruit
personally. He never forgot the conversation:

'Ah, Miles, isn't it? Delighted to welcome you. What school did you go
to, my boy?'

'Johnson Street, sir.' The CO received this information with a puzzled look. 'Oh – er . . . who was your tutor?'

'Tutor, sir?'

'Your tutor at . . . er . . . sorry, what school did you say it was?'

'Johnson Street, sir. In the East End of London. Near to where I live, sir.'

The Colonel was taken aback for the merest fraction of a second. Then he pushed back his chair, stood up, and smiling and nodding stretched out his hand to clasp Charlie's. 'I'm delighted, Miles, delighted to welcome you to the battalion!'

Charlie, who was not a fool, but knew his place, was highly gratified. He had spent a happy time with the battalion and was not in the least put out when the entire strength, with the exception of himself and the two others who had enlisted with him, was sent back from France to officers' training units in England. He thought that was quite as it should be. The casualties among infantry officers had been catastrophic, and where else was officer material to be found if not in the ranks of the public schools? Nevertheless, it had accorded him some mild amusement when the three remaining members of the battalion were drafted into the equally illustrious ranks of the Stock Exchange Battalion. After three years in the Army, Charlie had perfected the art of taking things as they came.

The same could not be said for the Australians who were encamped on the other side of the road from the 10th Royal Fusiliers at Strazeele. The Tommies were simultaneously shocked and impressed by their casual attitude to war – or at least to the Army. It could hardly be right for Aussie privates to address their Commanding Officer as 'Jack', but the Fusiliers heard them do so with their own ears. For their part, the Aussies were equally disapproving of certain rites observed by the 10th RFs.

Private C. Miles, No. 7322, 10th Btn., Royal Fusiliers

The Colonel decided that he would have a full dress parade of the guard mounting. Well, the Aussies looked over at us *amazed*. The band was playing, we were all smartened up, spit and polish, on parade, and that happened every morning. We marched up and down, up and down. The Aussies couldn't get over it, and when we were off duty we naturally used to talk to them, go over and have a smoke with them, or meet them when we were hanging about the road or having a stroll. They kept asking us, 'Do you like this sort of thing? All these parades, do you want to do it?' Of course we said, 'No, of course we don't. We're supposed to be on rest, and all the time we've got to posh up and turn out on parade.' So they looked at us a bit strangely and said, 'OK, cobbers, we'll soon alter that for you.' The Australians didn't approve of it because they never polished or did anything. They had a band, but their brass instruments were all filthy. Still, they knew how to play them.

The next evening, our Sergeant-Major was taking the parade. Sergeant-Major Rowbotham, a nice man, but a stickler for discipline. He was just getting ready to bawl us all out when the Australians started with their band. They marched up and down the road outside the field, playing any old thing. There was no tune you could recognise, they were just blowing as loud as they could on their instruments. It sounded like a million cat-calls. And poor old Sergeant Rowbotham, he couldn't make his voice heard. It was an absolute fiasco. They never tried to mount another parade, because they could see the Aussies watching us from across the road, just ready to step in and sabotage the whole thing. So they decided that parades for mounting the guards should be washed out, and after that they just posted the guards in the ordinary way as if we were in the line.

And that wasn't the end of it with the Australians. The rations used to come up and it was all divided out, a loaf to so many men, and in the barn we began to wonder where our bread was disappearing to. Well, we knew we wouldn't steal from each other, so it was a mystery. One morning we'd got up and were filing out of the barn after reveille to go for a wash, when there was a great rustle in the pile of straw in the bottom part of the barn, and two men appeared. They were Australian soldiers and they'd been hiding out there, and on this particular morning they made the mistake of coming out too soon. Well, *then* we knew where our bread had been going to. They didn't call it deserting, they said they'd just gone for a rest because they were tired of the people over the way. Sergeant Read was in a bit of a dilemma. He should have reported them, of course, but he was a good bloke, a very good NCO. He simply said to them, 'Right, lads, that's your last night's rest here. Out you go!' 'Oh, come on, cobber,' they said, 'have a heart!' 'Never mind the "cobber". Out you go,' he said. 'Do you see these stripes? Well, I've worked hard to earn these stripes. If I harbour you they go, and I'm not losing my stripes for anyone. Good enough, cobber?' So they took the point, and they just disappeared. We never knew what happened to them. As likely as not they just went back across the way.

Forty-eight hours later the 10th Royal Fusiliers were on their way to the salient. 25 June was a day of blazing heat, and it was hard going in full marching order with more than sixty-pounds' weight of kit on your back and your rifle slung on your shoulder. For Charlie Miles and the other runners it was somewhat easier, for they marched in front of the battalion wheeling their bicycles, and the beauty of that position was that their kit could be slung to their bikes. The runners were always in the vanguard. If it hadn't been for that, Charlie would never have disgraced himself.

He was the very first man in the line, on the off-side of the first row of runners as they marched four abreast up the road from Hazebrouck to Bailleul. His mate, Sid Smith, was on his right and from time to time they whistled or sang or talked. Mostly they just sweated and counted the kilometres as their feet began to swell and ache as they trudged over the rough *pavé*. The Colonel, the Adjutant and the senior officers clopped behind them on their horses, and the long line of marching men stretched far down the road at their backs. Suddenly there was the sound of clatter-ing hoofs and over the breast of the hill came an army limber travelling at an amazing speed, swaying dangerously from side to side and taking up most of the road. The team was galloping full tilt towards Charlie, and Charlie was badly scared. He stopped dead in his tracks and the battalion behind him had no alternative but to stop as well. It was an outrageous breach of march discipline, the whole battalion marking time except for Private Miles, who stood stock-still, transfixed. He was brought back smartly to reality by a blow across his back from the Adjutant's cane. 'Get on. Get on.' Charlie's humiliation was complete when the driver gained control of the runaway limber and a moment later trotted sedately past the 10th Royal Fusiliers, sufficiently in command of the situation to salute its commanding officer in the regulation manner by dropping his whip over the side. Charlie blushed scarlet. Sid Smith smirked and sneered under his breath.

But the day ended better than it had begun. The battalion, marching through Bailleul three miles ahead, smartened up to attention as they approached the town square, the band struck up, and as it played 'The British Grenadiers' Charlie Miles found himself leading the battalion past General Plumer. Behind streamed the thousand men of the battalion, eyes left as they passed the dais. At the very end of the column, mounted on two limbers, were the field kitchens, the chimneys of the boilers belching the savoury steam of the bully beef stew that had been simmering gently all the time the battalion was on the march. It was dished out in a field on the other side of Bailleul. There was plum duff as well and mugs of hot tea to wash it down, and a welcome stretch on the grass before the Fusiliers marched on to Dranoutre.

Dranoutre and the nearby village of Locre did not offer the legendary delights of Poperinghe, but in the rear of the salient there were worse places to be. There was the Frontier Café in Locre, which sold *vin blanc* at one franc a bottle, with the added attraction of a resident pianist. Paula was just seventeen, a cousin of the proprietor, and she was only too happy to entertain the soldiers who packed the café night after night. The snag was that her mother was there too. The piano was in a back parlour, and when the merry drinkers persuaded 'Mademoiselle' to play and crowded round the piano, Maman insisted that the door should always be kept open so that, between serving the drinks, she could keep an eagle eye on her daughter's virtue. Paula, with her short schoolgirl's skirt and her long hair tied back with a black satin bow, was in demand by everyone.

Less welcome was the presence of Marguerite, the six-year-old daughter of the house, who was everywhere in the café – clinging to khaki legs, sitting on khaki knees, begging illicit sips from the glasses of regiments of indulgent 'uncles' and picking up, parrotwise, some highly unsuitable English phrases. On the whole, Marguerite was an inhibiting presence and as the war went on she waxed and grew fat on the bars of chocolate which she was given as bribes to go away.*

The belle of Dranoutre was Victoria, who served in the local café and cut sandwiches in the YMCA on concert nights. The soldiers ragged and flirted with her mercilessly. At sixteen, Victoria blushed and giggled and didn't mind a bit. She had a soft spot for all the soldiers, but her particular favourites were the men of the balloons. The balloonists were regular habitués of the cafés at Locre and Dranoutre and their exploits were legion. If the Royal Flying Corps, buzzing in their fast, flimsy machines all over the sky above the salient, were the lords of the air, then the balloon boys swinging high in their baskets 600 feet above the earth were not far behind them in the glamour stakes. Time after time, the high crackle of machine-gun fire would draw the eyes of civilians upwards to the clouds in time to see a German aeroplane streaking off into the blue; the grey bubble of the balloon collapse and crumple; and two tiny white specks appear high above as the observers floated down under the canopies of their parachutes. The balloon boys basked in universal admiration and enjoyed not only office hours (for observations could not be made in the dark) which enabled them to lead a satisfactory social life, but during their working hours, from their vantage-points in the sky, they also enjoyed a grandstand view of the salient below.

Naturally they had to spend most of their time looking towards the

---

*Marguerite has had her revenge. Sixty years later, as the owner of the same café, she entertains a stream of old soldiers now anxious to enjoy her company and recall old times.

east, where the flashes of gunfire and the smudges of black smoke thrown up by exploding shells marked the semi-circle of the front line. It was the job of the balloon observers to plot the explosions and, if they could, to pin-point the location of the enemy batteries. But on quiet days there was time to look around. Away to the left a narrow ribbon of yellow beaches bordered the sea, but from the coastline in the west to the guns in the east the countryside had almost disappeared beneath the paraphernalia of the armies. Wherever you looked, there were crawling khaki columns, and great clouds of dust thrown up by the wheels of the limbers and wagons that moved in endless convoys along the roads. Camouflaged tents stretched as far as the eye could see across the meadows, among grey patches of huts that seemed to spring up overnight like mushrooms. The balloon observers saw the brown churned-up fields full of horses and transport lines; the fields of glistening white marquees – each marked with a red cross – which were the casualty clearing stations; great dumps of stores; aerodromes; wagon parks; and everywhere, on almost every open space, ant-like battalions of men swarming across the earth, training and practising, parading and exercising, as busy and disciplined as their hard-pressed officers could contrive. Looking down on the salient from 600 feet at the press of activity below, there seemed hardly room to place a pinhead between the swarming armies.

Yet, here and there, there was a cluster of green, a yard of hops, a field or so of crops or grazing land around a battered farmhouse that some long-suffering peasant farmer tilled and cursed and hung on to like grim death. Life had to go on, livelihood had to be won somehow, but it was not always easy. The civilians and the military, pursuing their very different objectives, did not always see eye to eye. Pastor van Walleghem committed his complaints to his diary:

15 June. It is truly painful to see how the English destroy the crops. There are so many bare fields around the village, and still it often happens that they set up camp on the cultivated fields, ignoring the abandoned ones adjoining. Many farmers have had their meadows taken away from them quite suddenly. I have thus known farmers who one day had sufficient fodder for a stable full of animals, and the next day not even enough for one goat. . . . If the farmer dares to complain, they only laugh at him and say he should not remain on his farm. Requests for compensation prove quite impossible, for if the complainant cannot indicate the unit to which the offenders belong, his claim cannot be considered. However, if he attempts to obtain the identity of the unit, he is accused of spying and told he has no right to go into such matters. Either way, he cannot win! . . . It is shocking the

way the potato fields have been pilfered by the soldiers. Two farmers have lost the whole crop. A third apprehends a soldier in the process of digging up some potatoes. The latter tells him that he has been sent by his officer. The farmer then seeks out the officer, who admits to this and simply adds, 'to pay after the war'. All the farmers of Dickebusch who have planted crops this year bitterly regret it. . . . Fresh troops have arrived on the farm of Cyriel Lamerant and have occupied the last remaining corner of grass, although there was ample space just beyond, where two batteries had just left. Also troops in the meadow of Remi Onraet. . . . Owing to the large number of horses and soldiers (and an Englishman is not happy with just a few drops), much water is consumed and has now become very scarce, in spite of the numerous basins and wells laid on by the Army.

The soldiers had their side of the story. Coming out of the line, or coming into the salient after many days' march on dusty roads, they badly wanted a bath. Hot baths were hard to come by in the salient, but it did not seem to the soldiers that an all-over wash, a shave, a clean-up in cold water ought to be classed as the height of unattainable luxury. Water (of which a little later there would be all too much) in the summer of 1917 was scarce. There had been a low rainfall and the Belgian owners of the wells were anxious to conserve what they had. The Tommies wanted water by the bucket, by the hundred buckets, and a couple of companies could drain a well dry in a scant hour of merry ablutions. So, with what they regarded as simple providence, a substantial number of Belgian farmers chained and padlocked the wells in the yards of their farms.

The Tommies were livid. They were dirty, they were lousy, they were uncomfortable; furthermore, they were here, in this benighted spot, risking, their lives (or about to risk them) to save 'plucky little Belgium'. If the 'plucky little Belgians' thought they could make a profit by charging them for a few splashes of water, they were very much mistaken. Convinced of the justice of their cause, the troops invariably resolved such disputes by simply shooting away the padlock and helping themselves. The only resort the Belgian farmer then had was to apply to 'Monsieur le Clams'. The lot of 'Monsieur le Clams', as the Belgians referred to the Army Claims Officer, was not an enviable one.

There were a dozen or so 'Messieurs le Clams' in Belgium, usually officers who were also linguists and had, therefore, been allocated the task of mediating between the sitting tenants of the salient and its unenthusiastic defenders.

Since 1877 it had been laid down by law that any damage done by the British Army in billets should be made good. It was almost impossible not to do damage in billets, for the troops were not only accommodated in camps but in farmhouses, barns, outbuildings and homes the length and breadth of the back areas.

The sympathy of 'Monsieur le Clams' tended to lie with the troops. After all, the civilians *were* being paid rent by the Army, not just for the billets but for the land which had been appropriated, and while the rent was not lavish it had been fixed high enough to cover at least some of the incidental and unavoidable damage. Of course, there were Tommies who, lurching back from a jolly post-pay-parade evening at the local *estaminet*, accidentally broke a bar of a farm gate, or a few window panes. There were Tommies who laid siege to the virtue of young daughters of the house. There was the odd one who felt sure that no one could possibly grudge him a few potatoes, dug up illicitly after dark, to supplement his ration of Maconochie's stew. There were Tommies who, believing that Madame was charging an extortionate price for the carefully-measured glasses of wine or cider that she would supply on application, awarded themselves their money's worth by drinking the barrel dry when her back was turned.

As almost every farmhouse did a brisk trade supplying coffee and fried eggs and chips to the men, and chickens, eggs and cream to the officers, the soldiers were convinced that the Belgians were making a huge profit out of the war. The Belgians themselves, looking gloomily at their spoiled crops, their trampled land, their ever-diminishing shell-pocked acreage of fields, doubtless considered that if they could make a few francs on the side it was no more than their due.

Day by day, the padre at Dickebusch passed judgement on the behaviour of the troops and recorded the verdict severely in his diary. One thing puzzled him. He could understand the disputes and even, on occasions, see both sides of an argument, but what he couldn't understand was the meaning of a certain two-syllable word which he heard hourly on the lips of soldiers wherever he met them:

> I have looked it up phonetically in my little English dictionary (fah-ke) and I find, to my surprise, that the word 'fake' means 'false, unreal or not true to life'. Why the soldiers should refer to us in this way is difficult to understand, and yet everywhere one hears them talk of 'fake Belgium' and 'fake Belgians'.

Meanwhile, across the length and breadth of the churned-up fields of 'fake Belgium', the soldiers worked and trained, grumbled and waited and, off duty, applied themselves to the business of enjoying themselves as best they could.

Chapter 8

Those who had a few francs to spare and were fortunate enough to get a pass would make for the nearest village. Even a few centimes to spend in an *estaminet* would buy a cup of coffee that you could nurse all evening, enjoying the sing-songs and the company. But there were always huddled groups left behind at camp whether they had money or not. They were the card players and the gamblers. Day after day, week after week, month after month, in and out of the line, whenever there was a moment to spare, the card players set up their schools. They played nap and pontoon, whist, bridge, poker and brag. The greasy, dog-eared rectangles of pasteboard were scrutinised, breathed over, dealt and redealt far into the night. The stakes were astronomical, and some lucky players were millionaires several times over. But no one ever expected to be paid. To the card players, the game was the thing. Card playing was officially discouraged; most officers turned a blind eye to it. In any case, the really serious gamblers preferred Crown and Anchor, and that was strictly forbidden.

Rifleman W. Worrell, No. 6905960 12th Btn., Rifle Brigade

The Crown and Anchor men were the kings. They were the men who sat with their bottles of *vin blanc* and treated the people around them. They were the men with the money. We were in bivouacs at Dawson's Corner, near Elverdinghe, and the 12th Battalion Crown and Anchor king there was a Pioneer Corporal. These blokes were usually chaps who were at Battalion Headquarters. Very few of the fighting troops ran the boards. The troops were there to be mugged. This Pioneer Corporal was a Lancashire man with an immense nose. He had two boards running when we were out of the line, and he would run one himself and he would employ somebody to run another. If one board lost its money, that was shut down immediately. Not that it often happened like that! Now and again we had a lucky streak – but not too often.

If you were unlucky at Crown and Anchor there was always the chance of winning a franc or so on a louse race, for lice were in plentiful supply. With thousands of men living in close and insanitary proximity, it was almost impossible to avoid becoming infested. 'Chatting' was an interminable occupation. All over the salient, in quiet periods, in the trenches and out of them, bare-torsoed soldiers could be seen sitting in the sunshine minutely examining their khaki shirts. The trouble was that the lice laid their eggs in the seams, so that no matter how hard you shook the shirt, no matter how many of the irritating pests you plucked off and cracked on your thumbnail, no matter how meticulously you washed, there was always a new generation ready to hatch out with the heat of your body as soon as you put the shirt back on again. The 'remedies' were almost as numerous as the pests themselves. Some soldiers favoured running a lighted candle up the seams, others turned their shirts outside in, in the hope of getting a few minutes' peace before the lice managed to penetrate to the other side of the coarse material. Disinfectant powder arrived by the hundredweight in parcels from home. Some methods were more drastic.

Rifleman W. Worrell, No. 6905960 12th Btn., Rifle Brigade

Every company had a sanitary man, and ours was called Dan. Dan, Dan, the sanitary man. Every sanitary man was called Dan, regardless of what his proper name was. We were in the reserve line at Ypres and it was fine warm weather and we were all very 'chatty'. Somebody had a brilliant idea. Dan was coming along as he always did with a can of creosote spray on his back, pumping it up and spraying the trenches and making them smell beautifully antiseptic. Why shouldn't we get our shirts sprayed as well? We wondered that nobody had thought of it before! So we pegged our shirts up and when Dan came along we asked him would he please spray our shirts, thinking that this would kill the nits. The whole of my section had our shirts beautifully sprayed. We left them in the sun to dry off and then later, of course, we had to put them on again, because we were on a carrying party up the line. They were very long, these army shirts, great long tails to them that you tucked well down into your trousers and between your legs.

Well, off we went on the carrying party at dusk. It was still a very warm evening, although it was dark, and we were carrying loads of wire stakes miles up the duckboards, sweating and straining all the way. It was a lively night for shelling, but it wasn't the shelling that worried us because, as we sweated, the creosote got into the pores under our arms and in all the tender parts of our bodies. Were we uncomfortable! We were on fire! When we got back, the whole of my section were walking bow-legged with our legs wide apart and our arms held up, we were so very, very sore. We got back to the reserve line and showed our Sergeant. 'We'll have to go sick,' we said. 'Look at us, blisters here and blisters there. You can't put a pinhead on us for blisters!'

We didn't get a bit of sympathy, and no chance of going sick either! The Sergeant had a good laugh. 'It serves you right,' he said, 'it serves you right for trying to be clean. You ought to be "chatty" like the rest of us.' And after that we were.

Lance-Corporal J. Wilson, No. 52764, 12th Btn., Durham Light Infantry

There were baths at Poperinghe and one or two other places, but with so many troops there it could be weeks before your turn came. So, when we were out of the line, one of our officers thought he'd fix things for us. He got a working party to dig a big hole in a meadow and filled it with water, just two or three inches of water, and we all stripped off and got in naked. Well, we didn't half jump about! He'd told the orderlies to tip disinfectant into the water. One minute we were sitting down in the 'bath' and the next we were all out dancing around like a bunch of naked dervishes. He fixed it all right. He nearly fixed us for good!

In Poperinghe the sugar refinery had been taken over and the legend DELOUSING STATION painted on the wall in letters two feet high, and there were also baths in the brewery.

Rifleman W. Worrell, No. 6905960, 12th Btn., Rifle Brigade

There were three huge vats in the brewery and between them there were planks. The first vat was full of hot, dirty, soapy water. The next one had hot water, not quite so dirty. The last one had cold water, fairly clean. You started at one end and you stripped off. You tied your khaki uniform up in a bundle and tied your boots to it and your cap. Your underclothes were taken away to the fumigator. Your khaki was also supposed to go in the fumigator, but it didn't usually do so. You went up and there were ropes across the vat, so you pulled yourself across on the rope to the other side, climbed out on to the next plank into the next vat, jumped in there, washed the worst of the dirt off, and then into the last vat. When you got out at the other end, you picked up a towel, wiped down and then looked around.

'Where's my hat?' It was the only way you could find your own bundle, with your hat and identity disc attached to it. Then you were issued with underclothes. If you were lucky you got some that nearly fitted you, but, of course, I was the wrong size for that and it would always happen to me that I got huge underwear. They were all Long Johns in those days and by the time I'd done them up they were right around my chest, and I'd also have to take about three folds in the bottom of the legs. That would be topped by a vest hanging down below my knees. On the other hand, a fellow who was a six-footer would be issued with a set so small that he could hardly get into it at all, so we had to swop around as best we could. Sometimes the language got pretty fruity. We had some laughs. The odd thing is that you forget the bad times. It's the happy memories, the silly things that stick with you – like prancing about in that ridiculous underwear.

Poperinghe was the Metropolis – the nearest thing to the bright lights that the blacked-out salient offered, and to the troops it seemed to offer everything. Affectionately they called it 'Pop'. Admittedly the long-range shells did fall there, but they fell mostly around the station, often just when troop trains were arriving or leaving. Irregular though the trains were, you could almost believe that Jerry had a time-table and sent his shells over accordingly. Sometimes a stray would fall on the town, but this did not happen often enough to scare away either the civilian population or the soldiers who flocked along the streets enjoying the varied delights of 'Pop'.

The officers thronged into the town as well, for in 'Pop' there was Skindles Hotel and officers' clubs where a man could write or read in peace, enjoy a reasonable meal and, if he were lucky enough to have a 24-hour pass, a decent night's sleep in a real bed. 'Pop' also had Talbot House (known by the gunners' signalling code as Toc H) where similar facilities could be enjoyed by anyone. It was run by the genial Reverend Tubby Clayton on democratic lines which were particularly appreciated by officers who had friends or brothers in the ranks, and by rankers who had friends or brothers who were officers.

Just across the Gasthuiststraat from Toc H was a shop much patronised by the troops. Oddly enough, it was an undertaker's. One of the windows on either side of the entrance still displayed the gloomy trappings of the funereal rites, but it was the goods displayed in the other window, constituting the sideline of Mr Schaballie, that attracted the Tommies. Early in the war they had practically cleaned out his stock of funeral candles, and he was quick to see that there was a good trade to be had in supplying their

Captain Martin Greener (*on the left*), who worked on the Hill 60 tunnels before
the Battle of Messines.

Left: Gunner Jason Addy, 4th Battalion, Tank Corps, of the crew of *Delysia*, which attacked at St Julien on 22 August.

Below: Lance-Corporal (later Quartermaster-Sergeant) Joseph Pincombe (*front row, fourth from left*), who tried to deliver the rations to the 1st Battalion, Queen's Westminster Rifles, when they were fighting for Glencorse Wood.

Above left: 2nd Lieutenant Jimmy Todd, 11th Battalion, Prince of Wales' Own West Yorkshire Regiment, who was the only officer of the battalion to emerge unscathed from the Battle of Messines.

Above right: 2nd Lieutenant Alfred Angel, 2/4th London Battalion, Royal Fusiliers, who lost an eye at St Julien and was ever after known as "Nelson".

Right: Captain Alan Goring MC, 6th Battalion, Yorkshire Regiment, one of the vanguard who made the crossing of the Steenbeek possible.

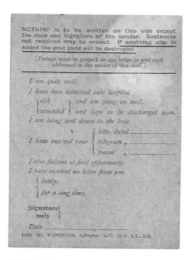

Above: Field Postcards crossed the Channel by the boat-load ... and postcards from home travelled to the field.

Left: 2nd Lieutenant Paddy King, 2/5th East Lancashire Regiment, who was cut off from his battalion for two days in the first abortive attack on Passchendaele, 26 October.

Above left: Private Victor Fagence, 11th Battalion, Queen's Royal West Surrey Regiment, who went over the top at the Battle of Messines.

Above right: Out of the line, postcards were on general sale. "France" to the Tommies meant anywhere on the Western Front.

Left: Rifleman George Winterbourne, 1st Battalion, Queen's Westminster Rifles, who was captured in the fighting at Glencorse Wood.

Above right: Private Charles Miles, 10th Battalion, Royal Fusiliers, who was a flyweight, and later a bantam-weight, boxer of great skill.

Above left: The aftermath of war: Charlie Miles and a legless friend in 1923.

Right: Private W. G. Bell MM (*extreme right*), 9th Battalion, Army Cyclist Corps, who did more labouring on working parties than cycling.

Above: Private Frank Hodgson (*back row, third from left*), a stretcher-bearer attached to the forward aid post at Tyne Cot during the battle for Passchendaele.

Right: Gunner Walter Lugg M M. On the first day of the battle (31 July) it took him eight hours to help his wounded friend a quarter of a mile back through the mud to the forward dressing-station.

Above left: Major George Horridge MC, 1/5th Lancashire Fusiliers, who was in support of one of the many fruitless attacks on the Frezenberg Ridge.

Above right: Private Harold Diffey, 15th (London Welsh) Royal Welch Fusiliers, who inadvertently captured a German prisoner, in a pillbox at Langemarck.

Right: Rifleman Tom Cantlon, 21st Battalion, King's Royal Rifle Corps, in hospital blues. He got lost with No. 3 Platoon on the way up to the Battle of Messines.

wants. So, in addition to candles, Mr Schaballie now stocked the solid methylated blocks that fuelled the tommy cookers; thick black Belgian tobacco; biscuits when they were obtainable; and assorted souvenirs, including the delicately-embroidered lacy postcards, that the Tommies loved to send home. Occasionally there were sweets and 'Café au Lait', a fairly expensive luxury much like coffee-flavoured condensed milk, which, added to hot water, produced a reasonably palatable drink. One particular consignment of souvenirs, dredged up from a box which had languished forgotten on a wholesaler's shelf since before the war, was snapped up by the Tommies and sold out in the space of a day. It consisted of a few dozen trashy metal brooches engraved with the name *Ypres*. They were sent off by the next post to mothers, sisters and sweethearts in England, not because of their beauty, but because the soldiers immediately recognised in them a subtle way of cheating the censor.

Now and again, there was an easy way round censorship. 'I am in the same place I was at Christmas,' one would write, or, 'I am in the place where Tom was wounded in 1915.' But if circumstances did not permit such subtleties the Tommies had to resort to more devious means:

2nd Lieutenant F. Kenchington, Royal Field Artillery

My own plan was to use the Field Service Postcard, which contained printed stereotyped messages, and you were only allowed to cross out those items which did not apply. You could not write anything except the name and address to which it was being sent. I calculated that the address side would not be scrutinised very closely and sent a card to Mr Y. P. Rees at my home address, where its significance was at once grasped. Later when we moved to 'Pop', another card to Mr P. O. Perring was equally successful.

In Britain field postcards arrived by the sack load, the boat load. A sergeant-major of the 13th (Service) Battalion, The Rifle Brigade, was astounded when an avalanche of postcards poured through the letter-box of his house in east London, where he was enjoying well-earned home leave. Every single man in his company had sent one. The messages varied but *Hope to be discharged soon* was a popular choice.

There was time for pranks in that summer of 1917, and for the young officers there was time too for tea parties, dances and even tennis parties with the nurses from the casualty clearing stations which were dotted about behind the lines. The three big ones around Proven were known facetiously as 'Mendinghem', 'Bandagehem' and 'Dosinghem'.

Sister Mary Pollock, Theatre Sister, 'Mendinghem', No. 46 Casualty
Clearing Station at Proven, Territorial Force Nursing Service

When the big pushes were on, the work went on day and night and it
was very hard going. Even when it was quiet we always had plenty of
casualties from shell-fire and gassing, but we got time off as well. We
were very much in demand with the officers, because there were
very few women around. It was the flyers that we liked best. Proven
was just up the road and we had aerodromes all around, and if you
were friendly with one of the boys and they went out on a flight at
night they used to say, 'Expect an envelope in the morning. I'll try
and drop one.' And we used to go to this field and they'd drop these
little weighted cellophane envelopes, flying fairly low, and there
would be a message in it. That's how they made their dates.

   We used to go to all the different officers' messes. We were very
snooty. We all kept to the officers. We used to go there and have
supper with them and play cards. For some reason we weren't supposed to dance, but we always did. They all had gramophones. There
would be at least one invitation to go to an officers' mess every day.
Of course, we couldn't all go at once, so the off-duty nurses took
turns. We had a very happy time in between the bad fighting. But we
needed it; we needed something just to keep our courage up.

   For the other ranks, excluded from the refined delights of socialising
with the nurses, there were the more robust pleasures of the cafés and
estaminets in Poperinghe. Night after night the Tommies crowded into
them, consuming huge quantities of eggs and chips (in the case of the
affluent colonial troops, up to nine eggs at a time) and *vin blanc* by the
gallon at one franc a bottle. It was poor thin stuff but its potency was
proved by the raucous roof-raising choruses that could be heard everywhere in Poperinghe as the evening went on. In these 'troops only' cafés,
inhibitions went to the wall.

Rifleman W. Worrell, No. 6905960, 12th Btn., Rifle Brigade

The cafés were our only opportunity of seeing anything of life. We
used to go into the Café des Alliés in Poperinghe. It was a popular
place because there was a little man with a squeeze-box there and he
knew all the right tunes to play. He'd picked them up from the troops
and some of them were pretty fruity. He'd start off very politely with
'Mademoiselle from Armentières' (and of course we had our own
words for that one) but the universal favourite was 'The Monk of

Great Renown', and, sooner or later, he got around to '*Après la guerre fini*':

> *Après la guerre fini,*
> *Soldat Anglais parti,*
> *Mademoiselle in the family way,*
> *Après la guerre fini.*★

In the streets outside the cafés the Military Police patrolled.

Private W. G. Bell, No. 4640, 9th Btn., Army Cyclist Corps

One of the cafés had a piano in it and I used to play a lot and amuse the lads. I was playing away and they were putting the glasses of *vin blanc* and *vin rouge* on the lid of the piano and I was drinking it down. I was all right while we were inside, but when turning-out time came and Mademoiselle said '*Allez*' it was a different matter. When I got outside into the air the road just started to go round and round and up and down. I remember staggering around, still singing. I was happy!

A couple of my mates got hold of me and took me back to the billet. I remember going up the wooden stairs into the loft among the hay, and I remember having a candle in the neck of a bottle, and I remember lying down, and drunk as I was I remember a voice shouting up the stairs, 'Put that light out.' I also remember saying, 'I'll put *your* light out if you come up here.' The next minute I was under arrest. It was the sergeant-major who had called up and he wasn't a man to stand any nonsense. He called out the guard. I got the fright of my life when I saw them standing there with fixed bayonets. I was marched up the road and thrown in the stable we used for the 'nick', and next morning I was up for orders. I had to go before the major. Drunk on active service. He gave me a real dressing-down, then he said, 'Since you are out at rest, I'll take a lenient view, otherwise I hope you realise it would be the extreme penalty.' I presumed that he meant 'shot at dawn'. Anyway, I was scared stiff. 'I'll give you the maximum,' he said. 'Twenty-eight days' First Field Punishment.'

First Field Punishment was no joke. It meant that you had to parade in full pack and go up and down the road at the double. Everything was done at the double. *About turn, left, right, left, right, about turn, left, right, left, right*. It was all done under the Military Police

---

★Words were fitted to a haunting tune which, many years later, became a 'hit' again with new words and a new title, 'Under the Bridges of Paris' ('*Sous les ponts de Paris*')

and it was hard going, because you had a full pack, tin helmet and all your stuff, sweating up and down the road. Then you took your pack off and it was up against the wagon wheel. They marched me into a field and twice a day I was strapped up against the wagon wheel of a General Service limber for an hour in the morning and an hour at night. My wife wrote out, 'What's happened? My money's stopped.' They did that. They stopped your pay and your wife's allowance immediately you went on to punishment. She went to our headquarters in London and asked why she wasn't getting her money. 'Your husband's been misbehaving himself,' they told her. There was nothing she could do about it. That was the worst of all for me. It was such a disgrace and it was terrible being strapped to the wheel of this limber. It wasn't so much that it was uncomfortable, though you did get hot and cramped, but I just felt such a proper poppy show. All the chaps looking at you. You really felt the disgrace. Before my twenty-eight days was up, we got orders to move up the line. So, being in the Army Cyclist Corps, I finished my last few days riding a bike and carrying another one on my back. That was my punishment.

It seemed to the colonial troops that the British Army was obsessed by discipline. *They* would never have stood for it. There were cases where Australian troops, incensed by the sight of a man undergoing Field Punishment, cut him loose again and again, and threatening the MPs – who had the unpleasant duty of tying him up – with loaded rifles, dared them to truss him up again.

A great many officers shared their opinion, and army records began to show a disturbing number of sentences imposed by courts martial which were (in the opinion of the hierarchy) ludicrously trivial in relation to the offences. The mutinies in the French Army had made some staff officers uneasy, and they feared too that the more casual attitude of the troops from the Dominions would have a deleterious effect on the more docile British troops under their command.

As the guns boomed around the salient in preparation for the coming offensive, a meeting of senior staff officers was convened. The main item on the agenda was the lack of discipline shown by the Canadian soldiers, and the conversation turned to their deplorable habit of failing to salute superior officers. What could be done about it? The discussion continued for more than forty minutes until General Plumer, who had been growing increasingly restive, broke in abruptly. 'Well, gentlemen, I don't think there's much wrong with the saluting of the Canadians. Nearly every Canadian *I* salute returns it.' There was shame-

faced silence and Plumer rustled his papers together. 'If that's all, gentlemen. . . .'

General Plumer had other problems to concern him and so had General Gough, for he was in command of the force which was to make the
long-awaited thrust that would break the salient.

Chapter 9

General Plumer's Second Army, having conquered the ridges and therefore secured the right flank of the salient, was to sit tight until after the
main attack in the salient itself. This was to be the job of Gough's Fifth
Army, now disposed along the line from Zillebeke, round Ypres and along
the canal bank to Boesinghe. Haig confidently expected that Gough's
army would be astride the ridges in a week. Meanwhile a force from the
Fourth Army, under General Rawlinson, was despatched to Nieuport, just
down the coast from German-occupied Ostend. Its purpose was to launch
a seaborne attack on Ostend and the ports to the north, as soon as Gough
was able to penetrate far enough inland to swing round and attack the
coast from the rear. On the extreme left of the salient, between Boesinghe
and Dixmude, there were to be simultaneous attacks by the French and
the Belgians.

The land beyond Dixmude petered out into impassable swamp, where
the situation had been static ever since King Albert had ordered the
floodgates of the canals to be opened in 1914, in a last desperate effort to
stem the German advance. So the waters spread over a large area of land, a
stagnant, insurmountable barrier between the opposing armies, although
the Allies had managed to retain a toehold around the coastal town of
Nieuport. Nieuport was literally the end of the line. On his daily inspection of the trenches, 2nd Lieutenant 'Paddy' King of the 2/5th East Lancashire Regiment always made a point of going right to the end of the very
last trench which abutted on the beach. It appealed to his sense of humour
to feel that, for a few seconds at least, he was the last man on the Western
Front. At such moments, in that time of misunderstanding and confusion
before the offensive, he was probably the only man on the Western Front
who knew exactly where he was and what he was doing. But to a disinter-
ested observer, like Pastor van Walleghem, there was an unmistakable air
of purpose behind the lines.

Pastor van Walleghem

9 July 1917. There is more and more talk about the impending offensive, we see many extensive preparations here, and learn the ones of the neighbouring sectors; additional railways are being laid all around. Guns are being brought in and the ammunition depots are being enlarged and new ones established. Soldiers and officers alike tell the civilians that it will be terrible and continuous. They must break through at any cost, and in a few short weeks Flanders will be delivered. Also the newspapers make mention of the importance of the coming offensive. The people are full of hope, but those nearest the front fear the bombing which will precede the battle. Under the circumstances, a farmer from Vlamertinghe requests permission from the military authorities to move his livestock owing to the danger of the coming offensive. Instead of obtaining this he received a visit from the Gendarmes: 'What? An impending offensive? How do you know that? How dare you give away military preparations?'

The Belgian civilians could hardly refute the evidence of their own eyes and ears. It was perfectly obvious to them that an offensive was imminent. The soldiers, pouring into the salient in previously unheard-of numbers, could hardly fail to be aware of it. Senior officers were naturally *au fait* with the hundred detailed pages of the plan of attack and, thanks to German Intelligence, the enemy was almost as well informed. If anyone doubted that, it was plain for all to see in a report from the War Correspondent of the *Frankfurter Zeitung*, published on Sunday, 1 July:

The mine battle in Flanders was conceived not only as a menace to Lille but also as a breakthrough on the whole Yser front. There is no adequate reason to suppose that General [*sic*] Haig will content himself with what has been achieved. . . .

In connection with the considerable increase of activity of the English from the sea against the Flemish coast, the renewal of an ambitious land operation with far-reaching strategic aims is doubtless to be expected. I think I am betraying no secret when I say that for a long time past we have contemplated these things in a state of preparation.

The German information was correct in every particular. There was just one thing they did *not* know, and that was that the War Cabinet in London had not only failed to give the go-ahead for the offensive but

were still doubtful if it should take place at all. Haig was not aware of that
either. There had been an appalling failure of communication and everyone concerned was proceeding on false assumptions. The War Cabinet
assumed that Sir Douglas Haig had clearly understood the final agreement
which had been reached at the end of the June meetings – that he had
been given approval to continue his preparations but with the proviso that
the offensive would only be undertaken if the French were able to partici-
pate actively in it. The Cabinet had undertaken to 'sound the French out'.
The politicians believed that they had made it clear that they reserved the
final decision to themselves, and that it would be based on their assess-
ment of what the French were able and willing to do.

It had been agreed that Albert Thomas was to do his best to persuade
the French Cabinet to throw in all their resources and attack simultaneously with the other Allies; but a fortnight after Haig had returned to
France, the Paris Conference had still not taken place and the time and
energy of the War Cabinet itself was almost exclusively taken up with
endless and frustratingly pointless discussions on the situation in Mesopota-
mia. Meanwhile, on 1 July, Haig had received a visit from General Anthoine, who informed him that the French would not be ready to attack on
25 July, the date that Haig had set for the beginning of the offensive. He
asked for a postponement of three days. Reluctantly Haig agreed. It is
reasonable to suppose, or at least to give him the benefit of the doubt by
supposing, that Sir Douglas Haig assumed that General Anthoine's request
for a delay implicitly embodied that commitment of 'wholehearted support' on which the politicians in London had insisted, and that there was
now no obstacle to proceeding with the offensive which, for so long, had
been the corner-stone of his strategy. The tragedy was that the strategy
was based on assumptions which, by July 1917, were no longer wholly
true.

*The offensive in Flanders would relieve the hard-pressed and demoralised
French armies in the south?* The French were now well on the way to
recovery and rapidly recuperating both in morale and in strength.* *A victory in the west would stiffen the resolve of the Russians in the east?* The
Russian front was crumbling and moving towards total collapse which

*Haig may have been led to believe that the situation of the French Army was
more serious than was the case, for as he revealed (although in retrospect, ten years
later), he was under constant pressure by the French insistence that he should
attack and keep on attacking in Flanders. He may too have been influenced by
eyewitness reports by people such as General Trenchard, who, while inspecting
airfields in the French sector, was appalled at the lack of discipline and morale
among the French troops.

nothing could now avert. *The war could not be continued unless the Channel ports were captured and British shipping losses reduced?* Thanks to the introduction of the convoy system in May, the shipping losses had already dropped dramatically and 300 submarine-chasing destroyers, nearing completion in American shipyards, were expected to be in operation within weeks.

No one in London thought it necessary to draw the attention of the C-in-C to the significance of these developments. The War Cabinet had other things on its mind. With the increasing number of air raids on London, public morale was showing signs of becoming shaky. There was a suggestion that two squadrons of fighter aeroplanes should be taken from the Western Front and brought back to defend London against attack from the air. Haig refused point-blank to allow any such thing. Every gun, every aircraft, every man was needed on the Western Front. Flanders too was being bombarded with bombs.

Faced with the knowledge of the coming offensive, but not knowing exactly when it would take place, there were only two things that the Germans could do. All around the salient they mounted raid after raid on the trenches, hoping to capture prisoners or papers which would reveal the vital information. Reconnaissance aeroplanes reported enormous concentrations of troops and equipment in the back areas. And, knowing that a missile dropped virtually anywhere was likely to hit some target which would impede the preparations, the Germans stepped up long-range shelling and sent every available bomber to blast anything and everything that moved between Ypres and the sea.

Pastor van Walleghem was concerned with the sufferings of the civilians.

12 July. Bailleul bombarded today, killing civilians. Also another painful accident happened tonight. German planes overhead from 21.30 to 22.30 dropping bombs at Ouderdom. The English guns shoot at them. Unfortunately, one of the English air shrapnel shells lands on the house of Artur Tahon, who now lives along the Abeele road just outside Reninghelst. The occupants were sitting round the table. The shrapnel shell pierced through the roof, through a chest full of clothing, through the ceiling, and then comes below and drills straight through the child sitting on its mother's lap, slices off the mother's right thigh and goes through the floor-boards, finishing up almost one yard underground. Small Albert Tahon, aged only eighteen months, is killed instantly. The mother, thirty-two years of age, is taken to Couthove and dies the next morning. I have never seen anything as sweet and at the same time painful as that poor little child. It was laughing heartily when its small body was pierced and death

was so instantaneous that the poor little lamb's facial expression never changed.

Sister Mary Pollock at 'Mendinghem' recalls,

Sister Mary Pollock, Theatre Sister, 'Mendinghem', No. 46 Casualty Clearing Station at Proven, Territorial Force Nursing Service

We had a lot of refugees at that time and a lot of them wounded, and we quickly had to put up marquees for them because we couldn't put them in with the wounded soldiers, but we had to care for them just the same. I remember the woman with the severed leg although they didn't bring her to the hospital. She was taken to a little cottage a bit down from the station. There were French people still living there and they were relations of hers. The surgeon and I went down to see her and she was in agony, poor thing. He said, 'Give her some morphia and keep watching her. We can't move her, but you come down as often as you can.' Of course I was as busy as I could be, but I did run down the hill a few times, really just waiting for her to pass out. She just passed away. It was the best thing she could have done, really, because gangrene would have set in.

All the casualty clearing stations were as busy as they could be because on that same night, 12 July, the Germans attacked for the first time with mustard gas. 'Mendinghem' alone took in over a thousand cases over the next few days, for the effect of the gas was not necessarily immediate. It was a dark oily fluid which not only emitted noxious fumes but seeped into the earth and clung and hung in the crevices and furrows of the churned-up soil. Days later, soldiers who had crawled out to listening-posts beyond the front line, or who had thrown themselves into shell-holes for cover, would crawl out, their uniforms burnt through, their bodies covered with agonising blisters. Even quite far behind the fighting line, to the ribald and callous amusement of their comrades, men squatting in convenient shell-holes suffered severe burning and even sloughing of the genitals. At No. 11 CCS at Godwaersveldt (a jaw-breaker which the troops preferred to call 'Gert wears velvet') there were casualties even among the girls who were nursing the gas victims.

Staff Nurse C. Macfie, No. 11 Casualty Clearing Station, Godwaersveldt, Territorial Force Nursing Service

I'd just arrived with another nurse from the south, because they needed as many staff as they could get with the big stunt coming, and it was just a couple of nights later that the mustard gas cases started to come in. It was terrible to see them. I was in the post-operative tent so I didn't come in contact with them, but the nurses in the reception tent had a bad time. The poor boys were helpless and the nurses had to take off these uniforms, all soaked with gas, and do the best they could for the boys. Next day all the nurses had chest trouble and streaming eyes from the gassing. They were all yellow and dazed. Even their hair turned yellow and they were nearly as bad as the men, just from the fumes from their clothing. And all the time, of course, the bombs were falling, night after night.

The men were very good. In a way it must have been worse for them just lying there. The beds all had folding legs, and there were sandbags piled a foot or so up the sides of the ward tents. On a moonlit night the CO, Colonel Humphries, would come round and say, 'All down on the floor tonight, we're expecting Jerry over', so we had to turn the legs in and lower the beds to get them down below the level of the sandbags, to save the soldiers getting shrapnel. I was terrified when the bombs were dropping. We were all terrified – patients and nurses – we were all shaking. I remember one night when I was on duty and these bombs were dropping all about, I said to the doctor, 'Oh, I wish I didn't shake so!' And he just looked at me and said, 'Oh, be quiet. We all shake.'

The British bombardment began on 16 July. From Dixmude to Bailleul, through miles of tented camps, men slumbering on groundsheets felt the earth vibrate beneath them. In the casualty clearing stations and in base hospitals miles from the line, surgical instruments in their steel trays began to tinkle gently, incessantly. A Tommy grasped Sister Macfie's wrist as she bent over him to dress his wounds. 'Listen, Sister. Do you hear it? It's started.'

Late that evening, after dark, Catherine Macfie went with two other nurses and an orderly to the nearby vantage-point of Mont des Cats. The salient was an arc of flame. All around, like sunlight dancing on water, the countryside flickered and rippled with flecks of fire, as the shells flashed and roared from the muzzles of more than 3,000 heavy guns. Beyond a patch of darkness, a straggle of fireflies in the distance marked the forward positions of the light artillery standing wheel-to-wheel behind the line. The old moon had died and the first slim crescent of the new was still three nights away, but the jagged ruins of Ypres were silhouetted – now red, now green, now starkly black – against an ever-changing backcloth of light. The SOS rockets rose and flared and died as the shells rained down on the German lines and defences beyond the salient. In the British trenches and in the German the front-line troops sweated and crouched in the quivering earth, hands pressed to their ears. Around them the air whipped and swirled as the storm of steel roared past on the wind.

Sheltering in their concrete dug-outs the Germans were better off than the Tommies in their exposed trenches, for in response to the SOS signals from their front-line troops German shells were raining down on the British positions, and the screaming in the air was echoed by screams from the ground and cry after cry of 'Stretcher-bearer!' As the nurses, awed by their glimpse of the inferno in the salient, hurried down from Mont des Cats to prepare for the arrival of the first of the inevitable convoys of wounded, Lloyd George was presiding over a dinner party at 10 Downing Street.

The guests were Lord Curzon, Lord Milner, General Smuts and Colonel Hankey, Secretary to the War Cabinet. It was an uneasy meeting, for the opening of the preliminary bombardment had taken the politicians by surprise. They had agreed, undoubtedly, that Sir Douglas Haig should continue preparations for the offensive. They had not fully realised that his preparations had gone quite so far. To all intents and purposes, the offensive had already started. Should it, could it, be stopped?

All through dinner, and later over the port, the brandy and the fine cigars, the Cabinet went over the old ground and the old arguments. No one, least of all the Prime Minister, was happy about the offensive, but eventually a reluctant agreement was reached. It was decided that Sir Douglas Haig should be allowed to begin his offensive, 'but not to allow it to degenerate into a drawn-out, indecisive battle of the Somme type. If this happened, it was to be stopped and the plan for an attack on the Italian front would be tried.' *

A meeting of the War Policy Committee was arranged for Wednesday, almost two days later. Not until then would the informal agreement, which had been reached over the dinner at Downing Street, be confirmed.

It was well after midnight when the guests left. Outside, the evening bustle of the streets had long since faded to a murmur. It was a moonless night, so no Zeppelins would come to disturb the peace of sleeping Londoners. However, through the still air of the warm summer night, it was just possible to hear a faint drumming, like thunder in the far distance. It was the sound of the guns, 120 miles away at the front in Flanders. Exploding in their thousands on the land beyond the salient, each salvo meticulously aimed at a different grid on the closely-drawn artillery maps,

*The Supreme Command, 1914–1918, Lord Hankey (George Allen and Unwin Ltd, 1961).

the shells were systematically pulverising the earth into a tormented moonscape of hillocks and craters. Over this terrain the infantry would have to advance.

The role of the short-range field artillery just behind the front was to protect and support the infantry, but many of the batteries now moving into position behind the line were adding their voices to the bombardment. Major Rory Macleod, who had just arrived in the salient, was given command of C.241, a battery situated just north of Brigade Headquarters at the Reigersburg Château, a quarter of a mile or so behind the canal bank. On 20 July he wrote to his parents:

As you know, I have taken over a new battery. It is not really the best time for taking one over, as life will be too strenuous to keep an eye on it at first. Every night the battery has to fire 600 rounds on the roads and tracks probably used by the enemy. To give the remainder of the battery some rest I put this on to a different section each night. By day the battery carries out various bombardment tasks with other batteries.

I have a fairly comfortable dug-out myself, with a little room where I can put things. My hours are fairly regular. On account of generally being up most of the night, owing to gas, I get up and have breakfast about nine. After that I generally walk round the position, and see how they are getting on with the work, and supervise it. In the afternoon I generally go to the OP and stay there till the evening. Then I always have a good deal of office work and correspondence to deal with, besides issuing orders, making out reports, etc.

The weather today has been fine but very muggy. I was quite tired after my walk this morning. It looked like rain two or three times during the day, but none fell.

The walk to the observation post was exhausting at the best of times, for it was situated more than a mile away at Hilltop Farm on the other side of the canal and the journey over rough ground was heavy going. Hilltop Farm was no longer a farm, but a complex of tunnels and dugouts on the breast of an almost imperceptible rise beyond the canal. Immediately in front of it ran the front-line trenches, and the observation post itself was in a trench. In the flat-lands of the salient it was not always easy to find a suitable vantage-point near enough the front line from which the targets and ranges could be accurately pin-pointed. With some ingenuity, the French had solved the problem.

Out of the trench grew a tree, which had long since been shattered by shelling. Nevertheless, an obstinate remnant of its barkless trunk still stood ten feet high. One dark night the French engineers had cut it down, dug out its remaining roots and erected an exact replica made of steel. The entrance was in the trench itself. Inside, a ladder led up to the narrow ledge on which the artillery officer sat cramped and hunched, hour upon weary hour, with his binoculars trained on enemy territory, which was visible through a narrow slit in the side of the 'tree trunk'. The firing pattern, the ranges and targets, had been arranged before he left the battery, and two telephonists, squatting in the trench below, relayed his corrections back to the guns.

It was the first time Rory Macleod had ever made use of such an observation post, and when he climbed into it he had a nasty feeling that it was also going to be his last. As he squeezed himself on to the narrow ledge in front of the observation slit, the tree suddenly lurched and took a distinct tilt to starboard. If any sharp-eyed German observer had happened to be looking at the 'tree' it would have been only a matter of moments before they opened up on it. But luck was on Major Macleod's side and it stayed with him on the journey back.

Major R. Macleod DSO, MC, C. 241 Battery, Royal Field Artillery

An eleven-inch shell burst about four yards away. Fortunately it was in water (it burst in the canal as we were crossing it coming back from the OP). Luckily it only soaked us. It was a very heavy shell and it threw up a column of water of a hundred feet at least. The Germans were shelling the canal area night and day. They knew from their observations that we had bridges across the canal. Of course, they knew that the offensive was coming and they knew too that in that part of the sector, north of Ypres, we'd have to get vast numbers of troops and materials across the canal before we could attack. So they kept pasting it, especially at night. Every morning I had to cross it to get to my OP, and every morning it was a shambles of broken wagons and dead horses and bodies lying all over the place. Their guns knew just where the bridges were because of movement on the tracks that approached them. But there were two causeways across the canal and another camouflaged causeway which we hoped the Germans wouldn't spot. It was covered with nets with sheets over them to look like the water below, and we were absolutely forbidden to use it or the camouflaged road that ran up to it until the night of the attack.

Sapper W. Mathieson, No. 50048, 96th Company, Royal Engineers, 20th Division

We built these roads. By the middle of July we'd been at it for weeks because as soon as the infantry went forward they had to get the guns up to cover them. We built the road of beech slabs, gorgeous beech slabs three inches thick, and we had hundreds of tons of them. We were always short of concrete but we were never short of timber. We laid three slabs long-ways and then two cross-ways and then we covered them with metal. Of course, it all had to be done at night and all the materials cleared and the work camouflaged before daylight. We could only go as far as the canal bank. As soon as the attack started, we were to cross just behind the infantry and start pushing the road up further on the other side, so they could haul up the guns and supplies. There were three companies of Royal Engineers attached to every division in the sector and we were all doing that, at it every night as soon as darkness fell, and knocking off just before dawn the next day – and of course we had hundreds of parties from the infantry to help us.

'*The Army's flowing with milk and honey,*' groused the weary working parties, envious of the tradesmen's pay, '*We do the work, the REs get the money.*'

Driver L. G. Burton, No. 113755, 40th Division, Motor Transport, Army Service Corps

If the attack was going to work at all we had to get big loads of supplies right up to the front line before the offensive. I was with a motor lorry ammunition column and our job was to get the stuff up. We took up everything – shells, rifle ammunition, Mills hand-grenades, mortar-bombs, duckboards, narrow-gauge railway-line sections, wood, and loads of large gas or liquid-fire cylinders. Day and night we worked from dumps to depots and depots to dumps near the front fighting line. We used to go through Ypres at night with no lights on our lorries, of course, as the road was under enemy observation from the various hills around. But there would be plenty of Very lights from the fronts going up and down continuously all around us, the flashes from our own guns and Howitzers in the ruins, and enemy shells bursting among the wrecked houses and roads. It was just fumes and dust and smells all the time, and sometimes there was gas too, sometimes incendiary shells. You could see them glowing red among the brick-ends.

It was so important to get the ammunition and supplies up that we were taking chances and running the lorries right up to Hellfire Corner, on the other side of Ypres on the Menin Road. I'd been the last to set off and when I got to Hellfire Corner it was chaos. A salvo of shells had landed in among the convoy. The lorries were scattered all over the place and even those that hadn't been directly hit had run off the roadway, in among all the bricks and debris, and the drivers were sheltering in the ruins. I got out and walked down the road to find our sergeant in charge.

We decided to try to get the lorries back on the road facing home, which meant that we had to start up the engines by hand and manoeuvre them round in among the shambles on three-point turns. The shells were simply thundering down, but some-how or other we managed to get any lorries that hadn't been knocked out back on to the road, lined up facing Ypres. We'd just thrown the stuff off them anyhow and left it for the carrying parties to get to the dumps. The road was littered with bodies and debris and shell-holes all over the place. However, at last we were ready to go, lined up, and my lorry having been the last to get there, I was the first in the convoy going back, with the sergeant sitting beside me.

Just as we were about to try to get out of it, some soldiers ran up and banged on the door. They'd found one of our drivers very badly wounded and they were carrying him to the roadside, so they shouted for us to wait a minute while they put him on the lorry. The sergeant had the wind up and yelled back at them that we couldn't wait, we had to get out of it quick. I just gave him a look and jumped out of the cab. After all that, I couldn't drive away and leave one of our boys wounded, laid out at the roadside. I dropped our tailboard and got the men to lift our man into the lorry, leaving the back down, and they shouted to me that there was an aid-post just down the road on the left in the ruins of an old convent.

We set off, bumping down over the terrible surface of the road, and sure enough I came to a small signpost with a red cross and an arrow on it. We carried our chap down a small pathway and we found the dressing-station in a cellar, with hurricane lamps and stretchers on the floor and men waiting for ambulances to fetch them. The sergeant sat in the cab all the time. He was nearly foaming at the mouth by the time we eventually started off. When we got back to the lorry park the sergeant put in his report. He got the

Military Medal. You should have heard the lads when they heard about that.

Far away from the inferno of the bombardment in the Headquarters Château near St Omer, Sir Douglas Haig was also foaming at the mouth. It was 19 July and he had just received a letter from General Sir William Robertson, whom up until now he had considered to be his main friend and ally in the War Cabinet.

It pointed out that official approval had not yet been given to his plan, although it also expressed the hope that this would be forthcoming 'in a day or two'. Haig was flabbergasted. 'In a day or two', to be precise in exactly one week from today, the offensive was due to begin. When the 'approval' finally reached him two days later it was couched in terms of such misgiving that a man of lesser confidence might have been utterly demoralised. As it was, Haig was indignant and aggrieved not only that his preparations had been allowed to proceed thus far without the support of the Cabinet, but that the grudging words of the 'approval' made it perfectly obvious that the War Policy Committee had no confidence in the strategy of its Commander-in-Chief.

Gloomily, Haig summoned a meeting of his commanders to discuss the final details of the plan, and the results of that meeting did nothing to raise his spirits. For several days past, the salient had been covered by drifting mist, and deprived of its eyes the Army had been unable to complete the aerial observations it desperately needed before the attack. Uneasily, fully aware that he might be making the wrong decision, Haig agreed to postpone the attack for three more days. Zero day would now be 28 July. On 27 July came another bombshell. The French were not yet in position, and at this late date Gough, commanding the Fifth Army, was reluctant to proceed without them. And so Haig agreed to yet another postponement.

Zero hour was finally fixed for ten minutes to four on the morning of 31 July. These two fatal postponements allowed the guns an additional full week to continue the bombardment which originally had been planned to last for seven days before the attack. Day and night they thundered on. A thousand miles away a depression was forming far out in the Atlantic. A cool air-stream was moving slowly towards northern Europe, and there was rain on the wind.

Part 3

The Rains Came

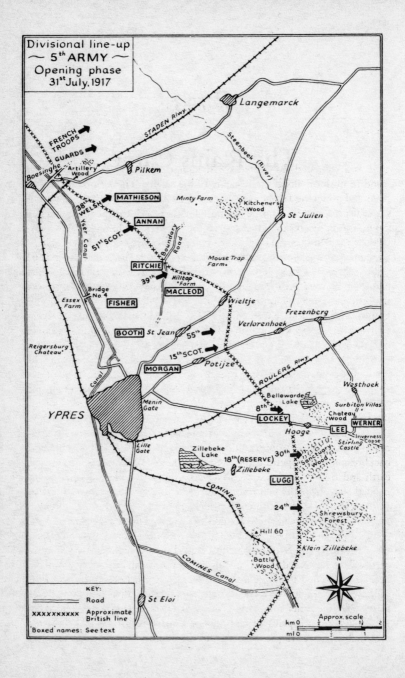

Divisional line-up
~ 5ᵗʰ ARMY ~
Opening phase
31ˢᵗ July, 1917

Langemarck

STADEN Rlwy.

FRENCH TROOPS
GUARDS

Boesinghe

Artillery Wood

Pilkem

Steenbeek (River)

Minty Farm

Kitcheners Wood

St Julien

38ᵗʰ WELSH
MATHIESON

Yser Canal

51ˢᵗ SCOT.
ANNAN

Boundary Road

Mouse Trap Farm

RITCHIE
39ᵗʰ
Hilltop Farm
MACLEOD

Bridge No 4

Essex Farm

FISHER

Wieltje

Frezenberg

BOOTH
St Jean
55ᵗʰ
Verlorenhoek

Reigersburg Chateau

Canal

15ᵗʰ SCOT.

MORGAN

Potijze

ROULERS Rlwy.

Westhoek

Menin Gate

YPRES

Bellewarde Lake

8ᵗʰ
LOCKEY
Hooge

Surbiton Villas
Chateau Wood
WERNER
LEE
Inverness Copse

Lille Gate

Zillebeke Lake

18ᵗʰ (RESERVE)
30ᵗʰ
Sanctuary Wood
Stirling Castle

Zillebeke

LUGG

COMINES Rlwy.

24ᵗʰ

Shrewsbury Forest

Hill 60

Klein Zillebeke

N

Battle Wood

COMINES Canal

St Eloi

KEY:
———— Road
xxxxxxxxx Approximate British line
Boxed names: See text

km 0   1   2
ml 0   1

Approx. scale

Chapter 10

Taut as a clenched fist poised for the knock-out blow, the Fifth Army stood in position along the knuckle of the salient. The ration parties had been and gone, the last hot meals dished out, and 6,000 gallons of strong, sweet tea slopped into outheld mugs. The last fiery tots of rum scorched down a hundred thousand gullets to soothe the clutching, knotted muscles. As the minutes ticked towards zero, an omniscient presence, able to pierce the darkness of the cloudy night, might have discerned the outline of the salient by a straggle of rising steam as the army emptied its bladder before going over the top. Then they waited for the whistle, bowed under the burden of 80lb of equipment – rifle, haversack, gas-mask, water bottle; bombs, ammunition, entrenching tools; and down the back of every fourth man, the pickaxe or shovel that would send him ramrod-straight into the battle, unable to crouch and dodge the enemy fire.

Behind the jumping-off positions the guns leapt and spat fire as the gunners slammed round after round into the breech. On the left of the salient at the canal bank in front of Pilkem Ridge, the engineers could hardly make themselves heard above the din as they shouted orders to the pioneers and working parties. Ever since dusk they had been working on the mammoth task of throwing causeways over the canal, so that the guns, horses and supply wagons could follow the infantry across. It was hard, backbreaking work getting the scooplike, open-fronted skips, heavy with earth and rubble, to the water's edge. Skill as well as muscle-power was needed to transfer the centre of the weight so that the skip would tilt up and cascade its load in the right place. There was no room for mistakes, and no time to spare to shelter from the shells that burst all around.

Squatting in the open outside a gun store in the dubious protection of the canal bank, Bill Mathieson of the 96th Field Company, Royal Engineers, was being spared the task of bridging the canal; but only because he had been detailed to go over as OC's orderly, just behind the attacking infantry, to survey the route of the supply road that must be driven forward on the other side as soon as the troops advanced. Knowing Major Storey, whom Bill privately considered to be a terror, he had a shrewd idea that the order to proceed 'behind the infantry' would be interpreted so literally that they would be grazing the heels of the advancing troops. It would not be pleasant, although Bill had the slight consolation of knowing that, here on the extreme edge of the salient, zero hour would be slightly later than elsewhere and there was a chance (although it wasn't much of a hope) that, by the time they got going, the Germans' attention might have been distracted by the attacks on the adjoining sectors.

At the time Bill was hardly in a position to know that he himself (with some hundreds of his comrades) was directly responsible for the delay. In order to throw bridges and causeways over the canal to carry the advance, the engineers had first had to cut away the canal banks. The Germans, in their listening-outposts on the other side of the canal, had mistaken the noise of this operation for the sound of tunnelling. Remembering Messines, they had wisely evacuated their front-line positions and retreated to the steel and concrete security of a second line a thousand yards behind. Four nights previously, in the course of their stealthy patrols into No Man's Land on the eastern side of the canal, the Guards had discovered this interesting fact and had moved into the trenches, after an operation of consummate ease which involved little more than announcing their presence to the skeleton force of Germans manning the outposts. So the Guards, at the extreme left of the salient next to the French sector, now had the advantage of being already at their first objective. In order to give the other divisions time to catch up, it had been decided that zero hour, on their front, should be delayed by thirty-four minutes.

The Guards were to attack one minute after the sun rose at 4.23. The time had been precisely worked out at GHQ. The staff officers agreed, as they pored over the map, sliding their fingers over an inch or so of glossy parchment, that in thirty-four minutes exactly, the troops in the neighbouring sector (the 38th Welsh Division) would have caught up level with the Guards in their advanced position. The trouble was that the troops would not be advancing over glossy parchment.

At the best of times a foot-slogger trying to cross a ploughed field in the country around Ypres would find it hard going across the furrows of heavy clay. And the showery weather of the last few days had laid a film of mud over the ground, so that the men slipped and slithered as they ran forward through a turmoil of mounds and craters. In trying to circumvent them, in trying to find a foothold in the slippery, clinging mud, it was impossible to keep direction, never mind keep in formation. Even without the German shells, which as soon as the attack started had begun to fall on the advancing infantry, it would have been difficult going.

At first they made astonishingly good headway. In keeping with their reputation, the 51st Highland Division were going across like terriers intent on flushing rats from a hole. In the vanguard of the attack, through the bursting shells and fountains of thrown-up earth raining back on them, the 4th Battalion of the Gordon Highlanders were plunging forward towards the first objective. Watching through binoculars from the top of the canal bank, three young officers of the 1st/9th Royal Scots, waiting to lead the second wave across, marvelled at the progress of the Gordons. To be more precise, two of them, Jock Gellatly and a subaltern called Campbell who had newly joined the battalion, stood marvelling. The third, Jim Annan, waiting prudently with his men in the lee of the bank as they waited to cross in the second wave, kept yelling at them to come down. The battalion was almost ready to move off when the shell came over. Lieutenant Campbell was killed outright. Jock Gellatly's arm was gone, but he was alive. There was time – just – for Jim to see him carried into an ambulance, already full of wounded from the shelling. Jock, at least, was out of it. As Annan moved his platoon on to Bridge 4 to cross the canal, another shell screeched overhead and exploded on the spot they had just left. Jim Annan glanced back over his shoulder. There was only a cloud of dust where the ambulance had been.

Lieutenant J. Annan, 1st/9th Btn., Royal Scots

Our objective was as far as we could go. The Gordons were doing well. They were advancing away ahead of us, so we only got a few stray 5.9 shells on the way across. We didn't have a single casualty until we got to Minty's Farm. It was a strongpoint, an outpost, fortified by the Germans and bristling with machine-guns, but the Gordons had taken it. They took it with the bayonet, like wild things, and when we got to it the dead were lying all around. Germans, grey against the mud, all mixed up with the dead Gordons lying there in their kilts. But they'd taken it all right. They'd even set up Battalion Headquarters there, and moved away on ahead. Of course the Germans had every one of their own positions marked on the map and registered by their artillery, so that if they had to get out of them and give them up they'd have the guns on them right away. So, just as we were coming up to Minty's Farm, the shells started falling all around. We got a slashing there all right.

As we were struggling up to it one of the boys got hit with a huge shell fragment. It sliced him straight in two. He dropped his rifle and bayonet and threw his arms up in the air, and the top part of his torso fell back on to the ground. The unbelievable thing was that the legs and the kilt went on running, just like a chicken with its head chopped off! One of my boys – I think it was his special pal – went rushing after him. He had some mad idea of picking up the upper part of the torso and chasing the legs to join him up. I shouted him back and he was wild with me because he wanted to help his pal. He couldn't realise that he was beyond help.

I had a terrible job keeping the men bunched up, to keep contact, and just past Minty's Farm, for the very first time I saw a man going berserk with the shelling. He came running back towards us just like a spectre waving its arms, and shouting and yelling, 'Mother! Mother! Mother!' I left the platoon – I shouldn't have done that, but I went a little way towards him and got hold of him and said, 'Come on. Come on over here, till we see to you.' But he was like a mad thing. He just shook me off and ran on yelling, 'Mother! Mother!' completely off his head. That was the last we saw of him. We had to get on. It had taken us half a day to get that three miles. It might have been half an hour or half a year for all you noticed the time going.

Some way ahead, John Ritchie, who had gone over in the first wave with the 6th Gordon Highlanders, literally stumbled across a pal of his from the same street in Inverurie. In their schooldays Jock Marr had been the butt of much chaffing directed at his huge buck teeth. Now, in the clamour of the battle, looking down at the dead boy, at the terrible scarlet hole where his mouth had been, Ritchie thought, 'If it hadn't been for those teeth sticking out, he might have got away with it.'

The 39th Division started their attack from the front line in front of Hilltop Farm, and Sergeant Bill Booth of the 11th Royal Sussex Regiment was making progress half-left to the first objective, the capture of Kitchener's Wood. They had practised the attack over and over again on the training grounds in the south near Armentières, at a place called Jesus Farm. The training area had been specially selected, so their officers informed them, because it closely resembled the country over which they would actually attack. The practice attacks had taken place in growing corn, with 'Kitchener's Wood', a mile behind the enemy front line, represented by the lopped-off branches of trees stuck into the ground.

Now, leaping, stumbling, slithering between the churned-up craters, dodging the bursting shells as he went towards the real Kitchener's Wood on the breast of the Pilkem Ridge, Booth could see not the faintest resemblance, try as he might, between the practice and the real thing. Nevertheless, on one of those days of practice attacks in the summer sunshine, Sir Douglas Haig himself had given them his blessing. The soldiers advancing towards the tapes that represented the enemy lines in the trampled cornfield had seen a group of cavalry approaching.

Sergeant W. Booth MM, No. 390, 11th Btn., Royal Sussex Regiment

As they got closer we could see that it was Sir Douglas Haig. We were told to get down. As he arrived at our front he halted. I was Platoon Sergeant so he called to me to come to him. I explained to him all the details of the attack. He nodded. He smiled. He seemed to approve. 'Very good,' he said. 'Wish all your men the best of luck.' Then he was gone.

Now, at the head of his platoon – shouting at his men to keep up, stopping to hoist up an overladen Tommy who had tumbled on the rough, slippery incline, diving into the shelter of shell-holes as the explosions burst around them, and floundering onwards through a storm of machine-gun bullets – Bill Booth cast his mind back to his moment of glory in the cornfield and wished that Sir Douglas Haig could see them now.

The eighteen-pounder guns of Major Macleod's battery, C.241, at Reigersburg Château, had been firing all night on an 'interdiction task'. This meant aiming at the roads and tracks leading to the enemy front, to deepen the barrage and prevent the Germans bringing up supplies and, more important, reserves to their troops, who were hard-pressed by the punishing bombardment on their front line. Even while the firing was still going on, Macleod had managed to have the gun positions broken down so that the battery was ready to move forward as soon as the word came that the first objectives were gained and being consolidated. When it came, the drivers were standing by ready to 'limber up' the horse teams to the guns, the officers mounted their own horses and the battery was ready to go.

On the canal, the camouflage nets had been whipped off the bridges and now they were teeming with mule trains, with messengers, with men and materials streaming forward to the battlefront and, streaming back, a straggle of wounded and stretcher-bearers. Beyond the incline of the ridge, fumes of gas and cordite lay like a second stratum below the heavy rainclouds that were gathering above the battle. Now that the enemy guns had pulled themselves together and settled down after the initial attack, they were not only firing on the advancing troops but sending heavy shells further back to disrupt the advance of the reinforcements. It was a mile from the canal bank to the top of the hill. For Macleod and his cavalcade of guns and horses, advancing diagonally, it was close on two miles. They rode through the bursting 5.9 shells as if they were on parade, strung out in order of march.

As they breasted the rise and looked beyond, Macleod looked back. A stream of gun batteries, nose to tail, stretched back right to the canal bank. A moment later, disaster struck. Just as C Battery was crossing the reserve trenches, the access bridge which had been hastily thrown across the night before collapsed under the weight of a wagon. It took an interminable half-hour to haul it out again and repair the bridge. In the cratered, muddied ground, there was no way of dispersing, so an entire brigade of artillery stood still on the wooden track, presenting the enemy on the ridges beyond with the finest target of the day. The Germans, perhaps, had their hands full with targets nearer at hand, for the British infantry were still making progress. Pulling into his position a little way out in what had been No Man's Land, sweating from the effort of controlling his terrified horse as it bucked and reared and whinnied in the blast of an exploding shell which had almost thrown its rider out of the saddle, Rory Macleod had no time to take in more than a general impression of the scene.

A shallow indentation ran just behind the breast of the hill rising to Kitchener's Wood away on the half-left. Taking advantage of this slight cover, the batteries pulled in one after the other until the shallow end of the valley was as thick with gun-barrels as bristles on a brush. The ground in front of them sloped gradually down to Admiral's Road (in No Man's Land, until that morning) and then to a hump-backed ridge. Behind it were the formidably fortified ruins of the hamlet of St Julien, and although machine-guns were still spitting busily all around it, the next wave of troops were already on the other side, making for the road ahead that linked the villages of Zonnebeke three miles to the right and Langemarck barely three miles to the left. The towers of the two village churches had long ago been shattered and turned into nothing more than grid references on the maps of British artillery officers, and the villages themselves were mere heaps of rubble. But they were visible, and their names had been bandied about so easily in the briefings before the attack that hardly a soldier on the field would have believed his ears had he been told that Langemarck and Zonnebeke, by the end of this day's fighting, would seem as unattainable as the mountains of the moon.

The guns were barely in position when the SOS signals began to go up from the vanguard of the advance as the Germans massed for a counter-attack. A few minutes later it began to drizzle and a grey Scotch mist rolled over the battlefield. One by one the landmarks disappeared from view, until even Kitchener's Wood on the rising ground a scant mile away was only a darker smudge on the grey curtain that blotted out the horizon. Only the coloured SOS rockets could pierce it. In response, the grim-faced gunners sent round after round, barrage after barrage, of shells, trying to break up the German counter-attack, shortening the range as the troops fell back; and when yet another breathless runner brought back new information on the position of the infantry, shortened it yet again. The artillery officers knew that things were not going well. Before the afternoon was out Major Macleod, checking his dump of shells, realised that, in answering the SOS signals which had come so thick and fast, he had almost run out of ammunition. He sent a message back to the wagon lines. He must have more ammunition and he must have it soon. By four o'clock the rain had turned into a steady downpour that lashed and spattered and bounced and trickled into the earth. On their open site, unprotected by the sandbagged pit of a permanent gun position, smacking up showers of mud with every recoil, the guns were ever so slowly sinking.

Struggling back to the signallers, who were working under a groundsheet in a shell-hole, to send back a signal for beams to shore up the trails of his guns, the Major found that his feet were sinking too.

As early as 8.30 that morning, after the taking of the first objective, rumours of jubilation and success flew enthusiastically around the country behind the salient. They went from Regimental Headquarters to wagon lines, from wagon lines to *estaminets* and from the *estaminets* into the ear of almost every civilian between Brielen and Bailleul, including that of Pastor van Walleghem.

> 31 July. Rumours speak of an advance of five miles. However, we are able very soon to conclude with certainty that the attack is successful. We hear that some horses have been brought in to take the guns further forward and at 9 am we see a procession of English cavalry coming from Westoutre, heading for the front. They pass for two hours on end, and we admire their beautiful horses and the lavish and good equipment.

With jingling harness and shining accoutrements the cavalry regiments trotted towards the front. It was the crux of the Army Commanders' plan that, as soon as the infantry had advanced, the cavalry would sweep through, galloping up on to the dry ground of the ridges which Haig had been misled by his Intelligence reports into thinking had a firm, sandy surface. Exactly the kind of ground which was ideal for cavalry campaigning. All things being equal, cavalry and infantry together would be on the Passchendaele Ridge in a week, or perhaps in eight days. It was unfortunate that all things were far from being equal.

After the first heady hours of the morning when the news of successes and captured objectives had poured back to Fifth Army Headquarters,

messages of a more disturbing nature began to trickle through, even
before the weather deteriorated. For the army had come up against an
unexpected obstacle which, in planning their strategy, the army staff had
entirely failed to take into account, for the very good reason that they
knew nothing about it.

The fact was that, apart from a few strategically situated fortifications
and machine-gun posts dotted about the German front lines, the Germans
regarded their forward lines as mere outpost positions. Their real defences
lay further back where, concealed by the folds of the first low ridges, they
had built a fortress which they believed was impregnable. There were
large shelters with walls and roofs many feet thick, so that the bulk of the
troops could be withdrawn during a bombardment and emerge unscathed
when the attack started. There were groups of strongpoints, from which
twenty men manning machine-guns could spray lethal fire into the lines
of the infantry approaching in open order. Sandbagged and camouflaged,
hidden in woods and crouching close to the ground, the pillboxes were
undetectable from the air. All round and between them were tiny dug-outs
bunched just above the earth, almost invisible in the mud and shell-holes
but big enough to house a machine-gun or a sniper.

It was little wonder that the soldiers, as they advanced intent on their
objective, rushed past them without noticing until they were caught in
their fire. It was little wonder that the soldiers in the second wave were
mown down by a blizzard of bullets almost as thick as that which had
caught the vanguard unawares. It was little wonder, too, that the Lewis-
gun teams setting up their guns on the rim of a shell-hole to answer the
fire were hard put to see where it was coming from. After the initial
capture of the first thinly-held German line, the infantry was shocked to
discover that it was storming a citadel.

On the Frezenberg Ridge, the Scots of the 15th Division suffered the
greatest deception, for their preparations and staff work had been of the
most meticulous and they had every reason to believe that their task
would be easily accomplished. A week previously, on two successive
nights, they had mounted a raid on the enemy trenches. They called them
'raids', but they were actually battles in miniature, supported by heavy fire
from the divisional artillery pounding the enemy front lines, and by a
heavy concentration of machine-gun fire.

Both operations were highly successful. The raiders had pinpointed
potential trouble spots, and had even captured some enemy machine-guns
together with their unfortunate crews. They had captured, moreover,
several scores of German prisoners who had shown no reluctance at all to
throw in the towel. Some prisoners had talked, so the redoubts beyond the
first objective would come as no surprise. According to the prisoners, the

trench systems linking them had been badly mauled by the bombardment
and they were thinly held. But the 15th Division did not know what lay
behind the area the raiders had penetrated. They did not know about the
forts at Beck House and Borry Farm.

As Orderly Runner to Acting-Captain Campbell of the 10/11th Battalion Highland Light Infantry, Bill Morgan saw more of the battle than
most, for although he went over with the first wave – rifle and bayonet at
the ready – until more permanent communications could be established,
his job was to run back and forth between his Company and Battalion
Headquarters to carry back the news of their progress.

Private W. Morgan, No. 24819, 10/11th Btn., Highland Light Infantry

We went over behind the creeping barrage and I went over with
Sergeant McCormack on one side and Captain Campbell on the
other. Sergeant McCormack was the greatest man on earth. He got
everybody as calm and collected as you could get. He said to me,
'Now come alongside me and try and keep that bunch of boys
alongside you. You stick close to me, as close as you can and you'll be
all right.'

Verlorenhoek was our first objective. It had been a village but it
didn't look like anything at all, just buildings practically levelled. We
just walked across. Mind you, the din was terrible, and there were
machine-guns in front of you, at the side of you and our own
machine-guns on elevated sights at the back of you spattering bullets
over your head. But we got to that line all right, with a bit of fighting,
and the Jerries came out mostly with their hands up. We just swept
over them. There was still a bit of barbed wire in front of the German
lines and people tended to bunch up, but old McCormack was there
all the time and he kept us going. 'Now boys, keep in line. Don't go
past me. Keep in line.' He was shouting all the time and looking back
if anyone was straggling. 'Come on now. What's wrong? Keep up.'
He had a rare way with him. Didn't seem to have a nerve in his body.
He kept the whole thing going in our sector and all the officers left it
to him. He was the best man, and they knew it.

When we got up to the village it looked just like red brick ruins,
but inside it was reinforced concrete and the machine-guns were
spattering out of gaps in the walls. They were sweeping all along the
front. Of course, a lot of the lads were getting it and dropping as we
went. But we took the village. We took it between us, with a lot of
the boys running up with bombs and the rest of us with rifles and
bayonets. We went right through and on to the second objective.

That was Frezenberg, maybe another thousand yards ahead. We were fighting all the way now, because they had machine-gun posts all over the place and I really started to use my rifle. If you were held up a minute, you just had to throw yourself down and shoot at whatever was shooting at you. By now the dead and the wounded were lying all about us, our boys and the Germans, and at the back of us there were stretcher-bearers running around. Every Company had its own stretcher-bearers so that they could get the boys back as quick as they could. But they couldn't keep up with the wounded.

When we got to Frezenberg the boys went with their bombs at these pillboxes and we went for the trenches. I saw a lot of the lads using the bayonet, but I didn't have to use mine, though the place was packed with Germans in shell-holes and trenches. I got to the top of a trench and there was one Boche just in front, looking up at me. I can see him now. He had glasses on, and I pointed my rifle and bayonet at him and he just said, 'Oh, no, no, no, no.' And he put his hands up. 'Right,' I said, 'right you are. Up this way.' He looked just like a little clerk chap or maybe a schoolmaster and I knew perfectly well as soon as I looked at him that he was going to surrender. So even when he didn't come up beside me immediately and turned round towards this thing like a dug-out at the side, I still didn't fire at him. He shouted down this dug-out, '*Kamarads. Kamarads.*' The next minute a whole bunch of them came out with their hands up. Luckily at this moment McCormack came along and I shouted to him, 'Would you look at this lot I've got here!' He just pointed at them to go back and off they went, meek as lambs, which was a relief to me! Two of them could have done for me, never mind a dozen.

Captain Campbell called me then to go back to Battalion Head-quarters. He scribbled on a paper and gave it to me and he said, 'Just tell them that we're getting on fine, Morgan. If you happen to lose the message, tell them that we're getting on fine. We're over the first two lines.'

Back across the battlefield. Back through the clouds of cordite, the crashing explosions, the sniper fire, the crackling machine-guns. Dodging the shell-holes, sidestepping the bodies of wounded and dead, detouring to avoid the hottest spots where the succeeding waves were still mopping up and flushing the enemy out – even back at the first objective, where machine-guns and snipers were still firing from hidden hollows in the tumbled earth.

Bill Morgan could move, sure-footed and easily, across the slopes and summits of every hill around Balmoral, for his father was head gillie on the Invercauld estate, and Bill had been stalking the deer and travelling the hills for almost as long as he could remember. He knew the art of conceal-ment, he could leap burns and stay steady on scree and heathered bog, knowing instinctively where to place his feet with their ground-gripping gillie's tread. It was a help – in spite of the thundering, crashing, all-pervading noise that numbed concentration. Bill Morgan sang, to shut it out. He sang 'Dark Lochnager' at the top of his voice. He roared it out, over and over again. He could hardly hear the sound of his own voice, but he could hear the song in his head. It took him well over an hour to get back to Battalion Headquarters, and almost two hours to return.

Private W. Morgan, No. 24819, 10/11th Btn., Highland Light Infantry

By the time I got back, the battalion was away up towards the next objective. As I went on, over the place I'd left them, over the ground where I knew they must have crossed to get to the third line, there was nothing but dead bodies lying all around. There were shells exploding everywhere and bullets flying around as if the devil him-self was at the guns, and when I got up to the front there was this terrible fighting. I could see troops in front of me crawling and jumping up and crawling again and dodging into shell-holes. Away ahead, it was all smoke and explosions and bullets flying out of Lewis guns like streams of fire all around these buildings they were attack-ing. I couldn't see anybody belonging to my lot at all.

Eventually I managed to make my way forward a bit and I found Sergeant McCormack with Lieutenant Burns. We were really held up at this place but the bombers were at it, attacking it from the flanks. There were boys there with buckets of bombs, and one lad in particular I saw crawl up to the wall and reach up and chuck bombs in at the window of the gun emplacement. They were all going at it, hammer and tongs. They were still going at it when it started to rain. They were still going at it an hour later, and by that time we were practically up to our knees in water. Lieutenant Burns said to me, 'You'd better get a message back, Morgan, and let them know what's happening. We must have reinforcements.'

We were standing in this wet shell-hole and he was just handing me the message when the machine-gun bullet got him. He fell right over on to me and we both went right down into the water. I managed to pull him a bit up the side of this crater and laid him down and knelt down beside him. His eyes were open and he looked straight up at me and he said, 'I'm all right, Mum.' And then he died. He was younger than me. I was twenty. Sergeant McCormack

crawled across, and looked at him. Then he looked at me. 'Get back
with the message, Morgan,' he said.

This time, although Battalion Headquarters had moved up into a captured German pillbox in their old front line, it took Morgan even longer
to reach it. By the time he did, the 15th Scottish, with a superhuman
effort, had managed to take the complex of formidable strongpoints
strung around Borry Farm and Beck House and had even pushed patrols
beyond them in preparation for the taking of the next objective. But the
Germans were massing for a counter-attack. The ground that Morgan had
to traverse on the way back was already turning into liquid mud. The
bodies of the dead soldiers. were scattered, sodden, where they had fallen
on the ground, and although as a private and a humble orderly runner
Morgan was no tactician, it was perfectly obvious to him, as he struggled
forward towards the fighting, that his Division was in trouble, for he was
being fired at from behind. The fact was that the flanks of the 15th
Division were in the air, because, on either side of them, neither the 55th
nor the 8th had quite managed to keep up with their advance.

Chapter 11

But it was only where their sector met the sector of the 15th that the 8th Division was making slow progress. The battalions in the middle were forging on. They were attacking, directly in front of Ypres, from the old front-line trenches on the lower slopes of the Hooge Ridge, flanked by Railway Wood on one side and the Menin Road on the other. The German trenches were only a hundred yards away at the top of the ridge. Between the two lines the ground was pitted and cratered not just with shell-holes but with mine craters as well, for miners on both sides had been active here in the earlier days of the war. Hooge was a strongpoint, hotly contested, for it was the very tip of the salient, the furthest point of penetration. On top of the ridge the German trenches ran through what had been the pleasant property of a country gentleman.

The small estate was bounded by the Bellewarde Ridge rising gently, almost at right angles, from the low ridge of Hooge. In the hollow where the slopes met was a lake, surrounded by ornamental shrubs and trees. A wide tree-studded paddock swept from the lake to the château with its high windows, steep gabled roofs, marvellously wrought balconies and the terrace flanked by stone urns. Beyond the broad gravelled drive that swept round to the entrance on the Menin Road stood the stables, the kitchen garden, the pleasure gardens, and to the east was a small private wood. Such was Hooge in the parish of Zillebeke in 1914 when Baron de Vinck and his family had hurriedly vacated it when the first shells began to fall unpleasantly near.

Now, Hooge, in the very fulcrum of the line of the salient, hotly fought over, constantly bombarded for the past two years, had totally ceased to exist. The trees in the wood and round the lake had been reduced to leafless shattered stumps. Beyond the site of the stables, two vast mine-craters, which could have easily accommodated two battalions of soldiers, glowered from the bare earth. As for the château, the stables, the outbuild-ings, not a single mound of rubble, not one stone, not one brick remained to show that they had ever existed. Only a dozen or so camouflaged pillboxes and strongpoints were scattered across the cratered, gas-soaked bog – long since swept clean of all vegetation – that stretched from the lake to the Menin Road where it breasted the rise. Hooge was in the forefront of the German defences. On 31 July it was the first objective of the 8th Division, straight ahead of them as they attacked.

W. Lockey, No. 71938, 1st Btn., Notts & Derbyshire Regiment (The Sherwood Foresters)

It was a terrible sight, really awe-inspiring, to see the barrage playing on the German front lines before we went over. It was an inferno. Just a solid line of fire and sparks and rockets lighting up the sky. When the barrage began to lift we went over like one man towards what had once been the German front line. It didn't exist. There was not a bit of wire, hardly a trench left, that hadn't been blown to smithereens by our barrage. We were moving uphill over the Hooge Ridge to skirt the Bellewarde Lake, and then we were supposed to cross the Bellewarde Ridge and make for Westhoek, which was our objective.

We weren't so much running forward as scrambling on over fallen trees and shell-holes, and although our own barrage was going in front of us the German field artillery was firing back, so there were shells exploding all around. The chap on my right had his head blown off, as neat as if it had been done with a chopper. I saw his trunk stumbling on for two or three paces and then collapsing in a heap. My pal, Tom Altham, went down too, badly wounded, and Sergeant-Major Dunn got a shell all to himself. The noise and the din were unbelievable, but apart from the shelling and a bit of machine-gun fire we met very little opposition until we were going up the Bellewarde Ridge. Then a fellow on my left was hit in the leg by a bullet that had come from the rear. When we turned round we saw two Germans with their heads sticking out of a hole, up went our rifles, but, to our amazement, the Jerries didn't stand their ground. They threw down their arms and ran towards our lines with their hands up.

On the top of the ridge we came to a big dug-out, deep in the earth. Some of the boys shouted down, but there was no reply. Just to make sure, they chucked a Mills bomb down and the Jerries replied to *that* all right! Out they came, those of them that could still move, and there were about forty filing out one after the other with their hands up. We left an escort with them and pushed on. In fact, we pushed on so fast that we reached our first objective about half an hour before the scheduled time and even went past it. Our officers had to signal us back because we were getting into our own gunfire, which was supposed to be falling in front of us in this creeping barrage. Now we were deeper into the German lines, even beyond

their second line, so there were bits of trenches and dug-outs, not too
badly shattered. We got into a bit of a trench that we'd just cleared of
Jerries and saw the smoke and explosions.

On the ground all around us it was simply carnage. Bits of bodies
and knocked-out guns lying all over the place and in front of us were
the bodies of about thirty German soldiers, all tossed about anyhow,
who had probably been caught in the barrage of our guns as they
tried to get away. There were some chaps in our lot who would do
anything for souvenirs, so, while we were waiting for the barrage to
lift, they got out of the trench and started searching these bodies for
anything they could get. They were after watches and buttons and
things like that, and they'd go through their pockets as well for wallets
and money, cigars, even photographs. Anything they could say they
took off a German.

Well, these chaps were turning over the bodies, rifling them, not
bothering about taking cover, when all of a sudden a shell came over.
There was this tremendous explosion and the whole earth in front of
us went up. We ducked down in the trench with mud and earth and
debris showering down on top of us. When we got up, and looked at
where our chaps had been, they'd got the full force of the explosion
and there they were, lying there – dead Tommies and bits of Tommies
lying all tangled up with the dead Germans. A couple survived, badly
wounded, so someone crawled forward and pulled them back to wait
for the stretcher-bearers.

The barrage lifted and on we went, those that were left of us. Just
charged straight ahead, clearing out the trenches and dug-outs as we
went with bombs and Lewis guns and, of course, the rifle and
bayonet. But as we got further into their lines there was more and
more machine-gun fire, not just from their positions ahead of us but
coming from outposts all round about. Of course, we more or less just
had to go ahead for the next main objective and leave it to the people
behind to clear them out, though we knocked out what we could,
especially when they were holding us up. But the fellows coming up
behind us had a really rough time. We got into our position on the
Westhoek Ridge, took over some trenches and dug-outs, and another Division was supposed to pass through us and carry on the
advance.

While we were waiting, it began to rain. The battalion that was to
pass through our line were the Royal Irish Rifles and when they
reached us they were in a bad way. The majority were either knocked
out or wounded by the German machine-guns. Three or four of
them stumbled into our part of the trench and every one had bullet-

wounds in the arms and legs. They were dragging along another boy, a young lad, only about eighteen. He'd been hit by an explosive bullet that passed straight through his right cheek and blew away the whole of the left cheek. It was a terrible sight. His tongue was sticking out through this great hole in his face. He kept calling for water. It ran out through the hole in his face as fast as we gave it to him.

We couldn't get the wounded away, not from that point, for there was nothing between us and the Germans. They were pasting us with shells and machine-gun fire and the rain kept pouring down. The trench began to fill up with water.

In the same sector the tank *Revenge* and its crew were in action again. Going up to the attack, through Ypres and swinging right to go up the Menin Road, the boys were not entirely happy. The showers of the last few days had softened even the few patches of virgin territory that lay within the salient; and in the sector they were making for, where the notorious Hooge Ridge had been churned up by almost three years of continuous shelling, they knew that they would find conditions far from good.

They were not the only ones who were worried. Major Fuller, Staff Intelligence Officer of the Tanks, on the basis of the information he had been able to piece together, had taken the trouble to prepare a map of the ground beyond the salient over which his tanks were expected to attack. Where he knew that the ground was likely to be too marshy for tanks to manoeuvre with any degree of safety and success, he had coloured the area blue. The extent of the blue patches, far in excess of the white, appalled even the map's author. Nevertheless, he had sent it to Haig's GHQ, so that the Commander-in-Chief could judge the conditions for himself. The map had been intercepted by Haig's obdurate Chief of Intelligence, Brigadier-General Charteris, who promptly returned it with the well-known reply, 'Pray, do not send any more of these ridiculous maps.' He is also reported to have remarked to an aide, 'I'm certainly not going to show *this* to the Commander-in-Chief. It would only depress him.'

Now the tanks were on their way.

Revenge's objective was Surbiton Villas, just beyond Hooge Château in the open country on the other side of Château Wood. The 'open' country was the length of four fair-sized fields lying between Château Wood, behind the tanks in the direction of Ypres, and Glencorse Wood in front, in the direction of the attack. Half a mile away, on the left, Bill Lockey and the Sherwood Foresters were battling their way towards Westhoek Ridge. The tanks forged straight up the Menin Road in fine style past Hooge, past Château Wood, and arrived within sight of their objective some two hundred yards ahead of their infantry. Then they came to the bend in the road where the road bore off to the right. Now they were over the breast of Hooge Ridge, and ahead of them the ground sloped gently down to a hollow and rose again to where, at this point, Glencorse Wood lay behind the Westhoek Ridge. The scattered pillboxes of Surbiton Villas stood in the hollow half-way between the tanks and the bristling third-line German trenches that lay along the ridge in front of Glencorse. *Revenge* left the road and made for the objective in front of the infantry, a good two hundred yards behind. Almost immediately she was in trouble.

Corporal A. E. Lee MM, No. 220132, A Btn., No. 3 Company, Tank Corps

When we got to the furthest point of this little valley, one of our tracks broke through the soft ground and we went down into a deep hole. It was impossible to move the tank because she was lurched right over on to her side, one gun pointing to the earth and the other pointing to the sky. We were completely helpless. We didn't even have our unditching beam because that had been shot away on the road up. Looking through the slits of the tank we could see the enemy, just about a hundred yards away, and they were getting out of their trenches, running out of dug-outs and massing for a counter-attack. Well, our own infantry were more than twice that distance behind us, coming along in open order, and it was obvious that we would be overrun before they could get to us.

I had no intention of staying in the tank like a snail in a shell until the enemy winkled us out. We had machine-guns which could be taken out and used independently, and we had with us an Irishman, Pat Brady, who had joined us as a replacement for 'Connie' Banner, who had gone sick. Brady had been an infantry machine-gunner, and he was the only chap in the crew who was used to working in the open, so I said to him, 'How would you feel about getting out with me, get a machine-gun each and set them up and try to get these blighters as they come across? If we don't do something, we're done for this time.' Pat was an Irishman and his reply was typically Irish. 'Give me a drink of rum,' he said, 'and I'm with you!'

We got out of the tank on the blind side away from the enemy, and the lads handed us the machine-guns and a box of ammunition each. Pat went to the right and I went to the left and we crawled diagonally, dragging the guns and ammunition, to shell-holes quite a bit away in front of the tank, because we could see that *Revenge* was going to be in the centre of the attack. They started coming towards us. We waited – and it seemed like hours – until the Germans were at point-blank range. Then we let them have it. They were probably expecting fire from the tank and instead they were caught in crossfire from hidden positions in front. They were *absolutely* demoralised and broken up. The infantry arrived and took the survivors prisoner and we were all pretty pleased with ourselves.

Iron Rations came up just in time to join in the jubilations. We thought there was a chance that we might be able to get *Revenge* out so we tried to borrow *Iron Rations'* unditching beam, but it was jammed on top of the tank. We just couldn't budge it. I climbed up to try to free the beam and, while I was struggling with it, there was a direct hit on *Iron Rations*. The next I knew I was lying eight or nine yards away, completely unhurt. I staggered up and there was *Iron Rations*, a complete wreck. Everyone within yards was either dead or badly wounded. By some freak I'd been thrown off by the blast before the splinters had a chance to spread out. Somebody came to help me.

It took me a few minutes to realise that it was *Iron Rations* that had gone and that these were all my own chums lying there. The sponson and guns had taken most of the impact and the blast had driven forward into the tank, and in that enclosed space everyone was killed. The infantry were working away trying to consolidate the position in case there was another counter-attack. Some of them helped us get *Iron Rations'* unditching beam across (it had been blown off by the shell blast), and we managed to get *Revenge* out of her hole.

Just as we'd finished I saw movement out in front like a hand waving, and there in a shell-hole was this little bloke. He was a Bavarian sergeant and he was wounded. Not a bad wound, mind you. Just a machine-gun bullet in the leg! And I knew where he'd got that from. So, as either Pat Brady or myself was responsible, I helped him back to the tank. He'd very sensibly taken cover in a shell-hole until everything had quietened down. I carried him back to the tank and bandaged his wound. I had some chocolate in my pocket, so I gave him that and we had a good old chat in schoolboy French. He was a nice little bloke. He told me his name was Jeff Werner and that he lived at 25 Artilleriestrasse, Munich. In fact, he gave me a photograph of himself and wrote his name and address on the back. 'After the war,' he said, 'after the war, you come and see me. You write, eh?' I wrote my address on a piece of paper and he tucked it into his wallet. We didn't hand him over to stretcher-bearers, for things were still a bit lively and, it was ridiculous, but we almost felt by then that he was one of us! We took him back in the tank and dropped him off at a field dressing-station, shaking hands as if we'd all been to a party. Then we went on down the Menin Road, and back to base. We were finished for the day.★

At about the same time, on the other side of the Menin Road, Walter Lugg was beginning to think that he was finished for good. As an artillery signaller he had gone across with a Brigade of the 18th Division, and things had gone badly wrong. The four woods, Château and Sanctuary, Glencorse and Inverness, could be described as lying in the four quarters of a roughly drawn square, divided diagonally from top left to bottom right by the Menin Road. It was the 30th Division which led the attack, and they were ordered to proceed diagonally upwards, on a front that would take the four battalions of their 21st Brigade through the wood around Herenthage Château (known to them as Stirling Castle) and on through the lower part of Inverness Copse. Travelling in the same direction on their left, the four battalions of the 90th Brigade would cross the Menin Road at Clapham Junction and then fight their way across the open ground near Surbiton Villas to attack Glencorse. When it was captured, the 90th Brigade was to stop.

There had been thoughts of putting in a fresher division to make the attack in this vital sector, for the 30th Division was battle-weary and depleted by heavy losses, but it was decided that it was too late to effect the exchange. Instead, a Brigade (the 53rd of the 18th Division) was set behind the 90th, and as soon as word was sent back that Glencorse had been gained and consolidated, it would sweep through the captured ground and carry the advance on to Polygon Wood, paving the way to Zonnebeke and Passchendaele itself.

The commanders who had conceived this plan might have thought twice about it had they realised the full force of the opposition that lay ahead, for the woods were not 'woods' in any sense of the word. Three

---

★Only 48 per cent of the 134 tanks engaged in the battle reached their first objective.

It was only after the Second World War that Nick Lee met Jeff Werner again. He and his wife looked him up on impulse when they were on holiday in Munich. Werner, by then a Professor at Munich University on the point of retiring to the Rhine valley, was overwhelmed by delight. He would certainly have been in touch himself, he informed Lee, had it not been for the fact that his wallet, with Lee's address in it, had been stolen. The Werners and the Lees struck up a cordial friendship, and Frau Werner frequently remarked that her husband had never tired of saying how kindly he'd been treated by the English. Nick Lee has never thought it necessary to inform Herr Werner that *he* was the one who shot him in the first place – nor that he was awarded the Military Medal for doing so.

years of shelling had long ago destroyed most of the trees, and they lay across the sodden, pitted earth in an almost impassable tangle of twisted roots and mangled branches. But it was here, camouflaged among the few splintered thickets of barkless stumps that still stood miraculously vertical, that the Germans had concentrated their most formidable defences and manned them with crack *Eingriffen* troops of a very different calibre from their garrisons in the front line. Glencorse and Inverness were no longer woods. They were fortresses. They were also man-traps, waiting with steel jaws agape, ready to snap. But it was the 53rd Brigade of the 18th Division which walked straight into the trap, for a battalion of the 90th Brigade, sent ahead to blaze the trail, made a fatal mistake. They went to the wrong wood.

It took the 90th Brigade well over an hour of bitter fighting to break through the first German line running through the eastern edge of Sanctuary Wood. It was still barely dawn. The situation was chaotic, and in the confusion one battalion of the 90th (the one nearest the Menin Road) lost direction and strayed to the north. The wood they went to was Château Wood, which had fallen to the 8th Division in the first hour of the attack.

When the message was flashed back that 'Glencorse' had been taken, the waiting brigade of the 18th Division plunged forward through Sanctuary Wood into what, in reality, was a gap in the line. A mere four battalions of men were making straight for the untouched bastion of the Germans' second line of defence, and they didn't have a hope in hell.

By nine o'clock Divisional Headquarters had made sense of the situation, realised that a mistake had been made, and tried to recall the men. But by nine o'clock the men were already in the trap. The German shells had begun to rain down as soon as they cleared Sanctuary Wood, and now, as they battled forward over the Menin Road, they were caught by machine-guns firing in enfilade from the northern tip of Inverness Copse, which like Glencorse Wood was still firmly in German hands.

Gunner W. Lugg MM, C Bty., 53rd Brigade, 18th Division, Royal Field Artillery

I remember thinking that if we survived, it would be a miracle. We were all over the place, just taking shelter where we could. I was with Signaller Forsdick, a boy from Battersea who had been carrying a drum of cable with me, and after a while we realised that we'd been separated from our officer and the rest of the party. The Germans must have been very near by because we could hear the rifle bullets whizzing by, and all of a sudden Forsdick fell down. He'd been hit by

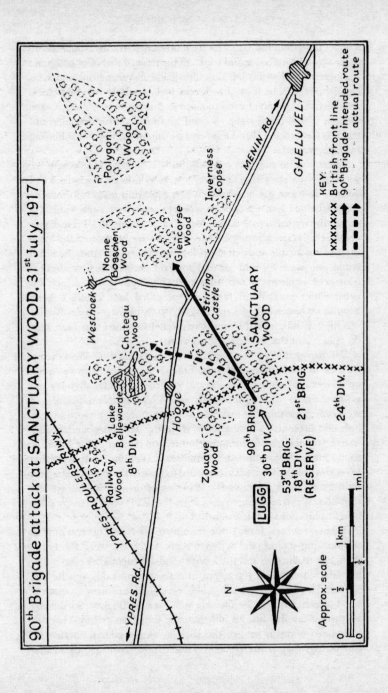

90th Brigade attack at SANCTUARY WOOD, 31st July. 1917

POLYGON WOOD

NONNE BOSSCHEN WOOD

GLENCORSE WOOD

INVERNESS COPSE

WESTHOEK

CHATEAU WOOD

STIRLING CASTLE

SANCTUARY WOOD

MENIN Rd.

GHELUVELT

Lake Bellewarde

HOOGE

RAILWAY WOOD

ZOUAVE WOOD

90th BRIG.
30th DIV.

21st BRIG.

24th DIV.

8th DIV.

YPRES–ROULERS Railway

YPRES Rd.

LUGG

53rd BRIG.
18th DIV.
(RESERVE)

N

Approx. scale

0   ½   1km
0   ½   1ml

KEY:
xxxxxxx   British front line
━━━▶   90th Brigade intended route
┅┅┅▶   actual route

a bullet fired from our rear. I carried him across to a shell-hole where there was a bit of cover and took off his tunic. The bullet had gone through just below his left shoulder-blade and come out under his collar-bone. Oh, he looked bad, very bad. He started spitting blood and his face was grey. I tried to console him by saying, 'Take it easy, old son. You'll be all right.' I eased his braces off his shoulder, and tried to staunch the blood a bit and tie an emergency field-dressing over the wound.

There was no point in carrying on. We hadn't a clue where we were, or where the rest of the party was, even if they had survived, so I decided to try to get him back. When the firing eased off momentarily I helped him up and managed to walk him a few yards. It's extraordinary the trivial things that stick in your mind. I remember vividly that with each step he took, blood oozed out on to the loose loop of his braces and fell drop by drop on to his trousers. From where we were I could see the forward dressing-station about a quarter of a mile to the rear, but I knew it was going to be a long job getting him back. Poor 'Dick', as we called him, couldn't speak beyond a whisper, and he kept hanging on to me for grim death as if I was his only link with this world. In a way I suppose I was. I just kept on telling him that he would be all right.

We managed to make progress, a few yards at a time. We'd shelter for a bit in a shell-hole, and then if the shelling seemed to be easing up we'd crawl into the next one and wait there for a bit, then try and get to the next one a yard or two away. After a couple of hours (and we'd only gone thirty or forty yards in that time) we got into a shell-hole and there was a youngster in it, crying. He was obviously in a state of terrible shock, he flung himself on us and threw his arms round my neck, shouting for his mother. I don't mind admitting that I was as windy as hell myself, but I said to him, 'All right, all right. Stay with us and we'll get you back.' He calmed down a bit, but we lost him later. We were trying to get on, but he didn't want to move once he'd found a hole in the ground.

We made it back. It took us ten hours to cover that quarter mile to the dressing-station, and when we got there we were absolutely drenched to the skin and thick with mud. Dick couldn't even whisper any more. When I got him into the aid-post dug-out he just squeezed my hand as if to say goodbye. I don't know how he made it, but I was happy that he did. He got back to Blighty. So did my brother-in-law. He was hit in Sanctuary Wood on 31 July. He must have been lying in one of the shell-holes we passed, because he had his right leg shattered and couldn't move at all. He lay in that shell-hole all night with water up to his neck, managing to keep conscious, otherwise he would have drowned. They got him out eventually, but he lost his leg. He was nineteen years old.

The rain teemed down mercilessly on the battlefield. By six o'clock the soldiers were standing up to their knees in mud and water in shell-holes and trenches; by eight o'clock, in places, they were waist-deep in a morass. The stretcher-bearers, in spite of the shells exploding all around, in spite of the steadily worsening ground, had worked manfully and performed miracles, but as the rain fell and the earth turned to liquid they were sinking knee-deep at every step. In normal conditions, even under fire, two men could carry a casualty from the line to the dressing-station. Now it took four, even six, men to haul a stretcher case to safety, and a journey of as little as two hundred yards could take two hours of struggle through the lashing rain and the sucking mud. When darkness fell – and it fell early on that wet and glowering evening – the first-aid men had to give up. There was no possibility of getting the wounded away. There they must lie, among the dead, sheltering as best they could from the bone-chilling rain, and hoping, if they were not beyond hope, for rescue in the morning.

As dusk fell dankly round the streaming eaves of La Louvie Château ten miles behind the battle, an orderly drew the curtains and lit the pressure-lamps in the room where the gloomy Corps Commanders had been summoned to confer with General Gough. Gough came hurrying in with his Chief-of-Staff, Neill Malcolm. 'Good evening, gentlemen. What a perfect bloody curse this rain is!'

Gough had already studied the reports. Everyone knew, so far as it was possible to know, what the situation was. The question now was, what could be done to improve it?

To their ears, the rumble of gunfire in the distance was no more ominous than the sound of the relentless patter of the rain in the tossing trees. The news of the first successes of the day, the capture of the first German lines, had been flashed to London, where in Fleet Street the headlines had already been set for the early editions of the morning newspapers.

GREAT ALLIED ATTACK
YPRES SALIENT WIDENED
FIRST DAY'S OBJECTS ACHIEVED

But it would have been more correct to say that the objectives of the first few hours had been gained, where they lay in the weakest outer perimeter of the German lines. On the left of the sector, the Guards had

done wonderfully well and had got right up to their third objective, a tiny
rivulet called the Steenbeek. But the enemy was ranged in force on its
other bank and the Steenbeek itself, under the torrent of water that
poured from the leaden skies, was stretching and widening, and dissolving
the ground on either side into a glutinous soup. In the adjacent sector the
51st Highland Division had also reached the Steenbeek and hung grimly
on to its position, in spite of shattering shell-fire and heavy counter-
attacks. The 39th had reached much further, as far as the Zonnebeke-
Langemarck Road, but had been forced to fall back to St Julien, leaving in
its wake a field of dead and wounded Tommies lying thick on the ground.
They lay thick on the Frezenberg Ridge too, where Borry Farm and
Beck House, gained at such awful cost in the afternoon, had been lost
again in the evening. They lay on top of the Westhoek Ridge. They lay
thickest of all around the Menin Road within sight of Glencorse Wood.

Recasting their plans, Gough and his commanders were under no illu-
sions. There could be no question of pressing home the advance. Tomorrow the troops would have to consolidate. Tomorrow, at all costs, they
would have to be relieved, for although the troops who'd taken part in the
initial assault had been told that they would be withdrawn at nightfall, in
the unexpectedly appalling conditions and the confusion of the front,
there was no way of getting reliefs up until the Engineers had managed to
make some sort of tracks to give them a foothold in the quagmire. Then
there were the guns. How were they to be moved?

On the open site on which C.241 Battery stood awash at Hilltop Farm,
Major Rory Macleod was not, at that moment, thinking of that particular
problem. His whole concern was to keep his guns firing, for enemy shells
were still thundering down on the infantry holding the ruins of St Julien.
The Germans were firing from permanent, sheltered gun positions with
solid dug-outs and shelters. At Hilltop there was no shelter at all. Not for
the guns, not for the men, not even for the ammunition – and the new
load of ammunition which had reached C Battery just an hour before was
already sinking into the mud. Each shell had to be dug up and cleaned
before it could be fired. It doubled the work, and the men were already
weary. Macleod intended to work out a rota whereby they could each
have an hour or two of rest in the coming night. There was no billet to
rest in, of course. Whoever could be spared from the guns must simply
make the best of it, and lie wrapped in a groundsheet somewhere between
the shell-holes, under the endless rain. Already they were soaked to the
skin. They wouldn't be dry again for a fortnight. Still, they were better off
than the infantry.

★

Less than two miles ahead in the inferno of shells exploding on the front around St Julien, the four Company Quartermaster Sergeants of the 1st Battalion, The Hertfordshire Regiment, were looking for their battalion. They were hours late, for the ground had been impassable in places, but they had kept on going with their small party because they were bringing up the Herts' supper – rations for 600 men.

CQMS G. W. Fisher, 1st Btn., The Hertfordshire Regiment, 39th Division

I saw my company off, with extra bandoliers of ammunition and so on, and I remember shaking hands with the officer commanding the company, Captain Lowry MC. He shook hands with me, and I looked at him and he looked at me and I knew he wasn't coming back, and he knew that I knew that he wasn't coming back. He said, 'I'll see you tonight up on the Green Line' – that was their third objective. I said, 'I'll be there all right.'

Normally, the rations went up on limbers, but the mud was so bad that we had to take them up in panniers on pack mules. The conditions were so bad that we saw some of the artillery people, who were taking their ammunition up that way, actually having to shoot some of their mules, for they were right up to their stomachs in mud. They just couldn't get them out. When we eventually got to what had been the first German line, the officer in charge of the transport said, 'Well, this is as far as I can take my mules. I am dumping the rations here. You must make contact with the companies and get carrying parties down to take the rations up.' So, he about-turned with his mules and off he went. There were four Company Quartermaster Sergeants, myself and three others, and we decided between us that two of us should go forward to try to find the battalion, one would stay with the rations, and the other one would try to find Brigade Headquarters to get some indication as to where the battalion might be. We tossed up for the different jobs and it fell to my lot to have to find Brigade Headquarters, so I set off. There was a most tremendous bombardment going on all the while. After a long time, I found the Brigade Headquarters. They were in an underground German concrete pillbox just in front of St Julien. I went down the stairs, saluted the Brigadier, told him who I was, explained the position and said, 'Could you give me any instructions, sir, that would help me to find the battalion?'

He just stood and looked at me. We were both standing on the steps, and the pillbox was rocking like a boat in a rough sea with explosions. After a while he said, 'I'm sorry, Quarters, I'm afraid there isn't *any* Hertfordshire Regiment.'

Of course, I was flabbergasted but a Company Quartermaster Sergeant doesn't argue with a Brigadier. I said, 'Well, sir, my problem is we've got rations for 600 men, including four two-gallon petrol tins of rum, can you give me any instructions as to what to do with it?' He thought for a moment or two, then he said, 'Well, Quarters, everyone's had a very hard day today so distribute it to anyone who happens to be about that you think could do with it – and then get back to your transport lines.'

We got rid of the rations to all sorts of people who were coming by – pack mules and transport people, artillery men, engineers, anybody at all. But we kept one two-gallon can of rum for ourselves for the trek back. It was five or six miles to the transport lines, through all the mud and rain, and we needed something to get our courage up to tell them that the battalion had been wiped out. We were all that was left. The few of us who'd been left back at the transport lines. About 10 per cent of the strength.★

The divisions which had been standing by, ready to go in to relieve the exhausted men out in the forefront of the battle, made hopeless attempts to get up the line, but after a little way they had to be withdrawn, and squelched their way back again to damp bivouacs in the rear. The engineers worked on. Bill Mathieson and Major Storey had been out all day on the Pilkem Ridge, surveying and marking a route over terrain that, in the course of the day, had turned from mud to swamp, so that the vital road could be built which would enable supplies and guns and even tanks to move to the new front line for the next attack. Miraculously, the road had been pushed forward a considerable distance beyond the causeway over the canal, but as Mathieson and Storey made their weary way back at nightfall, they were able to make out through the rain and gloom a terrible debris of shattered limbers and the bodies of men and horses, grotesquely strewn among the craters. In the half-light, little groups of stretcher-bearers were still wading through the swamp among the carnage. Limbers were still rumbling up the newly-built stretch of road, heavy with great loads of raw beechwood planks. Rain streamed from the horses' manes and poured off the ground-sheet capes of the Tommies and sappers who plodded behind, heads bent against the storm, as they went forward to carry on the work. Away to left and right, men were struggling to lay

★A few of the Herts eventually got back – a very few. Of the 650 who had attacked through St Julien to the Langemarck-Zonnebeke Road, 136 were killed and 400 wounded. The 1st Herts had temporarily ceased to exist.

duckboards in a tortuous track that snaked round and between the shell-holes, and all around them exploding shells sent fountains of mud and water roaring into the air.

Rifleman J. E. Maxwell, 11th Btn., The Rifle Brigade

By dusk, we'd been at that job for eight hours or more and the wounded were still coming down. Two of the RAMC people stopped just by our working party. They were carrying a young German private, obviously very seriously wounded. They laid the stretcher down on our duckboards and asked if anyone spoke German. Our lance-corporal said, 'Yes, I can speak a bit.' They were older men than us, and one of them said, 'Well, just have a word with this lad if you can, will you?' So he bent over the stretcher and said something to this boy. Some words of comfort in German. And the boy looked at him, and he said just one word, '*Mutti.*' Then he died. We knocked off, but I kept thinking about him. They were in the same boat as ourselves.

A mile and a half away in a captured German dug-out near the Steenbeek, Jim Annan and a handful of others were uncomfortably settling down for the night. They could have done with some of the rations that George Fisher of the 1st Herts was giving away to all and sundry in the murk a mile away, for no Company Quartermaster had reached them, and they were having to make do with iron rations – bully beef and hard square biscuits. They dared not show a light, for they were within yards of the Germans, across the Steenbeek, and the open gap which had been the Germans' rear entrance was now facing the enemy lines. It was a doorless aperture, framing a curtain of rain that changed from green to blue to silver to fiery red, against the backcloth of rocket flares and explosions. Gusts of rain blew in, drenching the crouching men inside, and over the lip of the aperture the muddy water trickled and splashed and plopped into the ever-deepening pool that covered the concrete floor.

Lieutenant J. Annan, 1st/9th Btn., Royal Scots Regiment

Uncomfortable! I should say it was. Our kilts were soaking, and when you sit in the freezing cold with a wet kilt between your legs it's beyond description. It was really only a two- or three-man pillbox. We managed to squeeze in five or six, so we took turns to squat in it for a bit, then we'd crawl outside and let some of the other fellows in. We had blokes wounded, badly wounded. We'd laid them on Jerry duckboards – because we'd no stretchers – but this entrance to the pillbox was so small we couldn't get the duckboards through. So there was nothing for it but to cover the men with groundsheets, lay them on the open ground in the shelter of the back wall of the pillbox, and post a sentry there to keep an eye on them. Then there was a lull in the shelling, and through the machine-gun slit on the back wall of the pillbox we heard this terrible kind of gurgling noise. It was the wounded, lying there sinking, and this liquid mud burying them alive, running over their faces into their mouth and nose. We had to keep heaving the duckboards up and trying to put some other stuff underneath, just so that the fellows wouldn't sink so much. We couldn't understand why, in the name of God, anyone had ordered an attack like that over terrain like that. It was impossible.

A hundred yards away, John Ritchie had not been fortunate enough to find a place in the dubious shelter of a flooded dug-out. When he and his mates had settled themselves on the slippery sides of a deep shell-hole, there had been a foot or so of water in the bottom. By midnight, it was up to their armpits. At least, remarked someone, it softened their supper for them, the ration biscuits so hard that they squeaked against your teeth. The thought consoled no one. Every man among them, every man along the confused line of the front, had been awake now for more than forty hours and had been marching or fighting for the last twenty-four.

The eight Corps Commanders, although reasonably sheltered in the comparative luxury of their headquarters' billets, also passed an uneasy night as they tried to make some sense of the situation on their fronts and worried about the outcome of the battle. At their meeting with Gough, it had been agreed that the attacks should proceed as soon as the reliefs could get in. On 2 August (and now that it was past midnight, that meant tomorrow) fresh troops would go ahead for the original objectives in the sectors where they had not been reached in the first assault. Then, on 4 August, the divisions now resting on the Steenbeek would attack the village of Langemarck. But it could only be done if the weather improved. First, it would *have* to stop raining.

As the miserable, grey dawn stretched leaden fingers over the Passchendaele Ridge and crept across the salient to Frezenberg, Bill Morgan, dozing in a shell-hole, awoke with the rain still beating down on his face. It was a large shell-hole, half-full of water, and half a dozen men clung cramped and exhausted to its sides. Opposite Bill was an officer of the Cameron Highlanders who had crawled in during the night. He lay at an awkward angle, his mud-coated legs sticking out from beneath a bedraggled kilt. There wasn't a mark on his body, but his head lay under the water. Bill could see his face quite clearly. The eyes were closed. He had slipped in and drowned in his sleep.

It was 1 August, the first day of what was destined to be the wettest August in living memory.

Chapter 12

It went on raining as if some malevolent deity had opened a tap in the heavens. It rained in sheets, in torrents, in cataracts. It rained as no man since Noah had ever remembered it raining before. It rained without stopping for four days and four nights.

The water falling from the sky on to the lower slopes of the ridges where the troops were grimly holding on to their ragged front line was augmented by water pouring from the high ground in front of them, in cascades that turned every stream into a torrent, every ditch into a watercourse and every trench into a creek of mud and effluent. It soaked into the earth and seeped up again from below as the Tommies who found themselves on open ground shovelled into the mud and threw up breastworks of slush for cover. They despaired of finding any dry ground, for no matter how deep they dug, it was mud, mud, mud that turned to liquid as soon as it was exposed to the rain, in trenches that filled with water as fast as the troops could bail them out with mugs and tin hats. But they had to go on trying to consolidate the line, to find a way of wedging a Lewis gun on the crumbling rim of some slimy hole, for there they were and there they had to stay.

In spite of the weather, the Germans were not content to sit in the shelter of their concrete strongholds but were throwing their men out into the morass in violent counter-attacks, supported by devastating machine-gun fire and terrible shelling from their positions up the hill. By some kind of miracle, a strong force of Germans managed to wallow across a porridge of churned-up mud and bodies between the Zonnebeke-Langemarck Road and St Julien, and retook St Julien itself. Later, at their last gasp and in a feat that was little short of miraculous, the bone-weary remnants of the men they had thrown out, managed to regain it. In most places it was stalemate.

The Army sat hunched, sheltering as best it could from the flying shells and rain that fell so heavily that Major Macleod, struggling towards his new forward observation post a thousand yards ahead at Oblong Farm, found it exceedingly difficult to register his guns on their objectives, for the simple reason that within five minutes his artillery map disintegrated and turned to pulp in his hands.

The Engineers worked on. The roads and tracks crept forward. The supply columns struggled as far as they could towards the line with materials for the roads, ammunition for the guns and rations for the troops – if they could get that far. Not many rations did reach the line. There were iron rations, of course, tins of bully beef in their haversacks and a reserve supply in the haversacks of dead comrades. There were sodden biscuits. There was the possibility of brewing tea on a tommy cooker contrived from a cylindrical cigarette tin filled with strips of wadding, judiciously soaked in methylated spirits before departure for the line. But there was only that possibility if you could find a match dry enough to light the wick. There were the wounded to be tended, cheered and comforted as they lay soaked, unconscious or quietly moaning. There was little enough that could be done for them. Like everyone else, they had no alternative but to wait until the reliefs came.

By midday on Saturday the rain had gone off. A watery sun was doing its best to sneak around the clouds. The relief had come up. Damp and weary, the boys were going out of the line.

The wounded, or those of them who had survived four days' exposure to the elements, were going out too, carried by comrades or stretcher-bearers on a four-hour journey through the swamp to the ambulances that would take them to the casualty clearing stations. It was not amazing that the casualties of the battle had been reported to be light, for only a fraction of the wounded had been able to crawl back or be carried from the field. Now the convoys were pouring in, and the nurses were rushed off their gum-booted feet.

Sister J. Calder, No. 19 Casualty Clearing Station at Remy Siding

In a camp hospital it's dirty because the ground is earth, there's no linoleum on the floor, nor wood. It was simply grass, we were walking on grass all the time – or rather it was grass before it turned into mud. And, of course, we were shelled and had shell-holes round about. It was that week at No. 19 that Matron fell into a shell-hole one night when she was doing a night round. We searched for her all over the place, because she was needed in the hospital and couldn't be found. Finally she was found dragging herself out of this shell-hole, a great deep one from one of those very heavy high-explosive shells. She'd been in it an hour and she'd just managed to prevent herself from being drowned, for it was full of water.

We'd had boys coming in all week, of course, and we'd been busy but the ones we got at the weekend were in a shocking state, because so many of them had been lying out in the mud before they could be picked up by the first-aid orderlies. Their clothes were simply filthy. They didn't look like clothes at all. We had to cut them off and do what we could. But it was too late for a lot of them, and many a one lost an arm or a leg that would have healed up right away if he'd been brought straight in. We felt terribly sorry for them but we had to try not to show our feelings, because it would never have done. We'd all have been sunk in gloom and then we'd have been no good to the men. But it was difficult when a man was very badly wounded, wounded in a very difficult place perhaps. It was hard not to show sympathy.

And there was always this extraordinary feeling of attraction between a wounded man and his nurse. I've never known anything like it. It was quite impersonal, but there was a sense of sympathy and understanding that was indescribable. In a civilian hospital – even an army hospital – the man had a home quite near and relations possibly, but the wounded man on the battlefield is miles away from his home and his family; he's in pain and he's amongst strangers, and I think that was why this sympathy went out from one to the other. And he somehow also had a sense of safety that he'd come to a haven where there was a roof over his head – though it was only a canvas one, at least he was having his wounds attended to.

If it was at all possible to move them, the men were sent down the line. All day from Remy Siding, from 'Mendinghem' and No. 11 CCS at Godwaersveldt, the hospital trains were loaded as fast as they could pull into the sidings, and sent off down to the base hospitals in the south. All week they had been receiving casualties in the clutch of hospitals around Boulogne and Etaples, and the 'Blighties' who were fit to travel, or even the lucky ones who might otherwise have been sent back to the front after two weeks' nursing, were being cleared out to make room for the inevitable flood of wounded after the next attack. The hospital ships had left low in the water with stretcher cases, their decks crammed with walking wounded, and by 4 August the hospital trains were pulling in every hour to Charing Cross Station.

It was Bank Holiday Saturday. Over at Victoria Station, in spite of the changeable weather, so many people were anxious to get away to the coast that supplementary booking offices had to be opened. Some holiday-makers had been queuing since five o'clock in the morning. The coastal resorts of Britain were packed and Blackpool in particular looked forward to a 'record' season. All weekend, as the papers reported, the seafronts of Britain's coastal resorts 'presented a very animated appearance'.

Londoners who were unable to get away for the holiday weekend packed into the Queen's Hall to attend a 'patriotic meeting'. The Prime Minister spoke. There was a display of the flags of the Allied nations, culminating in the ceremonial unfurling of the Union Jack. This was followed by a full rendering of the National Anthem, the solo verses sung by Miss Margaret Balfour. Many dignitaries attended, including the Archbishop of Canterbury and twenty members of the Government. They sang, 'Oh God Our help in Ages Past' and, as a grand finale, 'Rule, Britannia!' Meanwhile, a hundred or so miles away across the Channel, the Royal Scots, sitting on the Steenbeek beyond the Pilkem Ridge, anxious though they were to depart, were having considerable difficulty in getting out of the line. They knew the reliefs were there, but the trouble was that the terrain had changed so much since they went in that nobody could find his way back to Battalion Headquarters to guide up the reliefs.

Lieutenant J. Annan, 1st/9th Btn., Royal Scots Regiment

We sent out four runners to get to Battalion Headquarters at Minty's Farm, and every time, after an hour, the Adjutant rang up – because somehow or other we got a line laid – to ask, 'When is your runner coming up to take the relief out?' That happened four times, and still he was on the blower, kicking up hell and asking where the runners were. Well, we weren't too happy about it either! So I said, 'Well, the only thing I can do is have a go myself and see if I can get there.' I walked right to it and there were no landmarks at all. You couldn't say, well, I know that tree, or I can see half a house there, or anything like that. There was nothing. Just one morass of mud as far as the horizon. The runners had simply got lost, and I didn't blame them at all. I never knew before that I had a sense of direction, and in fact I was really surprised when I got there. But I did, and I managed to bring back the relief. Then we got out of it. We'd got as far as we could and held on, and we lived on iron rations for four days. We didn't think we'd done too badly.

My Lewis-gun team did best of all. I don't think there was one of them over twenty. We got them into a dug-out there and in spite of the mud they kept their gun in immaculate cleanliness, ready for anything. They were a great little team. They attended to it like a mother to a baby and the thing was absolutely like a new pin, even in all that mud. I never bothered or needed to examine it. I knew they were all right and ready for anything. They were marvellous, the whole bunch, the lads and the sergeants too. Sergeant

Runciman, and Sergeant Bruce, and Sergeant 'Ecky' Hume, and
Tommy Lamb in charge of the machine-guns, and all the boys
as well. They were still cheery, even after four days out among all
that.

And so, not quite so cheerily perhaps, the next lot of troops went in,
held the line, and waited for the next move.

For almost a week, between intermittent showers, the sun burned
hot on the salient, so hot that in places steam rose from the sodden earth.
At the front the gunfire abated a little as both sides recouped their
strength, and behind the line the Tommies, newly out of the trenches, had
time to dry off and spruce up for the inevitable kit inspections in every
camp.

Lieutenant G. Salisbury-Jones, 1st Btn., Coldstream Guards

It was one of the things we always made an effort to do. We got out of
the line, and almost as soon as possible we had an inspection to see if
the boots were clean, and so on, to get back into what I call peacetime
conditions. We were inspected by Sir Douglas Haig. He was delighted with what the division had done, which was everything that
had been asked of it. He also said that it did us great credit looking so
smart after we had only just come out of the line. So, of course, we
were very pleased, and I wrote home to my mother and told her
about it.

After the distributions of the great damp piles of letters and parcels,
which for the first time ever the Army had not been able to send straight
up to the men in the line, everyone was writing letters.

Dear Mum, Just a line to let you know I'm OK. . . . My Dear Mother
and Father, I'm sorry that I have not managed to write for a few days
but, as you may have seen in the newspapers, we have been rather
busy. . . . My Own Darling Wife, Thank you for your three sweet
letters which I received when I returned from. . . . Dear Old Girl,
Now don't get in a state when you see I am in hospital. It is nothing
but a scratch and I am quite OK, and full of beans. . . . Dear Mum –
Auntie May – Nellie – Ada – Gwen – thank you for the socks . . .
smokes . . . cake . . . toffee . . . pork pie . . . parcel from Fortnums. . . .

Private Harold Diffey was newly out of hospital, for a fortunate attack
of German measles had kept him out of the line when the 38th Welsh

Division went over on 31 July. He tried to make his letter home as tactful as possible.

Dear Mum and Dad and all at home,
   Thank you for your very welcome letter and parcel. What a surprise I got. When I wrote from hospital and said I would love some rabbit and pork like we used to have, I never thought you'd be having rabbit and pork at home the day you got the letter. As you say, it was a funny coincidence. I see you said it was Dad's idea to put it in an old Golden Syrup tin. Well, Dad, it was a very kind thought and I thank you very much. Unfortunately, by the time I got it, there was ferns growing out of the tin. Never mind, as the saying goes, it's the thought that counts.

A certain Mrs Worker had also lovingly packed a parcel for her boy, Johnny, who, far from home, was about to have his twenty-first birthday.

Guardsman J. Worker, No. 15756, 1st Btn., Scots Guards

She'd baked a birthday cake for me and packed it in a parcel, and she'd also put in something I'd asked for, which was a packet of disinfectant that would kill lice. It was called Paracitox. It tasted of carbolic, as I found out, because the packet had burst and my birthday cake was covered with this Paracitox – permeated with it. It tasted absolutely foul, but my mother had baked that cake and I was so sentimental that I couldn't bring myself to throw it away, and of course I was too ashamed to give any of it to my friends, so piece by piece I ate it, carbolic and all, rather than throw away cake that had come from my mother.

Dear Mum, Thank you for the parcel and the lovely cake. Also for the card and your good wishes . . .
But the postman, knocking at the door of 5 Kerr Street in Stockbridge in Edinburgh, brought a letter of a more disquieting nature:

*No. 2 Australian
General Hospital.*

Re: Pte. R. Harvey.   Ward K.   Bed 54
From Captain Hume Robertson.

Dear Mr Harvey,
   Your brave son has not escaped from the battle unscathed – he was wounded on the 31 July in the right arm and abdomen.

He is doing as well as can be expected. If you have not by the time this reaches you received any word from the Military to the contrary, you will know he still progresses to recovery.

I trust in God's goodness this will be granted.

He has every care and attention. He sends his best love.

Yours sincerely,
Hume Robertson
Chaplain.

At Nieuport, General Rawlinson's Army still waited to support the amphibious attack which would take place as soon as the troops could break out of the salient and wheel round to assault the coastline from the rear. Paddy King and some other men of the 2/5th Battalion, East Lancashire Regiment, took advantage of the fine weather to enjoy a little sea-bathing on what was, after all, August Bank Holiday Monday. They were within sight of the German guns at Ostend, and the Germans most unsportingly shelled the merry bathers while they were in the water. Rushing for the beach and the shelter of their trenches in the sand-dunes, they were further aggrieved to run slap into a shoal of stinging jelly-fish. There were no casualties from the shells, but the jelly-fish stings kept the MO busy for the rest of the afternoon.

The tide would be right for the attack on 25 August. Which gave the men in the salient exactly nineteen days to conquer the Passchendaele Ridge and advance seven miles beyond it.

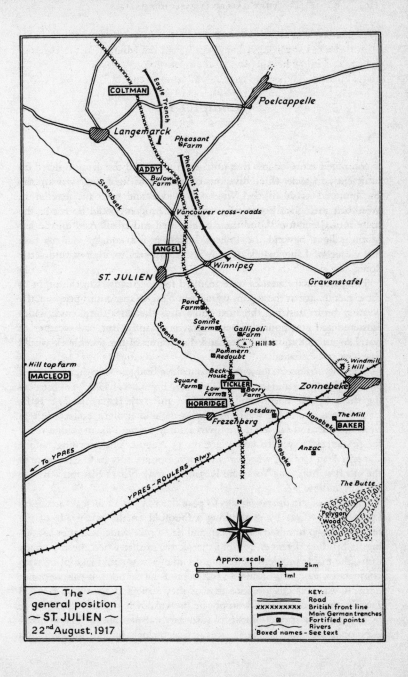

COLTMAN

Eagle Trench

Poelcappelle

Langemarck

Pheasant
Farm

ADDY

Bülow
Farm

Pheasant Trench

Steenbeek

Vancouver cross-roads

ANGEL

ST. JULIEN

Winnipeg

Gravenstafel

Pond
Farm

Somme
Farm

Steenbeek

Gallipoli
Farm

Hill 35

Pommern
Redoubt

Windmill
Hill

Hill top farm

MACLEOD

Beck-
House

Square
Farm

Low
Farm

TICKLER

Borry
Farm

Zonnebeke

HORRIDGE

Potsdam

Frezenberg

Hanebeke

The Mill

BAKER

To YPRES

Hanebeke

Anzac

YPRES-ROULERS Rlwy.

The Butte

Polygon
Wood

N

Approx. scale

0   1   1½   2km

0   ½   1 ml

The
general position
~ ST. JULIEN ~
22ⁿᵈ August, 1917

KEY:
——————— Road
xxxxxxxxx British front line
~~~~~~~ Main German trenches
▥ Fortified points
〰 Rivers
'Boxed' names - See text

Chapter 13

It continued more or less fine until 10 August, and the ground dried up sufficiently to allow three divisions of infantry to fight their way up the last hundred yards of the Westhoek Ridge and take the hamlet of Westhoek itself. But before any significant progress could be made, the bastion of Glencorse Wood must be stormed and taken. And on the left of the salient, beyond the Pilkem Ridge, it was equally vital to take the village of Langemarck. If only the capricious weather would settle down.

The preliminary attacks were planned for 13 August. On the night of the eleventh, just as the troops were assembling to move into position, the weather broke and for the next three days the skies thundered, winds blustered and rain poured down almost incessantly. But, bad weather or not, Langemarck must be taken and the swamp of the Steenbeek would first have to be crossed.

The only means of doing so was to make a bridge – or rather a series of pontoon bridges – and for the last week, the Engineers had been constructing them by the dozen. Bill Worrell of the 12th Battalion, The Rifle Brigade, was one of the weary men who, night after night, collected them from the REs and carried them up to a dump on the Pilkem Ridge, ready for the attack. It was to take place on 15 August. The morning before, Captain Alan Goring, who was a Platoon Commander in C Company of the 6th Battalion, The Yorkshire Regiment, took No. 11 Platoon across to 'do a little show'.

The idea of the operation was to pave the way for a full-scale attack on Langemarck village by establishing a foothold on the other side of the Steenbeek two hundred yards deep and half a mile wide; and after subduing its bristling defences, to hold the sector, so that when the big attack came, the major problem of getting the men across could take place with comparative ease two hundred yards behind the outposts. If this were not done, it was perfectly obvious that, as they struggled across the flooded ground, the soldiers would simply be mown down at point-blank range by fire from the strongpoints fifty yards beyond the morass. The preliminary operation was to take place at five o'clock in the morning, and

THE RAINS CAME

during the dark, rainy night, working parties had managed to lay a duckboard bridge across the Steenbeek and cut gaps in the wire on the other
side. 2nd Lieutenant Jelly went across first with 9 and 12 Platoons, and
Alan Goring followed with 11 Platoon in single file behind him.

Captain A. Goring MC, C Company, 6th Btn., The Yorkshire Regiment

Well, the first thing that happened was that I lost my platoon. I waded
across, got through the gap in the wire, turned round and there was
nobody there. I thought, My God! – what the hell do I do now. I
waited and waited, wondering what had gone wrong and eventually
they began to come through. What had happened was that they had
started to cross the swamp and, before they even got to this bridge
track, there was a bit of flooded ground about three feet wide. Well,
I'd hopped it, but of course my platoon went straight into it. Naturally, they thought they'd crossed the Steenbeek and lined themselves
up looking for me, but they were actually lined up in single file along
the bank. Fortunately they realised it and came on.

A Company on our right were instructed to go for a pillbox, and
so were the people on our left. Our objective was some German
strongpoints strung along a trench, which was really just a matter of
shell-holes. We took three platoons across – myself, Jelly and another
chap – and 10 Platoon we left in support. There was quite a bit of
opposition because the trenches were strongly defended, but we took
them, pressed on another fifty yards and started trying to dig in and
join up a few shell-holes. It was while the men were doing this that
Jelly was hit. We got him down into this little trench we'd dug and
there we stayed all day. The people on either side of us hadn't been
able to get so far, so we were in a little salient of our own with no one
on either side, both flanks right in the air.

We had a very busy time, for naturally there were snipers all around
us and bullets zinging about all over the place. I was left with just a
handful of men, all that was left out of those three platoons, so I
wanted to send a message back to see if we could get a bit of help
from the artillery. We had two pigeons in a basket, but the trouble
was that the wretched birds had got soaked when the platoon floun-
dered into the flooded ground. We tried to dry one of them off as
best we could and I wrote a message, attached it to its leg and sent it
off. To our absolute horror the bird was so wet that it just flapped into
the air and then came straight down again, and started actually
walking towards the German line about a hundred yards away. Well,
if that message had got into the Germans' hands, they would have

known that we were on our own and we'd have been in real trouble. So we had to try to shoot the pigeon before he got there. A revolver was no good. We had to use rifles and there we were, all of us, rifles trained over the edge of this muddy breastwork trying to shoot this bird scrambling about in the mud. It hardly presented a target at all.

Well, we did manage it but that still left the problem of trying to get a message back. We did everything to try to dry off that other bird. We had one man called Shuttleworth, a well-meaning chap, but very awkward. If there was a piece of barbed wire that everyone else had avoided, Shuttleworth fell over it. If there was a shell-hole that everybody else had skirted, Shuttleworth fell into it. Shuttleworth, anyway, was the one who suggested that if we had a tommy cooker with us we could have toasted the bird over that a bit until it dried off. Eventually, we did something nearly as ridiculous. We huddled round this bird and blew on its feathers. As a matter of fact we did get it dried off, but we made jolly sure it *was* dry before we sent it off with the message.

Then we settled down to keep the Boche amused for the rest of the day.

They made two or three movements towards counter-attacking, which we stopped. We did some sniping. I had a very good corporal named Wall, who was an excellent shot. Wall and I had a shooting competition. We took turns at the Boche in front of us while they were running about and moving up from time to time. That kept the troops amused and took their minds off the fire from the strongpoints directly behind us on our flanks. We were standing up to our knees in mud and it kept getting deeper. I crawled along from time to time to the other part of the 'trench' to see how poor Jelly was, and when it got dark I went along again to see if there was some way we could get him out and back. By this time, of course, you didn't have to take so much cover and I was just going to jump down into this little shell-hole trench when they said, 'Mind Mr Jelly.' I nearly jumped right on top of him. I could just see his face, otherwise he was all under water. They had three layers of packs under him for he was sinking all the time. I sent for the stretcher-bearers, but they couldn't get up. Jelly didn't mind. He didn't want to be moved until everyone else had gone.

By that time it was night and I thought, 'I don't like this idea of the Boche being behind me when it's dark.' So I went back and found a position perhaps fifty or sixty yards further back on a bit of a ridge, so that the Boche would be just in front of us. We crawled back and dug in there, and stayed there and held it until the main attack went through. After that, we were relieved.★

The 56th Division were sheltering in Sanctuary Wood getting ready for yet another attack on Glencorse Wood, and Corporal Storeman Joseph Pincombe was one of the men responsible for getting the rations up to his battalion, the 1st Queen's Westminster Rifles, from their base camp at Dickebusch. It was not an enviable task.

Corporal J. Pincombe, No. 40045, 1st Btn., Queen's Westminster Rifles

The first night we took the rations up was the night of the four-teenth. In normal times the rations included things like bacon and bread, beans, a ration of cigarettes and tobacco and, of course, the post – all the letters and parcels that had arrived for the Tommies since they'd gone into the line. But at Passchendaele that wasn't possible. We packed the sandbags with tins of bully-beef and tins of ration stew, and biscuits and sometimes a tin of jam for each platoon. There was water in two-gallon petrol tins and whatever happened, you didn't forget the rum. The transport men loaded the sandbags on to the pack animals and then the Captain Quartermaster called the roll. 'A Company?' 'Here, sir.' 'B Company?' 'C Company?' 'D Compa-ny?' 'Here, sir.'

We set off with the Transport Officer taking the lead at the head of the convoy. It was raining, and we all had capes over our uniforms and gas respirators at the ready.

We were just turning on to the road when a shell came right down on the cobbles of the road and knocked half a dozen of us flying. One horse was completely knocked out. When we picked ourselves up it was lying spreadeagled all over the road, and the rations it was carrying had gone too. But it had shielded us from the blast, so we re-formed the convoy and made for a fascine track on the right that led to Zillebeke through the flooded area where the gun batteries were sited. Going through them, the shrapnel and high explosives were falling so fast that you could hardly hear yourself speak. They were mainly salvoes of high shrapnel shells which burst on impact with the ground and sent shrapnel all over the area, covering it like an umbrella. You could hear the swish of the fragments splashing into the water beyond the track. When we got past the guns the track came to an end.

★2nd Lieutenant Jelly survived and was evacuated to base hospital in Rouen, where he later died. He was twenty-one.

We had a terrible time trying to find our way to Zillebeke. We knew we had to get there because the track ran from there up to Sanctuary Wood, but it was almost impossible. We spent about two hours going here and going there and getting into wrong positions and having to come back again. We had about half a dozen horses that were very badly wounded indeed, and the Transport Officer was very concerned, because horses are highly valued. It cost ten pounds for a horse, only a shilling a day for a man. He said, 'The horses are tired and a lot of them are wounded and we must get them back for treatment if we possibly can, so we'll dump the rations, and Pincombe and Reuter will stay here and sit on them until dawn. Will you do that?' So the Company Quartermaster Sergeant and myself said, 'Yes, sir.' 'Very well,' said the Major, 'and when it gets light you'll be able to find the battalion and distribute the rations in your own time as you find things.' Then they went off. 'Goodnight,' said the Major, 'and the best of good fortune to you both.'

We sat or lay on the dump all night, with a grandstand view of the shooting match on either side. When the morning broke I went across a bit of a rise in the country and there you could see Sanctuary Wood, quite near. There was no foliage there and from the back we could see the men just sitting about in broken trenches and shell-holes, some of them having a smoke, and we very soon got the rations brought forward and left them with the Orderly Corporal and his party to distribute them to the four companies. The men were all very quiet and calm. They were resting because they were going to make the attack on Glencorse Wood the following dawn.

The 1st Queen's Westminsters were to take part in the attack to clear Glencorse Wood and carry on to Polygon. This time it was up to the 56th Division to succeed where things had gone so badly wrong for the 18th and the 30th sixteen days previously. There had already been some attempts to clear Glencorse, none of them successful. D Company was to be in the forefront of the attack, leaving two companies in reserve, and one company further back in support. And they were part of a strong force of London regiments. Rifleman George Winterbourne, aged twenty but a veteran of several battles, was just as pleased not to be going across in the first wave. D Company of the 1st Queen's Westminsters were to be moppers-up, taking care of trouble-spots after the first and second waves had gone on, and consolidating and straightening the line. The line had already been moved slightly forward, for the jumping-off point was Jargon Trench, the place from which Jeff Werner had started off in the counter-attack on 31 July and walked straight into the sights of Nick Lee's machine-gun. Jargon Trench lay half-way up the rise between Surbiton Villas and Glencorse Wood, and it was now in the possession of the British.

Rifleman G. E. Winterbourne, No. 551237, 1st Btn., Queen's Westminster Rifles

We crept up the night before just after dark, but Jargon Trench was so broken up by shell-fire from previous attacks that we lay out in shell-holes at the back, and what a night *that* was! When the dawn came, the first wave went over and we could see what had been doing the damage. There was a pillbox in front, and I don't know what guns they had in it but they were covering a vast front, and as soon as you appeared they had you. We watched these London Rifle Brigade chaps going for it and dropping all over the place, but they bombed and they bombed, and eventually the machine-guns stopped and about a hundred Germans came out. They sent them back towards our lines and our infantry moved off, so it was time for us to go.

We got up and moved on, over this broken-up Jargon Trench and on up the slope. Beyond the trench it was soft going, but it seemed to be perfectly good ground – as good as any ground was around there at that time. All of a sudden I put one foot down and the next moment I was through the earth and in a bog up to my armpits. Well, our blokes were moving on so fast they didn't see what had happened. I was there absolutely on my own and sinking deeper and deeper, because the more I struggled, trying to get one leg up to get myself out, the deeper I went in. Fortunately the next wave came up and two runners of the 2nd London Fusiliers saw me and stopped. They got on either side and held out their rifles and that gave me some purchase to get out. There was no good shouting for help because there was so much racket going on and shells bursting all around that no one would have heard you. But I was lucky. My goodness, I was lucky! And I realised it a little later on. The two chaps who'd rescued me had to get on with the attack, so they left me and I hurried on to catch up with my lot.

They were held up, and we hadn't even got into the wood yet. We were going through all this awful ground that was just lakes of shell-holes filled up with water, with Jerry trenchboards here and there. In a lull in the shelling we heard cries, and there was a poor chap about fifty or sixty yards away. He was absolutely up to his arms in it, and he'd been there for four days and nights – ever since the last attack –

and he was still alive, clinging on to the root of a tree in the side of this shell-hole full of liquid mud. Lieutenant Whitby took three men over to see if they could get him out. But they couldn't get any purchase on the ground because it was all soggy round about. The more they pulled, the more they sank in themselves. Eventually, from somewhere or other, they got a rope, got it under his armpits and were just fixing up a derrick to see if they could hoist him out of it when we had to move on, because there was trouble up in front. All we could do was leave a man behind to look after him. It was another twenty-four hours before he was rescued.

A mile behind, Joe Pincombe was coming up the Menin Road with the rations.

Corporal J. Pincombe, No. 40045, 1st Btn., Queen's Westminster Rifles

We had to go through Ypres and up the Menin Road, because the battalion was in Glencorse Wood. The Menin Road was the artery of the battlefield. It was an extraordinary panorama, half frightening, half exciting. Everywhere, as far as you could see, there were spurts of earth from shells bursting and bursts of shrapnel and high explosive and men looking like ants in the distance. But as we got nearer we could see that they were stretcher-bearers coming through the mud to bring the wounded out. They were up to their knees in it, wallowing in it, struggling up carrying their stretchers to the field dressing-stations at the roadside. We could see doctors and orderlies outside, working in their shirtsleeves, even in the rain, and everywhere, all over the road and shoved to the side, were broken wagons, gun carriages and dead horses. You couldn't speak, the gunfire was so terrific, but you don't really hear the explosions individually – you just see them going off like geysers shooting up in the air. As far as you could see in front of you and to either side, there was nothing but mud, mud, mud for miles and just a few stumps of trees here and there and all hell let loose all around you. It was the first time I'd been out in the field when a battle was going on, and it was absolutely awe-inspiring.

Just as we passed Hellfire Corner we came on a young chap. Just about eighteen, I should think. He was staggering all over the road. Didn't know where he was, didn't know what he was doing, just walking back. I called to him, 'Chummy!' He didn't answer and I could see he was absolutely dazed and very disturbed. I also knew that we'd passed a Provost Marshal just a few yards behind. He was there to pick up deserters or spies or any strangers who shouldn't be there when there was an attack going on. And I realised that if this chap carried on on his own and was taken up by the police, it could be very serious for him. So I grabbed hold of him and said, 'You come with me.' He didn't know what he was doing and it was obvious that he was shellshocked. We walked behind the limber, and as soon as I saw one of these stretcher-bearers near by, because they were knocking about all over the road, I said to him, 'Now here, take this chap and look after him. Take him to the dressing-station there.' That made it official, so I knew the lad would be all right. He was from one of the battalions fighting in Glencorse and he must have turned and run. I don't know how he'd got that far. But I was pleased that I'd got hold of him, because I'd been in the line myself and, also, I used to write battalion orders on the Somme and almost every week there were men shot. The orders were to be read out to the troops, to stiffen them up. That's why they shoot the men not just to take their lives, but as an example to stiffen the troops.

I handed the lad over to the RAMC Sergeant, and I knew he'd be all right, so we pressed on to Hooge and got up to the high ground to the dump they'd made in front of Glencorse Wood. The Provost Sergeant was waiting there, a great man, we knew him as 'Bunny', and he was there all on his own. Just when we got up to him a runner arrived from Battalion Headquarters in the field. He was carrying a message which said that owing to the severity of the position in Glencorse Wood the reserves had had to go in and no men could be spared to collect the rations. If the situation improved, they might be able to send a party later. So we dumped the rations and turned and went back to get the rations ready for tomorrow. As we went back down the Menin Road the stretcher-bearers were still carrying and fetching the wounded from the field.

Things *were* bad in Glencorse, and most of the next day's rations would not be required, for the infantry were falling like corn before a sickle, and by nightfall those who survived would have been pushed back to where they started. All except George Winterbourne, long split up from the rest of his Company, for in the first chaotic hours of the attack a few men had actually managed to get through the wood and out of the other side; but although Polygon Wood lay tantalisingly in front of them across the open ground, they were in trouble.

Rifleman G. E. Winterbourne, No. 551237, 1st Btn., Queen's Westminster Rifles

We came out the other side of the wood and we were walking across this open ground near Polygon when, in the confusion, I suddenly found I was alone. I thought, 'Where is everybody?' I couldn't see a soul and I dived for the first bit of depressed ground I could see, which was a shell-hole. I had a look around very cautiously, and the shells were falling all about. Machine-guns were firing from straight in front and I noticed that they were firing in bursts. There must have been a bloke lying in front of me. I didn't notice him at all until he suddenly got up and dashed past me for another shell-hole. He never got there. They got him first. I thought to myself, 'I must time this bloke on the machine-gun.' So as soon as his burst finished I got up and dived for another shell-hole, and I made it. The minute I hit it, there was a great stream of machine-gun fire over my head, but he missed me.

In the shell-hole there were about a dozen other people, a couple of 2nd London officers and a wounded RB sergeant and two or three 2nd Londoners. We stayed there for quite some time and didn't know what to do, because we knew we were right out in front of the line. There didn't seem to be another soul around. The two officers went into consultation and it so happened that they had a pigeon. We sent a message back saying that we were completely isolated and that the prospect of holding this position all day seemed hopeless. But no help came. We held out for about an hour and then German infantry-bombers started coming up closer and closer and throwing bombs. The officers muttered away to each other and eventually one of them said, 'Well, I'm sorry, chaps, but it looks as if we're going to have to pack it in. You'll have to prepare to surrender. Now, first of all, has anybody here got a map?'

A couple of the lads did have maps, so they pulled them out and we scrabbled little holes in the side of the shell-hole and buried them. The officers got rid of some of the things they had, and then they told us to take off our equipment and put down our rifles, then we stood up in the shell-hole and put our hands up. We picked up the wounded sergeant and we all walked across to the Jerries. They took us back to their lines and put us in a dug-out. After a bit they walked us further back, and then they put us on one of their limbers and took us away.

The limber that took George Winterbourne back behind the German lines to Courtrai was one of a long convoy of British prisoners, the only

Allied troops who would pass over the Passchendaele Ridge *that* day, or for some months to come. They passed through Passchendaele itself about three o'clock in the afternoon, and at just about the same time a large staff-car swept through the gates of the château where Sir Douglas Haig had his headquarters and drew up, with an important flurry of gravel, in front of the imposing door. It carried an important passenger, General Sir William Robertson, and he was the bearer of a very particular and personal message from Lloyd George to his Commander-in-Chief. The purpose of his visit was to smooth over troubled waters and it took all his tact to do so, for so far as the Field-Marshal was concerned, Lloyd George had well and truly put his foot in it, and Haig was in high dudgeon.

At yet another conference held recently in London – and an international one at that – at which the advisability of switching troops and guns from France to the Italian front was canvassed and yet again deliberated, a vital question arose. What progress, if any was there likely to be on the Flanders front? It was 7 August, just a week after the big push, and although the communiqués had stressed the objectives gained and had slid over the fact that most of the originally-planned objectives had *not* been gained, it was all too clear that the first phase of the battle had been, at best, a semi-success and, consequently, a semi-failure. Was it early days to make such a judgement? Lloyd George did not appear to think so. 'I am afraid', he remarked, 'that we have put our money on the wrong horse. It would have been better to have reinforced the Italians.'

The remark had come to Haig's ears, and in order to smooth his ruffled feelings, Lloyd George had asked General Sir William Robertson to give Haig a personal message from him and, in a friendly way, to express Lloyd George's wholehearted confidence in his Commander-in-Chief. Haig was only slightly mollified:

> In reply, I told Robertson to thank the Prime Minister for his message, but what I want is tangible support. Men, guns, aeroplanes. It is ridiculous to talk about supporting me 'wholeheartedly' when men, guns, rails, etc., are going in quantities to Egypt for the Palestine expedition; guns to the Italians, to Mesopotamia and to Russia. Robertson agreed and said he was entirely opposed to any Italian venture.

Perhaps he was, for in the War Cabinet opinion was still split, and Lloyd George was in a quandary. As Colonel Hankey noted in his diary, 'The PM is obviously puzzled, as his predecessor was, how far the Government is justified in interfering with a military operation.'

This was the crux of the matter, and the real reason why Sir William

Robertson had come to see Haig was to report back on Haig's next objective. In other words the Prime Minister wanted to know exactly what was going on in Flanders. Sir Douglas Haig was in the happy position of being able to give him good news, based on the earliest reports of the day's fighting.

The 56th Division, as early as 9.45 that morning, had passed through Glencorse Wood and were going towards Polygon!

They were. But several hours had already passed since the soldiers who made that breakthrough had been either pushed right back out of the wood almost to their starting line; or, like George Winterbourne, were at this moment the object of curious scrutiny as they rattled on open limbers through the villages of German-occupied Belgium, towards Courtrai and the prisoner-of-war cage.

Langemarck had been taken. It had. But the original battle-plan had intended that Langemarck should have been attacked and captured on 2 or 3 August, almost two weeks before.

On the Frezenberg Ridge the troops of the 16th Division had got to Borry Farm and Beck House. They had. They had attacked across the field of dead bodies which had lain there since the disastrous attack two weeks previously, but Beck and Borry remained impregnable. The 16th retired in a rout, leaving a dreadful second crop of dead and wounded to lie among the decomposing casualties of a fortnight before.

The troops were advancing across the fields beyond St Julien and some had got as far as Winnipeg Farm on the Zonnebeke-Langemarck Road. Some had. The rest had died or drowned in the attempt.

Major Macleod's was one of the batteries which had fired the covering barrage for the attack – that 'creeping' barrage which had to creep so much more slowly now. It normally travelled forward 100 yards every four minutes, which was the time in which, in 'normal' conditions, the infantry was expected to cover the ground. But, other than in the military sense, the troops were not covering 'ground' any more. The barrage had been slowed down and the guns would now extend their range by 100 yards every *six* minutes to give the infantry a chance to catch up. It still wasn't enough. As the attack started, Macleod went to his forward observation post and watched it through binoculars.

Major R. Macleod DSO, MC, C.241 Battery, Royal Field Artillery

We had a tremendous barrage down that morning. All you could see, in front of the German line, were red and yellow flashes of shells bursting. The Germans must have been completely demoralised, because although their artillery was firing back on the infantry as they tried to get across, there was hardly any machine-gun fire coming from the German trenches. But there was no chance of the infantry getting across. I watched them gradually trying to work their way forward, struggling like blazes through this frightful bog to get at the Germans. However, they were up to their knees in mud, and by the time they got half-way across, it was virtually impossible for them to move either forward or back. Then when we lifted the barrage, the machine-guns started to pick them off.

I learned much later, after the war when I had access to the German unit records, that the Germans were so demoralised that they were all prepared in front of our infantry to come out and surrender as soon as our barrage lifted. But when it did, they saw the infantry struggling and realised that they couldn't get to them, so they went back into their shell-holes and started shooting them up. They just went down into the mud. It was a sickening sight. It made me feel quite ill to watch it.

Macleod might have felt even sicker had he known that it would be five weeks before the infantry succeeded in getting across the mud and craters of the one-time fields that lay between St Julien and the Zonnebeke-Langemarck Road. On the left, however, as Sir Douglas Haig had jubilantly informed Sir William Robertson, Langemarck *had* fallen; and the victory was due in no small measure to the men who had managed to cross the boggy Steenbeek two nights earlier and hung on to the precarious toehold at the foot of the rise where the Langemarck Road ran up to the village. But the taking of Langemarck was only part of a more ambitious plan. For the second objective, after the troops had cleared the 'green line' east of Langemarck, was to proceed to attack and occupy the strongly-held Eagle Trench some 700 yards beyond the village, and Eagle Trench was one of the most highly fortified German positions in the salient.

The task of bridging the Steenbeek, so that the infantry could cross it and forge ahead to Langemarck, had been given to C Company of the 12th Battalion, The Rifle Brigade, led by Captain Albert Rissik; and Rissik in turn was depending on his right-hand man, his Company runner, Corporal Greenwood. They made an unlikely combination. Rissik was a Public School man and a schoolmaster. Greenwood was a mill-worker from Lancashire, with such a broad accent that the Southerners in the battalion had difficulty in making out a single word he said. But between Captain Rissik and Corporal Greenwood, understanding was complete. 'We have a hot job on tonight, Greenwood,' Rissik had remarked earlier in the day. Greenwood was not perturbed.

Captain A. Rissik, 12th Btn., The Rifle Brigade

The carrying party with the bridges was due to leave at 8.30., so half an hour earlier, at dusk, the runner and I move down through Iron Crossroads. We go down the road to the branchless trees on the bank of the stream, and measure off some forty-five yards to the first position, No. 1 bridge. We wait rather tensely for a bridge to appear. Greenwood goes to the rendezvous on the road short of the stream. Could they all make it down this well-strafed road? Absolutely deserted; but before long this bank would be rustling with assembling troops. As I wait, Very lights, shells and machine-gun fire divide the darkening minutes. Then a gigantic camel looms above me where I am seated on a tree-stump. It is the twelve-legged No. 1 bridge *and* Greenwood, thanks be. They prop it on end, and as I wade across the stream it is lowered on its rope. It is firmly tied down on both sides. Greenwood has gone back to guide in bridge No. 2.

One by one, to my great relief, all the bridges loom up in turn. We have them all in position two hours before zero.

The infantry crossed over and fought their way to Langemarck. By early afternoon some of them had even fought their way to Eagle Trench 700 yards beyond. At four o'clock, at the very moment that a smart and shining orderly was serving tea in delicate china cups to Sir Douglas Haig and Sir William Robertson at GHQ, Rissik and five of his men took tea in the fortified ruins of a captured farm near Langemarck in which they had set up their Company Headquarters. The food had been scrounged by Corporal Greenwood, for no rations had reached them.

Corporal H. Greenwood, 12th Btn., The Rifle Brigade

The Captain sends me to the KRR's HQ, to find if our rations have gone there by mistake. But they haven't. Two wounded Tommies and one wounded German are lying in their pillbox. I return with this news and am sent back to Battalion HQ, taking Lewis with me, to find the Adjutant and ask for rations for twenty men. We get water, biscuits, jam, tea and sugar. With these I make tea for six of us and then have a rest. Afterwards Captain Rissik decides to go across to a German pillbox some seventy yards away, to use it if it is empty; but we find Germans there with a guard from the Shropshires. Four are wounded, one has dysentery, one is unwounded. The Captain talks to them in German. He tells them he will bring them part of our rations and some water. He gives each of them a cigarette and we return to take them back some rations. Then, Sergeant Greaves arrives. There was trouble at Eagle Trench.*

Captain A. Rissik, 12th Btn., The Rifle Brigade

Sergeant Greaves brought the message over half a mile of open country, heavily muddied, and he was sniped at all the way. He arrives panting, full of consternation. Our battalion is occupying only part of Eagle Trench where it dipped down at the right. The rest of the trench, a massive affair, a great mound built up to give at least eight feet of trench depth, is still in German hands; and our heavy guns are shelling the section we hold, under the impression that it is still held by the enemy. The men have had to evacuate the trench and fall back 200 yards.

Rifleman J. E. Maxwell, 11th Btn., The Rifle Brigade

Our people all climbed out except me. I was at the end of the trench, so I was the last. I was collecting my rifle – because it was a crime to lose your rifle, a serious crime – and I had to take up all my other things: pick, shovel and rifle grenades. I was just gathering all this up when a shell came over, just on the lip of the trench, and buried me right up to my neck. They dragged me out absolutely shell-shocked. The Lance-Corporal said, 'What's the matter?' and I simply couldn't speak. They sent a man to take me back, because I could hardly walk, and he half-dragged me back to the doctor's dug-out a bit in the rear. He just looked at me and put a ticket on to my uniform tied to a button. By the time I was dragged back to the first-aid dressing-station on the canal bank in a stream of other casualties, I couldn't walk at all; I simply fell down. So they put me on to a stretcher and took me in an ambulance to No. 62 Casualty Clearing Station at Proven. They tipped me on to a bed and by that time the mud and filth was all solidified round me like a suit of armour, and I well recall one of the nurses who was trying to strip me saying, 'Well, we can't get his uniform off. We'll have to cut it off.' So they did. Of course, there was nothing peculiar in that. They had to cut nearly every uniform off the blokes when they were brought in.

Next day the attempt to recapture Eagle Trench had to be given up. In the 12th Battalion alone, 1 officer and 31 riflemen were known to have

*From his diary.

been killed; 12 officers and 148 riflemen were wounded; 7 riflemen were missing; 1 in every 3 of the men who had gone into the line had come to grief.

Captain Rissik himself made one last valiant attempt, gathering the men who had evacuated the line, and after their own artillery had stopped firing on it led them back.

Corporal H. Greenwood 12th Btn., The Rifle Brigade

The 10th Welsh Battalion arrives to relieve us and we hand over the line. We make our way back over the Steenbeek stream, Stray Farm, Candle Trench, Caesar Avenue and over the canal bridge 6A. There we get an issue of rum. Captain Rissik gives me a cigarette and we have a smoke. The Captain tells me he is going on leave. I say that I am glad to hear this news.

General Gough spent the evening studying the situation reports from the different sectors of the front. When he had finished, he ordered a staff-car for ten o'clock to be ready to drive him south to Haig's headquarters.

At ten o'clock the following morning, having spent an uncomfortable night together in a cellar in Courtrai, George Winterbourne and his companions in misfortune – weary, filthy, bedraggled and only marginally drier – were marched into a hall to await interrogation. A German officer came in, immaculately uniformed, booted and spurred. He looked them up and down and remarked, quite affably, and in perfect English, 'Hello, what's this? Another English attack, is it?'

Another English attack, at least in the salient, was precisely what Gough intended to prevent, if it was within his power to do so. He put his case forcibly to Haig. He spoke of the terrible loss of men for every yard of ground gained. He stressed the difficulty of getting rations and ammunition up to the line. He spoke of the guns sinking into the morass. Of the terrible exhaustion of the infantry, and the impossibility of their being able to succeed in what they were being asked to do in conditions that were not merely appalling but hopeless.

When it came to the advance of infantry for an attack across the waterlogged shell-holes, movement was so slow and so fatiguing that only the shortest advances could be contemplated. In consequence I informed the Commander-in-Chief that tactical success was not possible, or would be too costly, under such conditions, and advised that the attack should now be abandoned.*

In spite of everything, in spite of the monumental losses, in spite of the fact that each success so far had also been half a failure, Haig remained confident in his strategy. Gough left him, more dispirited than ever. There was no going back. And no matter how sincerely Gough believed that there was little possibility of going forward either, his men were now irrevocably committed to the toil, the agony, the weary crucifixion of the long slog through the mud to Passchendaele.

*The Fifth Army, General Sir Hubert Gough GC, MC, KCB, KCVO (Hodder & Stoughton Ltd. 1931)

Part 4

'O Jesus Make it Stop'

Chapter 14

Pastor van Walleghem:

17 August. We hear little news concerning the results of yesterday's battles. If one broaches the subject with the officers, they know nothing, or they simply say that it was 'all right', which seems to indicate to us that things are not all right.

9.30 pm. Five German aeroplanes over Reninghelst, probably attracted by the bright lights of the cinema, theatre and canteens. The police always seem to be most strict towards the civilians as regards black-out, but are extremely lenient where the Army is concerned. Not surprisingly, five bombs were dropped near by, killing two and wounding three.

The troops had poured into Reninghelst from every camp and billet for miles around. Fresh out of the line, or waiting to go in, either way a concert would divert the mind from that other world of mud and flying steel just a few miles away. So the Tommies and Canucks queued up in the warm summer evening (for now that the attack was over, as if to set the pattern that was to persist with awful certainty for the next two months, the weather had improved).

Rifleman H. E. Lister, No. 2330, 12th Btn., The Rifle Brigade

It meant a lot to us when we came down the line, because there was nowhere to go, you see, it was all desolate. It made a great difference to the troops, though of course a lot of the troops didn't think of anything more than going in the *estaminet* and getting a drink. Captain Gilbey started the Very lights and he had men out of the whole division. When they weren't acting at night, they were doing such jobs as taking up the rations. They didn't go actually fighting, but they were all serving soldiers. There was one number that always used to bring the house down, and they always sang it. It was called 'Living in the Trenches' and it was sung by the comedian in full kit

with a blanket or pack, a French loaf, a couple of Mills bombs and a
couple of candles:

> Oh what a life, living in a trench,
> Oh what a life, fighting with the French,
> We haven't got a wife, or a pretty little wench,
> But everybody's happy in an old French trench.
> When we move to the attack
> You should see my blinking back,
> Rifle, sword and ammunition
> All in the Alert position.
> One smoke helmet, haversack,
> Fourteen bombs inside my pack.
> Iron rations, some dubbin for me boots,
> And Gawd help you if you don't salute.
> Everybody's happy, everybody's glad,
> It's the seventeenth bloody shell we've had.
> Whizz-bangs, coal box, shrapnel soar
> And a blinking mine underneath the floor.

It always used to bring the house down. It was so typical of what
we had to go through, but somehow making a joke of it when you
knew you had to go back to it made it all just bearable.

It was 'just bearable' because there was now a new attitude of fatalism
among the troops. If it had your name on it, you would get it. If it hadn't,
you would be all right. Meanwhile, a concert was a concert. So, as the
German planes circled the concert hut at Reninghelst and dropped their
bombs on the village, the troops sat on, merely clapping and stamping a
little louder to drown the sound of the explosions. But it was only bearable if you still had your nerve, if you had not yet been pushed quite to
the limit of endurance. A mile or so away at Proven the bombs were also
dropping, and in the big marquee that was the shell-shock ward at No. 62
Casualty Clearing Station, John Maxwell lay recovering from his ordeal of
the previous night.

Rifleman J. E. Maxwell, No. 445014, 11th Btn., The Rifle Brigade

The bombs were very near, and in the ward I was in some of the
patients went berserk. They were very, very bad cases of shellshock,
much worse than I was, and two of them in particular got up and ran
amok in the ward with their hands over their heads, screaming and

screaming and screaming. It was shocking as it was all in the dark, for they'd had to put the lights out because of the air raid, and they were charging around banging into things and this dreadful screaming going on all the time. The nurses were wonderful and it was amazing how they dealt with the situation, and after a while they managed to get the blokes calmed down and back to bed. Then the doctor came, after the raid was over, and gave them an injection.

A wound in the body would heal in time; a wound of the spirit was harder to cure. For the majority of the soldiers, sanity depended on not thinking ahead, of living for the moment and accepting each moment as it came. Their philosophy was simple. If you were a soldier in the line, you were either alive or you were dead. If you were alive, there was no need to worry. If you were dead, you were unable to worry. Therefore what was the point of worrying? If you could, you joked, and now that the war was into its fourth year even the deep soul-weariness of the interminable fighting was turned into a joke.

> 'How long are you in for, Bill?'
> 'I signed for seven years or Duration.'
> 'You're lucky! I'm Duration.'

It was the catchphrase of that August in 1917 – *Roll on Duration* – the classic response to the news that there was no jam in the ration sandbag, that two companies of your battalion had gone west in an attack, that there was no clean shirt to exchange for your lice-ridden one, that you were on a carrying party tonight, that you were going up the line in the morning. *Roll on Duration.*

The men working at the engineers' dump on the Pilkem Ridge shouted it several times a day, whenever a little railway engine puffed up the newly-laid track pulling truck-loads of supplies and ammunition. The REs had been quick to notice that its identifying number was ROD 1945. 'Roll on Duration nineteen forty-five!' they yelled with unfailing regularity, every time it hove into sight. After a while, the driver got fed up with the joke.★

Now that the lines had moved forward, the spidery narrow-gauge railway-tracks reached well up towards the front. The tracks were constantly being damaged by shell-fire, and the troops of the Light Railway

---

★ROD, in this case, stood for Railway Operating Division. Sapper Bill Mathieson, who recalled this incident, has never got over the coincidence that 1945 actually marked the duration of another war.

Sections were hard put to it to keep them operational. It was bad enough coping with the repairs that were the result of the attentions of the Boche, but when other accidents happened their fury knew no bounds. Tanks and limbers could obviously not be expected to go the long way round, so in certain places there were movable ramps which could be laid over the railway lines to let the traffic across. One tank commander, Captain Birks, had the misfortune to be crossing a ramp as an engine approached. He had judged the distance to a nicety, and all would have been well had it not been for the fact that the tank stalled as it was half-way across the ramp. The locomotive was too near to stop, and the resulting mess made the name of the Tank Corps stink throughout the Light Railway Section. Their locomotive was damaged almost beyond repair but in the collision it had obligingly knocked the tank over on to the right side of the ramp, and as the jolt had started the engine up again, the tank was able to go on.

It was 22 August – a date which does not figure prominently in the official annals of the battle for Passchendaele because the actions were not considered to be important enough to rank in history as a 'battle'. Nevertheless, the events of that night stayed in the minds of many men for the rest of their lives. One was Jason Addy. The other was Rory Macleod. It is also remembered by the survivors of four companies of the 13th Royal Scots and the 11th Argyll and Sutherland Highlanders, who were in support when the leading companies of their battalions set off again up the terrible Frezenberg Ridge in one more weary and desperate attempt to carry out orders by securing the fortifications of Beck House and Borry Farm. Two hours after zero, a handful crawled back. They did better than the Seaforths on their left, for none of them came back at all. Only beyond them was there the least measure of success, where the 7th Cameron Highlanders succeeded in sweeping the Germans off the rising gradient of Hill 35 and establishing a foothold on its crest.

It was a costly exercise. The strongpoints of Beck and Borry were still undefeated. The infantry had not been able to advance by so much as an inch the line that ran between Square Farm and Low Farm. Their ranks were horribly depleted, while, in the blood-soaked field beyond, some hundreds more men had dropped to swell the ranks of the dead. The results of this minor action were regarded at Headquarters as being disappointing. It was noted with regret that two companies of the Argyll and Sutherland Highlanders had lost all their officers, and that over 200 other ranks were killed, wounded or missing. The Argylls and the Seaforths were relieved. It would, unfortunately, not be possible to put them back in the field until fresh drafts of men were brought in to reinforce their ranks.

★

It had also been a bad morning for Major Macleod. Combined with the events of the night before, it added up to the worst twelve hours of his life. His battery, C.241, was due to support an attack of infantry and tanks with the object of securing some of the ground east of St Julien. It was to fire the creeping barrage that would cover the infantry in their advance. Major Macleod's task was to work out the barrage tables, a task involving meticulous mathematics and calculations, for every artillery officer was well aware of the fact that the infantry would pay for his errors with their lives. It was a long job. In order to maintain a constant rate of firing and allow for reloading, an individual firing-pattern had to be worked out for each gun. Rory Macleod worked at it during the late afternoon and early evening in a dug-out eighty yards behind the battery position, which was a mere sandbagged hole in the ground covered with a piece of corrugated iron. And the job was even more complicated than usual, due to the fact that a lucky shot from the Germans had knocked out one of his guns. So five guns would have to do the work of six. It took several hours to complete.

All evening, the guns of C.241 were silent and the men rested while other batteries waited, alert, for SOS signals from the front. At midnight, Macleod and Lieutenants Gascoyne and Allday were dozing in the dug-out when gas shells started falling round the battery.

Major R. Macleod DSO, MC, C.241 Bty. Royal Field Artillery, 48th (South Midland) Division

I shook Gascoyne and told him to put on his gas mask and go out and sound the gas alarm. He grabbed it and crawled out of the dug-out. It was like a football rattle – a terrible sound! And as he was doing this there was the most almighty explosion. I was lying on this stretcher thing facing the entrance. There was a bit of sacking hung over it and through it I saw this most tremendous sheet of flame. That was the last I knew for a bit. When I came to I was buried alive, covered with hot earth which smelt abominably. Allday and I managed to crawl out, and I was right on the edge of the most enormous crater. A shell had hit the high-explosive ammunition dump – three thousand shells – of our 4.5 howitzer battery just on the other side of the Boundary Road and fifteen yards behind us. The crater stretched right across the road, yards behind it and yards in front, right up to where our dug-out had been. Why we were not all killed I do not know. My next thought was to go and look for Gascoyne. I felt sure that we would pick him up in little pieces. But he'd also had a miraculous escape and there he was, still holding the gas rattle, staggering around, a bit dazed and slightly wounded but more or less all right. I sent him down to the dressing-station and I went with Lieutenant Allday to see what had happened to the battery. It was more or less a shambles. The two left-hand guns had been completely knocked out and several of my poor chaps had gone west. It was extraordinary that we, who were so near the explosion, suffered so little, while the battery, eighty yards from it, suffered so much. The blast and pieces of metal must have passed right over our heads.

I left Allday to clear up the mess at the battery, for we were due to start firing the barrage at 4.45 and, of course, all my barrage tables and orders had gone west because I'd had them with me in the dug-out. We were still being shelled by gas, so I plodded over to D Battery behind us. In their dug-out, wearing my gas-mask and by the light of a candle, using D Battery's copy of the orders and their barrage forms, I made out a fresh set of tables for my three remaining guns, which now had to do the work of the original six. I managed to get them finished off not very long before zero hour, in time to start the barrage.

Although the night was filled with the sound of shell-fire, and despite the clanking and rattling inside the juddering tanks as they tested the engines, Jason Addy and the crew of *Delysia* heard the explosion as the ammunition dump went up half a mile away. The line was still static, just east of St Julien, and the attacks of 22 August, both here and on Frezenberg to the right, were intended to push it forward so that it would be in line with recently-captured Langemarck. Almost every tank that could be scraped up was in the line to support the infantry. The crew of *Delysia* were newly trained, newly arrived at the front and all on the small side, for it was now the policy to recruit small men for the tanks – eight of them, after all, had to fit in. Addy was five foot two, a pawky Yorkshire lad, much teased for possessing an appetite as large as his frame was small. He considered himself lucky to be in D Company, for he felt that Corporal Hardy, the Company cook, was the best cook in the Army.

Hardy had come up himself that night, right to the front line in St Julien, to bring the boys their supper. Tonight there were hot rissoles in the dixies, made from hard biscuits which were soaked, mixed with bully beef, bound with eggs that Hardy had scrounged from somewhere, and then shaped into man-size portions. They were then rolled in more crushed biscuit crumbs and fried, sizzling hot, in bacon fat. They were still pretty hot now as the boys tucked into them – and there was plum duff to follow; biscuits again, but concocted by Hardy into a steamed pudding with the help of some sugar and a handful of raisins. There was even a hot jam sauce in a separate container to be ladled generously over each portion. Who cared about the flying shells, or that the feast had to be eaten by the reflected glare of Very lights and rockets! With a tot of rum for a *digestif*, the boys felt fit for anything.

A dozen tanks were to support yet another attack by the infantry across the blood-soaked ground that separated St Julien from the Langemarck-Zonnebeke Road a few hundred yards in front of the village. It was the same stretch of ground where Major Macleod had seen them bogged down in the mud less than a week before. The ground was drier now. The troops were fresher. And, although the enemy had strongly reinforced his line, they might just possibly make it. The tanks, however, could not risk going across the same ground.

Ten tanks were to go up the remains of the lane that had once linked St Julien with the crossroads; while the two others, commanded by Lieutenant Enoch and Lieutenant Knight, were to cover the sector further to the left, taking as their route the road which in happier times had been the main road between St Julien and Poelcapelle. It would be a bumpy passage, for beyond the British line it was pocked and cratered with shell-holes. Also, the retreating Germans had felled the vestiges of the leafless trees that had once lined it on either side. Their trunks now lay scattered across the length of the road, and over them the tanks would have to pass. The bombardment started. Zero hour came and the creeping barrage began. At the three remaining guns of Major Macleod's battery, the gunners worked dementedly to keep up the firing-pattern. Behind the curtain of shells the infantry went over and the tanks moved forward up the log-strewn road. Knight's went first, followed by Enoch's *Delysia*, with Jason Addy manning one of her guns.

Private J. L. Addy, No. 94804, D Co., 4th Btn., Tank Corps

When you're enclosed in a tank and there's that much racket, you don't know whether it's shells that's hitting you or what you're doing. The noise of the engine was tremendous, and we had to stand by with a pyrene fire-extinguisher and get ready to shoot it at the engine if it got too hot, because we had twenty gallons of petrol on either side of the tank and all round the sides there were racks of ammunition. If you had a fire in a tank you hadn't an earthly. Jerry was shelling back, and you could feel the blast of the shells as you were looking through the gun slit; and within your range of vision, you could see the infantry moving all around. You just kept your finger on that machine-gun button, trying to knock out the machine-guns that were going for the boys. Our officer, Lieutenant Enoch, was on the other gun and he kept giving directions – or screaming directions above the noise.

We were just coming to a place called Bulow Farm, which, of course, was a big pillbox, and the infantry were having a hard time there. Lieutenant Knight's tank was twenty yards or so in front of us and suddenly it just went *boom*. It was a direct hit from a heavy shell. The tank slewed right off the road, and we were just able to squeeze past it. We couldn't stop, of course, and in any event it didn't look as if anyone could possibly have survived that, so on we went to help with this scrap at Bulow Farm. It was unfortunate that it was a tank with six-pounder guns that was knocked out, but we did our best with the machine-guns to help the infantry bombers. And we got it! We took Bulow and even went on a bit further.

Then we turned to go back. We were still under terrible shell-fire, for the Germans were at it with their heavies and throwing over everything they'd got. Somebody shouted out, 'There's Jagger, on the side of the road!' Well, Jagger was the corporal of the tank that had got knocked out. Lieutenant Knight had been killed, and when we looked at the tank tipped off the roadside we could see his arm sticking out of the gun slit and his hand all twisted. But Jagger was standing there on the roadside waving us down, and we opened the door and he shouted in to us, 'I've got two wounded chaps here, can you take them back with you?' He had four wounded, actually, but we could only carry two in the tank. So we pulled in these two wounded chaps, laid them down on the floor on either side of the driver's seat and left Jagger to look after the two others.*

It was a terrible trip back for those two blokes, because we were lurching over all these felled tree-trunks across the road. It was a case of heave up – *bang*, heave up – *bang*, all the way back. And every time we banged down, those chaps were in agony. I'll never forget their faces. And it wasn't only the tree-trunks, for by now the road was a shambles of cartwheels and bodies. We had to go over them. You

*Lance-Corporal Jagger MM, D Battalion, awarded the DCM at Bulow Farm near St Julien on 22 August 1917. His tank received a direct hit killing his officer and sergeant. Under very heavy shell and machine-gun fire, he transferred a wounded member of his crew to another tank, returned and evacuated the remaining two wounded to a shell-hole. After handing over his Lewis guns to the infantry, he found that the two wounded had been buried by shell-fire, and he succeeded in digging them out with his hands and taking them to the dressing-station.

From the *Tank Book of Honour*, privately published for the Tank Corps. Although Jagger's citation refers to *one* wounded member of his crew, Addy insists that he took *two* aboard Delysia.

hoped they were dead but you had to go over just the same, you couldn't help it. Sometimes you'd see the wounded lying there. You can see they're alive, and you can see the expression on a man's face – he's terrified to think you're going to go over him. Well, you *do* go over him, because you can't stop, but we'd manoeuvre the tank so that the tracks would go on either side of him. There was plenty of clearance underneath the tank, but they were terrified just the same. You could see it.

We got back to St Julien, and lifted the two boys out and laid them behind a wall and went off to look for stretcher-bearers. When we'd handed them over, we camouflaged the tanks in their parking places and got on lorries that were waiting to take us back to La Louvie. We thanked God we weren't in the infantry.

Delysia was lucky that day – she attained her objective and returned. Of the ten tanks that went up the lane between St Julien and the Langemarck–Zonnebeke Road, six became ditched in craters before they were half-way across. The remaining four helped the infantry to capture a part of the line, and even a strongly-held pillbox known as Springfield. Then came the counter-attacks, and the troops were pushed back. But this time, not quite to St Julien. They had managed to advance the line by 300 yards, all along the line from Langemarck to the Frezenberg Ridge. The cost, in the front line, was a score of tanks and casualties of some 2,000 men. When the heavy German guns switched their attention to shelling the rear, there were more casualties in the gun-lines. The SOS signals had gone unanswered, at least from C.241 – for C.241 had ceased to exist shortly after zero hour when a direct hit knocked out two of Rory Macleod's three remaining guns. He signalled through to headquarters for orders and the reply came back: *Hand over your remaining gun to the adjacent battery, return and draw six more from Ordnance.* Sick and dispirited, Macleod ordered his small band of survivors to pack up and they started on the long trudge back to the wagon lines. At least it meant a week's respite from the battle.

The actions of 22 August were, of course, very minor. They were not destined to figure prominently in the official histories. But they were reported by the newspapers.

The Times, 23 August. *The following telegraphic dispatches were received from General Headquarters in France yesterday: 9.12 pm. Successful operations were undertaken by our troops this morning, east and north-east of Ypres, for the capture of a series of strongpoints and fortified farms lying a few*

hundred yards in front of our positions astride the Ypres–Menin Road and
between the Ypres–Roulers railway and Langemarck.

   Bitter fighting has taken place at all points. The enemy has again launched
repeated counter-attacks which have suffered heavy losses from our artillery
and machine-gun fire.

The *Times*, of course, could only print the information contained in the
communiqués it had received, and the communiqué did not mention the
fate of the Argylls, the Royal Scots or the Seaforths. Like Lieutenant
Knight and his tank crew, like the men who had fallen trying to get to the
Zonnebeke–Langemarck Road, like the men who had died at the guns of
C Battery, they were already merely figures in the appropriate column of
statistics.

   Field–Marshal Sir Douglas Haig studied the statistics with interest and
discussed them at length with his Chief of Intelligence, General Charteris.
Charteris had compiled other lists of statistics against which those of the
Allied armies could be compared, for they estimated the strength of the
enemy – the number of his guns, the number of reserves available to him,
the fighting strength and quality of those reserves, the number of Germans taken prisoner, and the estimated number of German casualties in
killed and wounded. The only ones which could possibly be accurate
were those showing the numbers of German prisoners captured by the
Allies. The others had been compiled by information gleaned by interrogation and by reports from spies. At best it was guess-work, sometimes
inspired, more often far wide of the mark. But Charteris backed his information to the hilt and Haig, having confidence in him, drew the conclu-
sion that if all else failed, the campaign could still be won by attrition.
Furthermore, he was assured that once the troops managed to get up on
to the Passchendaele Ridge they would find it 'as dry as a bone'. There
was still a chance, if the troops could only get forward, that they would be
in a position to attack the coastline when the tides were right in September. Even if that were not possible, the Passchendaele Ridge would be a
better place on which to stand for the winter than in the swamp half-way
up. Especially if, by gaining it, one had drained the enemy's life-blood and
absorbed all his resources, so that he would be too weak to strike a blow
elsewhere.

   It was about this time that a bitter joke began to circulate in the
depleted ranks of the infantry. Who, the soldiers wanted to know, would
take the rations up to the last man?

   It was about this time that people stopped saying, 'When I go on leave
–' and began to say, 'If I get out of this –'. It was about this time that
Gough himself observed that the heart had gone out of the Fifth Army.

It had lost more than its heart. Since 31 July the Army's casualties had been 3,420 officers and 64,586 from other ranks. Many were wounded or missing. More than 10,000 were known to be dead. One of the 10,000 was Ernie Gays. And his friend Jimmy Smith knew very well that he was dead, for he had buried Ernie himself. It had happened on a working party as that bloody August drew to a close.

Cyclist J. Smith, No. 21013, C. Co., Northern Cyclist Btn

We were always on fatigues in the Cyclist Corps. Well, you couldn't cycle in those conditions with nothing but shell-holes all over the place. So they had to do something with us. We were billeted in Spoilbank Tunnels – terrible place, damp and awful and always full of gas – and in August we went on working parties every night. We were up at Hill 60 digging cable trenches for the REs – and the Jerries were shelling hard, going for the guns, because it was full of batteries round there. And there were bodies where you walked, and often where you dug. The burial parties couldn't keep up with it. Well, we'd had heavy shelling that night but we didn't have many casualties. We managed to take cover. It was only when we got back that I knew Ernie had gone, because he was working on a different stretch from me. He was our only casualty. He was my best pal and I did feel bad about it – but I felt worse about the next night. Before we went in at night, we always used to line up in single file and the sergeant would come along and he'd split us up into groups of seven. He came along the line and counted off seven – seven – seven. Then, when he came to the end, there was myself and two other blokes left over. So he said, 'Right, you last three. You can bury Gays.' Oh, I felt bad, being detailed to bury my own pal. It was the hardest thing I ever had to do.

They'd laid him just at the side of this communication trench on Hill 60. I stayed with him while the other two chaps went to dig the grave, just by the side of the big mine-crater. When they came back we carried him over. I took him by the ankles, the other two took him by the arms and we laid him in and covered him up. I remember feeling a bit upset, for the grave was only about four feet deep. I knew he probably wouldn't be there for very long, because of the shell-fire. The place was getting churned up the whole time. I felt bad. You got very callous, seeing everything that was going on, but when it was your own pal – you couldn't feel callous then. After we buried him, we had to wait for the rest of the working party to finish. Then we got back to Spoilbank just before dawn. I couldn't go to sleep. I got up and wrote to Ernie's mother.

Ernie Gays was one of the last few statistics in the long columns that were totted up at the end of August.

Of the 22 divisions (each consisting of 12 infantry battalions) involved in the fighting, 14 had been hit so hard that they had to be withdrawn to be rested and re-formed.★

Haig now ordered Plumer's Second Army to turn its flank inwards and address itself to the higher reaches of the salient, while the Fifth Army concentrated its efforts on the left flank.

By the time August, weary and blood-stained, had dragged to a close, parts of Glencorse Wood alone had changed hands eighteen times. North of Langemarck the mighty Eagle Trench still guarded the approaches to the village of Poelcapelle. In front of St Julien the strongpoints guarding the Zonnebeke–Langemarck Road still held out against repeated attacks. While, on the Frezenberg Ridge, the Army looked out from the line between Square and Low Farm, across its field of dead, to the unattainable, inviolate fortified farms of Beck and Borry on the other side. On 6 September, they attacked them again.

It was not to be part of a full-scale battle, of course, for General Plumer refused to move until his preparations were complete, and that would not be until well into September. But Borry and Beck, on the Frezenberg Ridge, rankled like a thorn in the side. If the troops were to reach Zonnebeke in the first leap, then Beck House and Borry Farm must first be subdued.

The job was given to the 5th and 6th Battalions of the Lancashire Fusiliers, and while the 6th Lancs. attacked Beck House on the left, the 5th Lancs. were to attack Borry Farm. Or rather, four companies of the battalion were to be involved in the attack on Borry Farm and the trenches on either side of it. C and D Companies were to go forward while A and B Companies stayed in support. It was an arrangement which suited George Horridge and Bill Tickler very well indeed, for they were close friends. Tickler was to lead C Company into action, while Horridge, as commander of A Company, would support him from Low

---

★It is of interest that during the same period the Germans were faring no better. Of 23 German divisions defending the Passchendaele Ridge, 17 had to be withdrawn as unfit – and 9 replacement divisions had to be brought to the salient from the French front in Champagne, thus partially vindicating Haig's policy of 'attrition'.

Farm in the front line. Low Farm was a captured German pillbox almost exactly opposite Borry Farm, 400 yards beyond.

Captain W. Tickler MC and Bar, 5th Btn., Lancashire Fusiliers

We both kept watching the time and with five minutes or so to go I said to George, 'Well, I'm off now. See you later.' We shook hands and I crawled out of the pillbox and got into the trench ready to take the men across. The whistles went and we started off. We could see our objective very clearly indeed. It was a long straight trench running on either side of Borry Farm. We had only got a few yards when we saw the Germans running out of these pillboxes, Beck House and Borry Farm, and lining the trenches, and they started firing at us, rapid machine-gun fire. It was hard on the men – very hard. The officer can duck down, keep close to the ground, but the men were all loaded with picks and shovels down their backs, carry-ing bombs and ammunition and everything under the sun, and they were dropping like ninepins. You don't see a man going down. All you notice is that he's gone – half a dozen of them gone, and you know they're not funking it because they would go ahead if they could. It was criminal, because there weren't enough of us. That's how I felt as I went over, angry. I sent a message back by signalling lamp for stretcher-bearers.

Captain G. B. Horridge, 5th Btn., Lancashire Fusiliers

I couldn't give anyone an order because I thought, well, I might as well take out my revolver and kill them here, for they'd be sure to be hit the moment they went outside. So I simply said, 'Captain Tickler is signalling for stretcher-bearers.' There were two stretcher-bearers there. One was Holt, a Rochdale boy who had been a corporal, but he had lost his stripe through some misconduct. The other was called Renshaw. As soon as the words were out of my mouth Holt said, 'Well, I'm ready to go.' And Renshaw said, 'Yes, well, I'll go too.'

Holt went first. He crawled through the door and we pushed the stretcher after him. He stood up and got hold of the stretcher and put it on his shoulder, and just at that very moment there was a burst of machine-gun fire that knocked the stretcher right off his back on to the ground. He simply bent down, picked it up, put it back on his shoulder and off they both went. Neither of them was touched. I like to think that the Germans saw the stretcher and knew what they were about.

Captain W. Tickler, MC and Bar, 5th Btn., Lancashire Fusiliers

I'd lost a lot of men before I was half-way across, and by the time I got to the German line I was virtually on my own except for one or two chaps, and one of them was wounded. Things weren't looking very good just where we were, but I could see that over on my right some of the blokes of D Company were making a very good job of getting hold of this Borry Farm strongpoint. So I sent another message back, asking for reinforcements. Then we lay low and waited. Horridge sent out another platoon and I watched it coming across. Very few of them got to me.

There was a bit of a lull in the shelling, when all of a sudden I looked over and there on the edge of the German trench was one of my sergeants and a bunch of men, and he was just about to jump into the trench. I was lying behind this slight bank just a little way back, and I was so near that I could hear a German officer say, in perfect English, 'Right, put your hands up and put your rifles down.' So I screamed across at this bloke, 'What the hell are you doing giving yourselves up?' I didn't wait for him to answer me, I just let fly with my revolver. I was aiming at the German officers, but they were all mixed up together, these blokes, and the sergeant screamed back, 'Stop that bloody shooting!' The German officers scuttled into a dug-out and left the sergeant and the other blokes standing there.

Our men had just captured the pillbox of Borry Farm when I saw the Germans behind coming forward and massing for a counter-attack, so I sent a message to Horridge to send up the SOS signal.

Captain G. B. Horridge, 5th Btn., Lancashire Fusiliers

As soon as I got Bill Tickler's signal calling for the SOS, I got hold of a rifle and the rifle grenade with the SOS signal, which was a rocket that exploded two red and two green flares. I crawled through the hole in the wall and fired it up into the air. We waited. Ten seconds passed and it seemed like ten years, so I crawled through the hole again and shot off another signal grenade. About two seconds later our barrage started to come down. It was absolutely thrilling. Hundreds of guns in the rear opened up, and over the heads of our men there was a great curtain of smoke and shrapnel flashes. Even in the thick of it, I was absolutely thrilled to feel that I had brought this about and was virtually, at least for the moment, in command of the artillery.

Captain W. Tickler MC and Bar, 5th Btn., Lancashire Fusiliers

In spite of our artillery fire the Germans got Borry Farm back again. Lying there in a shell-hole in front of their line, looking to the right, I saw them bomb their way in and clear our men out. We hadn't enough men left to consolidate the position. So those of us that were left had to try to get back as best we could. The chap who was with me was hit. A bullet hit him right in the shin-bone. It was the most extraordinary, terrible noise. The bullet screams if it hits a bone, it spins round and screams, twisting. He wasn't badly hurt but he couldn't make it entirely on his own, so I set off trying to get back with him and looking for any of my other men as I went. It probably took us about two hours just to cross those few hundred yards, going from shell-hole to shell-hole. By that time it had quietened down a bit. The Germans didn't bother us much when we were going back.

Captain G. B. Horridge, 5th Btn., Lancashire Fusiliers

Tickler came in just before sunset, and when we had a rough count of those who had managed to get back, less than 40 men had made it out of the 160 he'd started off with. Bill Tickler was absolutely exhausted. I've never seen a man so worn out. He crawled into the pillbox and threw himself down on a wire stretcher-bunk and went straight to sleep. I went outside to see to the men and to watch the wounded coming in.

Then a most peculiar thing happened. A Scottish soldier had emerged from some ruined dug-out in No Man's Land when the stretcher-bearers were looking there for wounded, and someone brought him up to me. He was in the usual state, a bit the worse for wear and his uniform thick with dried mud. There were no Scottish troops that day anywhere near us, so I questioned him. He said that he had been there for many days, ever since a previous attack, that he had been left in No Man's Land and had then lost direction and didn't know which way to go to the British trenches. He had been living on the iron rations found on dead men and on water from their water bottles. It seemed perfectly reasonable so I simply told him to go off down the line. And then it struck me that, filthy though he was, the man was perfectly clean-shaven. It wasn't the face of a man who had been unable to wash or shave for the last ten days or so; it was the face of a man who had shaved that morning! In retrospect, and much too late, I realised that he could only have been a German who spoke English, wearing a uniform taken from a dead body, who had been lying out in a forward listening-post which had been overrun in the attack.

Even at that stage, Captain Horridge might have tried to pass on a warning had he not received a message that convulsed him with rage and put everything else out of his mind. He shook the weary Tickler out of a deep sleep.

'For God's sake, Bill, will you wake up and look at this bloody order DHQ has sent me.'

The order from Divisional Headquarters read, *You will send one officer and six men to bomb and capture Borry Farm pillbox. Should the men become casualties you will send six more, and then, if necessary, another six until the enemy post is captured. Lieutenant Pattinson will lead the first party.*

Horridge and Tickler were stunned. 'I'm damned if I'm going to send Pattinson out. I'm damned if I'm going to send *anybody* out,' Horridge exploded. 'If they think that six men with a bag of bombs could have done the job, why the hell did they send 280 men over the top in broad daylight against machine-guns to do the same job! I don't care if they bloody court-martial me. I'm not going to do it.'

It was perhaps fortunate that at this point the Commanding Officer made his appearance in person. The Colonel didn't say much. He simply asked to see the signals, and when he had read them he put them in his pocket.

'Don't worry. I'll see to this.'

Neither Horridge nor Tickler heard any more about the matter. Next evening the men of the 5th Lancs. were relieved and went, wearily, out of the line, leaving several score of their number lying in the charnel-house in front of Beck and Borry.

Chapter 15

Everyone who could be spared was given leave or rest of some kind in the brief space of time that was left before the offensive was renewed on 20 September, and fresh divisions practised the attacks over and over again. The infantry held grimly on to the hard-won length of the new line and repulsed the few counter-attacks launched by the Germans. The truth was that the German troops had been hit as hard as the Allies, and Ludendorf was encouraged by the unexpected quiet to allow himself to entertain the hope that the offensive was over. But peering into the darkness through the slits of wet pillboxes, or shivering in an open trench in the first chill winds of autumn, the fighting troops were more sceptical. Beyond the British lines they were aware of a constant movement, of a clanking and rustling, of muffled voices; and, shooting up their flares, they would see the front-line working parties frozen in the sights of their rifles and machine-guns.

The working parties were toiling as never before. They bridged the streams, repaired the roads and extended the winding miles of duckboard tracks up to the assembly positions. Yard by yard, the long supply roads stretched out until they reached all the way to Langemarck on the left and, on the right, past the great desolate craters of Hooge, through the skeleton of Château Wood and up to Westhoek. Now that the ground was drying out, there were assembly trenches to be dug in the pitted earth and, deeper still, trenches stretching beyond and behind the lines to carry the vital communication cables that would link the men in the field with Battalion Headquarters. In the two weeks before the new push, the men of the working parties bore the brunt of the battle. Of more than 10,000 casualties in the first fortnight of September, 6,000 were sustained by the engineers and almost 3,000 more by the 'PBI', reluctantly working under their orders.

One such casualty was Sergeant John Carmichael of the 9th Battalion, North Staffordshire Regiment.

Sergeant J. Carmichael VC, 9th Btn., North Staffordshire Regiment

We were on Hill 60, digging a communication trench, and I was detailed off with a party of men to get it done quick. I was supervising the job. We had men working in the trench and men working outside of it as well. One of the chaps was deepening the trench when his spade struck an unexploded grenade, just lodged there in the side of the trench, and it started to fizz. I was an instructor in bombing, so, knowing a bit about explosives, I knew that there would be seven seconds before it went off unless I did something. I couldn't throw it out, because there were men working outside the trench as well as the blokes in it. So I shouted at them to get clear and I had some idea of smothering it, to get the thing covered, keep it down until they were out of range. All I had was my steel helmet. So I took it off my head, put it over the grenade as it was fizzing away, and I stood on it. It was the only way to do it. There was no thought of bravery or anything like that. I was there with the men to do the job, and that's what mattered.

Well, it *did* go off. They tell me it blew me right out of the trench, but I don't remember that. The next thing I remember is being carried away. That's how I got this thing. . . .

'This thing' was the Victoria Cross. But it was several days before Carmichael knew anything about that. Both his legs were shattered and his right arm slightly injured, and he remembered nothing about the journey to No. 53 Casualty Clearing Station at Bailleul, nor of the first few days he spent there. Nor could he understand the fuss that was being made of him, or the flutter in the ward the morning that they told him he was to have a very special visitor – the General himself was coming to see him.

Sergeant J. Carmichael VC, 9th Btn., North Staffordshire Regiment

His name was General Williams, and he was very nice to me. They'd put me in clean pyjamas, and he patted me on the shoulder and called me 'my boy' and then he told me about the medal. I suppose I was pleased, but I've never been more surprised. And I was *more* pleased yet when my platoon came – the whole lot of them. I don't know how they did it, managing to come together, but they came into the ward and they lined up at the foot of the bed and every one of them saluted me. Oh, I was embarrassed, but it was a great feeling. It was very good of them. They said I'd saved their lives, but I was there and

I was in charge of them. I didn't think I was doing anything extraordinary.★

As soon as he was able, John Carmichael wrote home to his anxious mother in Airdrie, to tell her that he was recovering well. He didn't think it worth mentioning that he had won the Victoria Cross!

Another mother was anxious to have news of her son. As John Carmichael was lying unconscious in hospital in Bailleul, Ernie Gays' mother was sitting down to reply to the letter she had received from her son's friend, Jimmy Smith. He received it a day or so later.

> 44 Milligan Road,
> Leicester
> Sunday, 9 September 1917

Dear Friend,

I am addressing you as friend as any friend of my Boy's is my friend. I thank you for sending us word of how our Dear Ernest died. We had also a very nice letter from the Captain [Captain E. Johnston] the day before we received Yours. It is a dreadful thought to lose our Dear Boy in this way. We would not believe it till we had the letter from someone who saw him.

Did you see my boy after he died, could you tell us how he was? I should like to know what time of the day or night it happened (or thereabouts). Was he up the doings (are you allowed to tell us?) or was he on Sentry?

I am sure we are all the while thinking of you dear lads, hoping and praying for you to be kept safe, and then when these Awful tidings are sent us it shakes our faith. But then again when we get calm we know that God is still in his heaven and He orders all things for the best. I sent Ernie a parcel off on 21 August; if you should see anything of it, will you share what is good between

---

★Sergeant Carmichael's citation: *For most conspicuous bravery. When excavating a trench, Sergeant Carmichael saw that a grenade had been unearthed and had started to burn. He immediately rushed to the spot, and shouting to his men to get clear, placed his steel helmet over the grenade and stood on the helmet. The grenade exploded and blew him out of the trench. Sergeant Carmichael could have thrown the bomb out of his trench, but he realised that by so doing he would have endangered the lives of the men working on top. By this splendid act of resource and self-sacrifice Sergeant Carmichael undoubtedly saved many men from injury, but it resulted in serious injury to himself.*

you and his friends. I shall never forget you and hope you will write
often to me. So thanking you I close.

Yours truly,

Mrs Gays

PS. Write soon.

Ernie's parcel was still there at the dump and the boys shared its con-
tents between them. Then Jimmy Smith wrote to Mrs Gays, to thank her
and to tell her as much as he thought it appropriate that she should know
of the manner of Ernie's death. He was at least able to tell her that Ernie
had been buried, no matter how haphazardly. Although that fact was a
comfort to him, he could hardly expect Ernie's mother to realise its significance, for he hoped, as all the soldiers hoped, that the womenfolk at home
would never know the full horror of the carnage.* Throughout the Allied
armies there was a tacit understanding which amounted to a conspiracy of
silence.

Private G. Giggins, No. 32750, 62 Machine Gun Company

Well, the front-line dead — a lot of people won't like this — they're
simply dead. You can't do much about them. In most of the attacks, if
they were killed they just had to lie there until they disappeared
under the mud. That was the reason we had so many missing. When a
fellow gets hit by a splinter or shell, or even a bullet, he collapses at the
knees and usually falls face forward because of the weight on his back,
which means you've only got to have a few inches of mud and he
drowns in the mud. I was right behind the lines one day at Tor Top,
going down a track towards Zillebeke, and I saw a haversack, a very
good haversack, just lying there half in the mud. Now a machine-
gunner can always do with a haversack because ours get very dirty
and oily from carrying tripods. So I tried to pick the haversack up
and it was attached to a dead body. That was the sort of thing you saw
all the time. The thing was that you couldn't do anything for the
dead. It's surprising how heavy a man is when he's dead, and if you
were being pushed back, or even if you were just going out of the
line, you had enough to carry with guns and ammunition. The most
important thing is to get the wounded back, because they *do* stand a
chance.

*If Ernie Gays' body was recovered after the war, it was never identified and
presumably lies in the grave of an 'Unknown Soldier'. His name appears on Panel
154 (South Apse) of the Memorial to the Missing at Tyne Cot Cemetery: '20971,
Private Ernest Gays, X Corps Cyclist Battalion, Army Cyclist Corps. Aged 19.'

Quartermaster–Sergeant George Fisher, 1st Battalion, Hertfordshire Regiment, who on the first night of the battle delivered the rations to the battalion position, only to find that the battalion had ceased to exist.

Sergeant John Carmichael VC, 9th Battalion, North Staffordshire Regiment, who won his Victoria Cross on Hill 60.

Corporal Nick Lee (*on the left*) and the crew of the tank *Keep Smiling* – later the crew of the aptly-named *Revenge*.

Unteroffizier Jeff Werner, the German captured by Nick Lee at Surbiton Villas.

Above: C-in-C Field-Marshal Douglas Haig inspects the Signal Section of the 78th Winnipeg Grenadiers. Corporal Jim Pickard, who was at the taking of Passchendaele, is arrowed.

Right: Gunner Bert Stokes, 13th Battery, New Zealand Field Artillery, 3rd Brigade, who took part in the supporting bombardment in the final push.

Left: Colonel Roderick Macleod DSO, MC as a 2nd Lieutenant, Royal Field Artillery, who commanded C241 Battery for three months of the campaign.

Below left: Cyclist Jim Smith, who buried his friend Ernie Gays on Hill 60 and wrote to tell his mother.

Below right: Mrs Gays wrote back . . .

23/9/14   44 Milligan Rd
           Leicester

Dear Friend

I hope you will not think me too presuming but I feel I must write again and let you know we received your welcome letter of the 14th Sept and to thank you for helping to bury my poor Lad. I would very much like to know such a lot more, but I know you are not allowed to say much. But if ever

Above left: Rifleman Bill Worrell, the songster of the 12th Battalion, the Rifle Brigade.

Above right: 2nd Lieutenant Jimmy Naylor, Royal Artillery, who went over the top as a forward observer at the Battle of Messines.

Below left: Private Bill Smith, 2nd New Zealand Machine Gun Company, who escaped from the slaughter on the Bellevue Ridge.

Below right: The songwriter Sivori Levey, who was a 2nd Lieutenant in the 11th Battalion, Prince of Wales' Own West Yorkshire Regiment.

Left: The padres of the 34th Division. Seated cross-legged at the front is Stanley Hinchliffe, who went up to the line on the duckboards as one of his battalion.

Below: A gun-team of the 16th Canadian Machine Gun Company; Private Reginald Le Brun is seated with the gun.

Reginald Le Brun (*nearest camera*) with his machine-gun team in the reserve line at Passchendaele.

Taking ammunition up the line.

Sister Jean Calder (*in the centre*) of No. 19 Casualty Clearing Station, with VADs and nurses, photographed with a Belgian woman and her baby.

Driver J. McPherson, No. 2273, C Battery, Royal Field Artillery

You couldn't do anything about the dead, and there were so many bodies about that you got callous about it. All that time, before the push in September, I was up and down the Menin Road, up and down, up and down, taking ammunition on the backs of horses and mules up to the dump. They had to keep the Menin Road open, because it was the only way you could get up to that sector with horses and limbers, and it was shelled day and night. The Germans had their guns registered on it to a T, and the engineers had to keep filling up the shell-holes. They filled them up with anything. If a limber got a shell and was blown to pieces they just shovelled everything into the crater and covered it over, dead horses, dead bodies, bits of limber – anything to fill it up and cover it over and keep the traffic going.

I was a driver in the artillery and it was our job to get the ammunition up. We could only take limbers so far because of the shell-holes, so we had to go up the rest of the way with a walking squad, leading the horses. Each horse carried four shells, two on either side – and they were the big heavy ones with brass cases. We used to go twenty of us together, leaving the wagon lines at about three o'clock, up to the dump to get our shells, and we reached the guns about seven o'clock at night – if we were lucky enough to reach the guns. We sometimes thought it was a complete waste of time. The gunners never saw half the shells. With the weight of them they were just sinking into the mud, and it was a complete waste of ammunition because they couldn't find them.*

The bombardment started all along the front on 15 September. They called them 'practice attacks', laying down haphazard drum-fire on different sections of the line, just as if an attack were imminent, in order to confuse the enemy. And the gunfire reached a pitch it had never reached before, for all the guns of the Second Army were now trained on the right half of the sector and those of the Fifth were concentrated on the left. Many of the batteries in the centre of the salient were registering their guns on the mound of ruins that had been the village church of Zonnebeke.

Although Zonnebeke itself had long been pounded to rubble, it was 'fresh' ground. If the troops advanced at this point it would be a real

---

*This is borne out by the fact that every year the Belgian military authorities are called on to deal with munitions of all sorts which are still being unearthed from the land after sixty years. The average annual amount is 500 tons.

advance, and from Zonnebeke the road swung off to the left and ran straight to Passchendaele. But the troops on the right were attacking again at Glencorse Wood, and like the men on the left in front of St Julien, they would be attacking through the decomposing bodies of their fallen comrades.

On the grisly strip of land that still separated the British line from the German front on the old Zonnebeke-Langemarck Road, battalion after battalion had perished in successive attacks – the Herts, whose rations George Fisher had brought up in vain seven weeks previously; and the Scots, whom Rory Macleod had watched sinking and dying in the mud. During the night, Lieutenant Alfred Angel had brought his platoon forward ready to attack in the first wave. Their first objective was a small strongpoint just in front of the road, and they lay waiting for zero hour in shell-holes just fifty or sixty yards in front of it, crouched among the mangled remains of the dead.

Lieutenant A. Angel, 2/4th London Btn., Royal Fusiliers, 58th Division

Most of my boys were young Londoners, just eighteen or nineteen, and a lot of them were going into a fight for the first time. Regularly during the night I crawled round to check on my scattered sections, having a word here and there and trying to keep their spirits up. The stench was horrible, for the bodies were not corpses in the normal sense. With all the shell-fire and bombardments they'd been continually disturbed, and the whole place was a mess of filth and slime and bones and decomposing bits of flesh. Everyone was on edge and as I crawled up to one shell-hole I could hear a boy sobbing and crying. He was crying for his mother. It was pathetic really, he just kept saying over and over again, 'Oh Mum! Oh Mum!' Nothing would make him shut up, and while it wasn't likely that the Germans could hear, it was quite obvious that when there were lulls in the shell-fire the men in shell-holes on either side would hear this lad and possibly be affected. Depression, even panic, can spread quite easily in a situation like that. So I crawled into the shell-hole and asked Corporal Merton what was going on. He said, 'It's his first time in the line, sir. I can't keep him quiet, and he's making the other lads jittery.' Well, the other boys in the shell-hole obviously *were* jittery and, as one of them put it more succinctly, 'fed up with his bleedin' noise'. Then they all joined in, 'Send him down the line and home to Mum' – 'Give him a clout and knock him out' – 'Tell him to put a sock in it, sir.'

I tried to reason with the boy, but the more I talked to him the

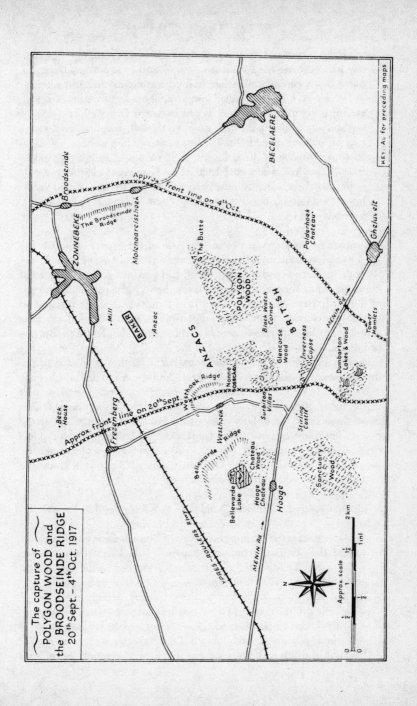

The capture of
POLYGON WOOD and
the BROODSEINDE RIDGE
20th Sept.— 4th Oct. 1917

KEY: As for preceding maps

BECELAERE

Gheluvelt

Broodseinde

Approx front line on 4th Oct.

ZONNEBEKE

The Broodseinde Ridge

Molenaarelsthoek

The Butte

Polderhoek Chateau

Mill

BAKER

Anzac

POLYGON WOOD

BRITISH

Black Watch Corner

Tower Hamlets

ANZACS

Glencorse Wood

Inverness Copse

Dunbarton Lakes & Wood

MENIN Rd

Westhoek Ridge

Nonne Bosschen

Surbiton Villas

Sterling Castle

Beck House

Frezenberg

Approx front line on 20th Sept.

Bellewarde Ridge

Westhoek Ridge

Chateau Wood

Sanctuary Wood

Bellewarde Lake

Hooge Chateau

Hooge

YPRES–ROULERS RLWY.

MENIN Rd

N

Approx scale

0   ½   1   1½   2 km

0   ½   1 ml

more distraught he became, until he was almost screaming. 'I can't stay here! Let me go! I want my Mum!' So I switched my tactics, called him a coward, threatened him with court-martial, and when *that* didn't work I simply pulled him towards me and slapped his face as hard as I could, several times. It had an extraordinary effect. There was absolute silence in the shell-hole and then the corporal, who was a much older man, said, 'I think I can manage him now, sir.' Well, he took that boy in his arms, just as if he was a small child, and when I crawled back a little later to see if all was well, they were both lying there asleep and the corporal still had his arms round the boy – mud, accoutrements and all. At zero hour they went over together.

For once the weather was not on the side of the enemy, although the signs had been ominous. However, after two weeks of comparatively dry weather, the drizzle and showers which had persisted for the forty-eight hours preceding the attack had only laid a slippery glaze across the surface of the earth. Beneath it there was a firm foothold, although the ground behind the German front was pounded into a mess of craters reaching almost lip to lip after the demented shelling of the last few days. But the drizzle ceased during the night and in the morning there was a mist lying over the salient. It was only a light mist, but it was heavy enough to put the Germans, for once, at a disadvantage. And the Allies had another ace in their hands, for the Australians, fresh from a long rest, were taking part in the battle. Part of their attack was to be from the Westhoek Ridge, down the slope to the shallow valley of the Hannebeke stream, and up the other side. On the extreme right of that sector lay Polygon Wood and just beyond, on the extreme left, were the ruins of the village of Zonnebeke, the objective of the British 3rd Division. Captain Baker was in command of the Company where the two sectors met.

Acting-Captain L. J. Baker MC, 2nd Btn., Suffolk Regiment

We were just on the right of the village of Zonnebeke as you looked towards the Germans, in front of Zonnebeke Lake. Our objective was a place called Le Moulin – at least, so it was marked on the map, but we couldn't see a mill or any sign of one. We'd had no trouble getting up and there were tapes laid to show us our assembly positions. People say that the morale of the Army had gone down in those days – well, it hadn't in our battalion. The idea of anyone refusing to go over the top was absolutely absurd. Of course, we were a regular battalion and although there were very few regular people left in it after the Somme, most of our troops were Suffolk men and we all had the same temperament – steady and slow, not dashing and daring. Reliable men.

Well, we did it. We made it. We advanced about a mile, thanks to the mist. The trouble was that we couldn't find this mill. I could see this patch of water and I said, 'Well, that must be Zonnebeke Lake and that must be the church, what's left of it' – for it was just a pile of rubble – but I can't see that windmill.' And then as I was looking round I saw a faint trace of a track with some white rubble at the end of the track, and that was it. That was 'Le Moulin', just on the edge of Zonnebeke. We had no trouble, just the usual fighting, and we also had a shrapnel barrage which burst on the top of the mist. You could see the flash going in front of us and it was very accurate, and we followed that all the time until we got to our objective. It was so easy that some people got wounded, because they went on so fast into our own barrage and through it.

On Baker's right the Australians were doing so well that they had the same problem.

Sergeant J. Stevens, No. 2795, 58th Btn., 15th Infantry Brigade, 5th Australian Division

It was just as though the battalion was carrying out an exercise during manoeuvres. There were only a few casualties, and we moved down into the dip and up the further slope through the 20th and then through the 18th Battalion, which had advanced well beyond its objective. Our colonel, Colonel Martin, had got to the first objective almost as soon as his leading platoons and set up an advanced head-quarters, and he observed that some people were pushing too far forward and were being caught in our own barrage. So he sent the order forward that we should re-align the position and consolidate it.

Acting-Captain L. J. Baker MC, 2nd Btn., Suffolk Regiment

On that occasion, we were told not to dig trenches when we got to our objectives, because by now they knew from experience that that would draw artillery fire. So we were occupying a string of shell-holes. But when I looked over to our right, I saw these Australians standing there in broad daylight and digging in for all they were worth. I dodged my way over to contact their Company Commander and got hold of him and said, 'Your chaps are digging trenches and you know we were told not to.' He said, 'Well, we've been ordered to do it and the boys prefer it.' There wasn't much I could do but I said to him, 'Well, you know, you'll be shelled and when you are I shall get it too. I shall get your "overs".' I had only just got back to my position when they had a hell of a blasting. It went on for hours, and when it stopped and I went back over to see them they were in something of a mess. But we all got everything we went for. Of course, the Germans tried to stage one or two counter-attacks during the four days we held the position, and we could see them coming down the slope and our SOS went up and . . . slap . . . down it came on the Hun – shrapnel, machine-gun barrage – the poor old Germans. That happened two or three times. The trouble was that once our SOS had gone up and our shells started coming down, then the Germans thought *we* were going to attack and they shelled us.

Inevitably we had casualties. The most unfortunate thing was that I accidentally wounded one of my own men. It was the same night, and it was bright moonlight and Jerry had started shelling gas. We had our gas-masks on and were squatting in this shell-hole when a runner chap came along with a message, and he was standing up there silhouetted against the moonlight. I shouted, 'Come down!' – but, of course, he couldn't hear me because of the gas-mask, so I pulled him by the leg. Unfortunately, as he fell down into the shell-hole, a bayonet leaning against the side went right through his thigh. It started to gush blood and I was absolutely horrified. I said, 'I say, I'm frightfully sorry about that!' Well, this chap was grinning all over his face and he said, 'Oh, that's quite all right, sir – it's a Blighty one, isn't it?' He was as pleased as Punch. Of course, I had to give him a note to the MO. I scribbled it on a piece of paper and said, 'This is *not* a self-inflicted wound. *I* did it.'

They called the fighting of that week the Battle of the Menin Road and by the standards which had been set since the campaign began on 31 July it was a success. Inverness Copse was cleared. At last the bloody stumps of Glencorse Wood were in Allied hands. A brigade of South African troops had swept over Beck and Borry. Most of Zonnebeke was taken, and the British had at last managed to cross the graveyard of their soldiers in front of St Julien and make their way across and beyond the shattered cobbles · of the Zonnebeke–Langemarck Road. The London boys had taken their objective. In the attack, Lieutenant Alfred Angel was severely wounded, lost an eye and was ever after known as 'Nelson'. The boy he had slapped in the shell-hole the night before received multiple gunshot wounds and did 'go home to Mum'. Merton, the fatherly corporal who had comforted him, was killed by the same burst of fire and never went home at all.

But the line had been advanced and, in places, by up to a mile. It was good, but for Haig's purposes it was not quite good enough, for on 23 September he was finally forced to cancel the amphibious attack on the coast which had been the corner-stone of his argument in favour of the Flanders campaign. The advance had been won only by throwing in a greater concentration of men and guns than ever before. But certain key areas were still holding out. On the right, Tower Hamlets beyond Shrewsbury Forest; in the middle, a part of Polygon Wood; while above Langemarck the mighty Eagle Trench still guarded the approaches to Poelcapelle. All three would have to be conquered before the Allies could start to move forward on the last lap towards the Passchendaele Ridge itself.

Eagle Trench was the big stumbling block. It had been one of the objectives in the attacks of 20 September, but it had resisted them just as it had resisted the efforts of the 20th Division to capture it on the day Langemarck had fallen almost three weeks before. It was a stronghold and the Germans had thrown in crack troops to defend it. In spite of their efforts, and in spite of the fact that, even after some reasonably dry weather, conditions north of Langemarck were still wet and marshy, some local attacks *had* succeeded, and parts of the formidable trench that snaked and curved through the muddy flats had been captured. But the centre, the most important part, was still in German hands. Behind its high ramparts of sandbags, supported by three massive concrete strongpoints forty yards to the rear, the German stormtroops who defended it resisted all efforts to eject them from their position, which they had been ordered to hold at all costs. The British were now beyond them on either side and, for once, it was the Germans who were in a salient. Ironically, this was partly the reason why it was so difficult to throw them out. An attack on such a narrow front supported by the usual artillery bombardment would cause as many casualties to the British troops in the line of fire as it would to the Germans. It was equally obvious that such a bastion could not be taken by unsupported infantry armed only with bombs, rifles and bayonets. A barrage there must be, and the only solution seemed to be to use a barrage of trench mortars firing lethal, short-range, accurate missiles. On the night of 22 September the trench mortar guns were brought up to the front and every available man was rounded up for the action. Captain Percy Coltman had been in hospital with trench fever and had just returned to rejoin his battalion.

Captain P. Coltman, 11th Btn., The Rifle Brigade

It was a Saturday afternoon when I got to the transport lines, and they said that the battalion was in the line and it was stunting the following day. It was our so-and-so luck that we always stunted on a Sunday and almost as soon as I'd reported I got a chit from the Adjutant, a man named Bosville, telling me to go up the line and join them. They gave me a guide and we set off as soon as it got dark. He was a *terrible* guide. Of course, it was a long way up; we had to go right up over this flooded ground and over the Steenbeek. Long before we got that far, the guide was in trouble. We were going up one of these duckboard tracks and every now and again I'd hear him say, 'Oh, my God', and with a great splash he'd slip off the duckboard and fall in a shellhole full of water. I don't know how many times I hauled him out, so at last I got so fed up with it – because it was very unhealthy at that point, there were shells coming over all the time – that I said, 'Look here, would you like to go back?' He said, 'Yes please, sir, I would, because as a matter of fact I'm night blind.' So he set off back and he hadn't gone fifty yards before he got a shell to himself. That was the end of him, I'm afraid.

I went on and eventually I found where the battalion was, and they had their HQ in a pillbox. I went inside and Davidson was sitting in a corner dozing; his upper denture was flopping about over his lower lip, he was so fast asleep and snoring. I woke him up and he said, 'Oh, thank God you've come, Colty.' He said, 'Look, come outside,' and when we got outside he said, 'Look over to the left there. See that bit of wood sticking up there?' I said, 'Yes.' He said, 'See that other thing sticking up over there on the right? Well, those are your boundaries and you're going over at seven with the right half of the battalion.' So I said, 'Well, where are they?' 'Oh,' he said, 'they dug in last night.'

I went forward and found them in one of these old German trenches we'd captured, and the first man I saw was Snarey. He was a runner I had, a mill-hand in Lancashire in private life, and he had not the slightest fear of anything. As a matter of fact he'd got a sword stuck in the wall of the trench, and he'd got his dixie and some shredded-up sandbag canvas and candle-grease alight in a tin, and he was heating up some pork and beans.★ Well, it was nearly time to go, so I said, 'Put that away, Snarey, no time for breakfast.' He said, 'All

---

★A foul-smelling but reasonbly effective substitute for the more sophisticated 'tommy cooker'. The method was to cover the bottom of an empty 'McConachie' tin with scraps of sandbag canvas, covered with shavings of candle-grease, and ignite.

right, sir.' But we went over shortly after that and I just happened to glance round to see that the men were keeping direction, and there was Snarey, rifle slung, and he was spooning his pork and beans out of his dixie with the lid of a Three Castles cigarette tin. I can see the green band round it now. And that's how he went over! He was a wonder, that chap.

The attack was preceded by the trench mortar barrage, and when they had fired the last round the gunners shot up a white Very light to signal the troops across. The bombing parties had crept forward under cover of the barrage, and the moment it ceased they bombed their way along Eagle Trench from either side while Coltman led his men in a frontal attack.

Captain P. Coltman, 11th Btn., The Rifle Brigade

We had very little trouble, we were attacking with swords – we always attacked with swords – but the bombing boys had done their job and the Germans were coming along the trench with their hands up.★ We got 102 Boche out of it, but I rather think not all of them got back to the cage. We had one nasty moment. They were coming along with their hands up and there was one evil-looking devil and he suddenly picked up a rifle that was lying on the parapet of the trench. Quick as a flash, he fired at one of my sergeants, who was standing on the parapet with a Mills bomb in his hand, marshalling them out of the trench. He shot him right through the ankle. My sergeant just lifted his foot and his face contorted a bit, then he pulled the pin out of the Mills bomb, waited about a second and a half and slung it at this Boche. I saw it happen. It hit him in the head and blew his head off. Well, it didn't take us long to clear them out after that, although we were a little bit busy for a time. And we cleared them out of the two block-houses at the back of the trench. In fact they started to run out of them when they saw it was all up in Eagle. We had set up a couple of Lewis guns by that time and we made it hot for them as they went. Of course, we had casualties ourselves. We lost quite a few men. As we were moving I jumped into a shell-hole and there was one of my boys there, down on one knee, ready to go on. As soon as the moment came, I shook him on the shoulder and shouted, 'Come on!' As I shook him his tin hat fell off and half his head with it. He had been scalped as he waited. I had to leave him where he was, for at this moment the Germans were massing for a counter-attack.

★In The Rifle Brigade, bayonets are traditionally referred to as 'swords'.

We could see them about 400 yards away forming up in a line, so we were working our way over across to reinforce the line of the 10th Battalion on our left flank. Luckily I was able to find two enemy machine-guns which they had abandoned on their way back, and I got some of the chaps on to them and we managed to stop the counter-attack. In fact by going a bit forward to stop it, we managed to get further than we had really been supposed to and we consolidated there, with Eagle Trench quite a bit at our back – and their block-houses too.

Eagle Trench lay 700 yards north of Langemarck. It had taken thirty-eight days to get there. The 11th Battalion was relieved on the night of 25 September. As the RBs slithered in single file along the three miles of duckboard track that would bring them to the canal bank (a journey made particularly unpleasant by heavy gas shelling which forced them to wear masks), far away to the south Sir Douglas Haig was entertaining the Prime Minister and his retinue to dinner at Advanced Headquarters. Colonel Hankey sat next to Haig during the meal, and later noted in his diary that 'he was rather preoccupied about tomorrow's attack, which has been somewhat dislocated by a big unsuccessful German counter-attack this afternoon.'

'Tomorrow's attack' was the Battle of Polygon Wood. By the end of the day, Polygon had been taken, the wounded were pouring into the casualty clearing stations and the prisoners were pouring into the cage.

It had been an interesting day for Lloyd George and his party, who had been able to keep a close eye on the progress of the battle from a safe distance of some thirty miles. Nevertheless, Colonel Hankey was probably not the only one to feel that they were right at the hub of activity.

26 September. There was a big attack that morning. All the time at the conference, messages were coming in from the front. Haig had a great map showing the line we wanted to reach, and it was very interesting the way first one bit was filled in on the map, then another, until by the time we finished (11.30 am) the picture was complete except for a small section, where two brigades had been held up.*

Haig must have been relieved to be able to demonstrate success. The small advance doubtless looked most impressive on such a large-scale map.

*The Supreme Command, 1914–1918, Lord Hankey (George Allen and Unwin Ltd., 1961).

The sad truth, however, was that by this time Lloyd George was virtually indifferent to the whole Flanders campaign. He had written it off precisely one month before on 26 August on receiving the news of Cadorna's great victory in Italy. That night he took the final decision to transfer his interest, together with large numbers of men and materials, to the Italian front. Now, although he was about to leave GHQ to visit Fifth Army Headquarters in the north, he was merely going through the motions. Haig had arranged the visit, and he had a particular reason for doing so. Since the opportunity of a coastal attack had been irrevocably lost, he was more than ever anxious to convince the Prime Minister of the effectiveness of his policy of attrition, and there was a satisfactorily large number of German prisoners in the cages available to be shown off. It had been arranged for the Prime Minister and his party to visit them.

Is it possible that he had also, perhaps unconsciously, planted the idea in the Prime Minister's head that Gough was to blame for the slow progress of the campaign in Flanders? Whether or not he had done so, Lloyd George had formed precisely that opinion and he made it clear that he had done so by an act of omission, which Gough interpreted as a studied insult.

> I saw him through my window in La Louvie Château walking past the door with General Charteris, who was Head of the Intelligence Service at GHQ. I was considerably surprised to see him, as I had received no intimation that he was coming into my Army area, much less to my own Headquarters. I asked one of my ADCs to find out what he was doing, and discovered that he was visiting some camps of German prisoners to see the deterioration in their physique – which I must say was not particularly apparent to me. I was struck by the discourtesy of the Prime Minister in actually visiting the Headquarters of one of his Army Commanders and not coming to see him, and I therefore let him pass on. It was an amazing attitude for a man in his position and with his responsibilities. He had never met me, and it would have been an opportunity of at least seeing for himself what manner of man I was, and of exchanging some ideas on the general position in which we stood. It was in fact his duty to do so. I have since understood that he blamed me for this Ypres battle and for its long continuation. But it is difficult to believe that a man in his position could be so ignorant of the system of command in an Army. Neither the inception of this battle nor its continuation was any more my responsibility than that of one of my Corps or Divisional Commanders. I merely received my orders from the Field-Marshal.★

★*The Fifth Army*, General Sir Hubert Gough GC, MG, KCB, KCVO (Hodder & Stoughton Ltd., 1931)

The clue to the misunderstanding perhaps lay in the fact that the Prime Minister was accompanied by General Charteris, no friend of Gough's, who was conducting the illustrious visitors on their sightseeing tour. They drove extensively through the back areas and through what Colonel Hankey described as

> ... the usual paraphernalia of dumps of ammunition, aerodromes, herds of 'tanks' like great mastodons, roads made of planks, etc. At a crossroads just outside Poperinghe a big eleven-inch shell whistled over our heads and burst a hundred yards away – too close to be pleasant. Our destination was a cage for prisoners brought down from the day's battle – containing a number of nerve-shattered, tired, unshaved and dirty men, who nevertheless sprang to attention as though under review by the Kaiser. [*The Supreme Command, 1914–1918*]

In order to underline the point that the Germans were beaten and almost at the end of their tether, someone had that morning given the order that the most unprepossessing and unfit of the prisoners should be segregated into a separate cage and that to this cage, and no other, the Prime Minister should be conducted. It really made very little difference. Lloyd George had decided to wash his hands of the campaign in Flanders. If Haig was determined that he would win the war by reaching Passchendaele, then let him do so. Lloyd George was no longer particularly interested.

Two days later, at a conference of his commanders, Haig was in an optimistic mood. He stressed that the repeated blows were rapidly using up the enemy's strength and reserves. He believed that the moment was near when the offensive might be pursued on a grand scale beyond the definite and limited objectives of the past few weeks. He believed that it would soon be possible to send in a force of tanks, and even cavalry. He had every reason to believe that a significant breakthrough was possible in the very near future.

It was almost October. The battle had now been in progress for two long months. The casualties amounted to 88,790 killed, missing and wounded. The advance, at the deepest point of penetration, was three and a half miles. In two months of anguished effort, with seemingly every circumstance against them, the troops had managed to get almost exactly halfway to the Passchendaele Ridge. And the nightmare had hardly begun.

Part 5

'We Died in Hell – They Called it Passchendaele'

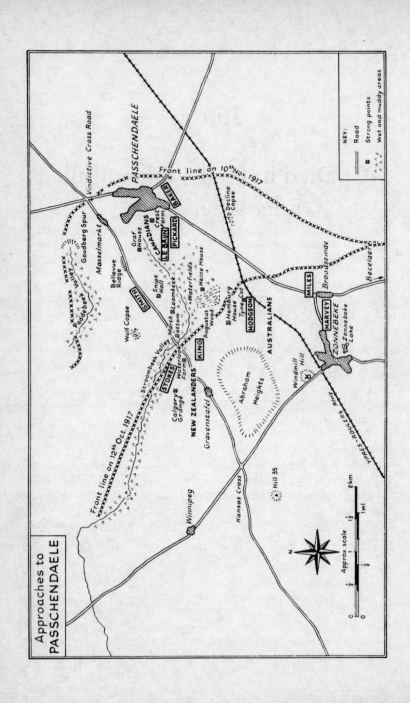

Approaches to PASSCHENDAELE

KEY:
Road
Strong points
Wet and muddy areas

PASSCHENDAELE

Front line on 10th Nov. 1917

BAKER

Vindictive Cross Road

Goudberg Spur

Masselmarkt

Graf House

Cross Farm

LE ROUN

PICKARD

Decline Copse

Bellevue Ridge

CANADIANS

Paddebeek Valley

Wolf Copse

SMITH

Snipe Hall

Loamkeek

Waterfields

Heine House

Bacelaere

Broodseinde

MILES

HARVEY

ZONNEBEKE

Zonnebeke Lake

Marsh Bottom

Hamburg House

Tyne Cot

HODGSON

Augustus Wood

Stroombeek Valley

Waterloo Farm

KING

AUSTRALIANS

STOKES

Calgary Grange

Gravenstafel

NEW ZEALANDERS

Abraham Heights

Windmill Hill

YPRES-ROULERS RWY

Front line on 12th Oct. 1917

Winnipeg

Kansas Cross

Hill 35

N

Approx scale

2 km
1 ml

Chapter 16

The deep bowl of land that, just two months ago, had lain beyond the salient had been narrowed now to a crescent of ridges, curving from Poelcapelle at one tip to the Gheluvelt plateau at the other. In the centre of the topmost ridge, girdled by strongpoints, was the tumbled brick-heap of the ruined village of Passchendaele. From horizon to horizon a cratered wasteland of mud stretched as far as the eye could see. It was just possible from the eminence of a balloon or aeroplane to pick out the scattered heaps of rubble that were the tombstones of dead farms and hamlets.

From the gates of Ypres to the heights of Passchendaele, from Boesin-ghe to Hill 60, the shell-craters now lay lip to lip, separated only by the slimy bridges of mud that snaked around their edges. The pitted surface of the salient was like a mammoth sponge, heavy with mud and water. Here and there, swollen by rain, dammed and diverted by the exploding earth, streams had pushed their way through the crumbling banks of the craters and linked a dozen or more into deep impassable lakes of liquid mud. On most of them and on the smaller shell-craters, as the exhaust of a car leaves an iridescent smear on a puddle, a film of red streaking the surface told all too clearly the fate of the men who had collapsed, wounded, into the morass. Often, as the troops passed by, a bubble would form and burst with a great sough as the air was expelled from some bloated long-dead body held in the mud below. For there were bodies everywhere, sunk in the marsh or lying on the surface among the remains of shattered limbers, of broken guns, of the dead hulks of half-buried tanks.

It was impossible to remove the dead, for as the armies inched and slithered and waded and fought their way up the slopes, they were still under observation from the German vantage-point on the ridge of Passchendaele. Exhausted and miserable, sharing much the same privations as their adversaries, almost worn out by the struggle to defend the tenancy of their portion of the shattered swamp, the Germans could still observe every sign of life in the marshes below. They could still pick out every inch, every yard of the ever-lengthening wooden tracks that straggled and meandered through the battlefield stretching closer and closer to their lines. They could still send down retribution from the guns behind them, secure in long-fixed positions. In daylight, the rats, as fat and bloated as the dead bodies they fed on, were the only living things that could move with impunity in the salient.

Corporal S. T. H. Ross, 39th Division, Signal Co., Royal Engineers

When you got beyond a certain line on your way up, that was the end of the world you came from and you just didn't bother to think about what was laid before you. You just did your job, and with any luck you came back. It's difficult to try to tell other people what it was like. It's not an easy thing to do. The salient was unimaginable.

2nd Lieutenant H. L. Birks, Tank Corps

The salient was a dead loss. I cannot think how the one or two senior officers there who had brains let the thing go on. Of course, they were helping the French out which makes a big difference. One doesn't know what the higher strategy was. But from the tactical side it was sheer murder. You had this Ypres-Yser Canal and you got the strangest feeling when you crossed it. You'd almost abandon hope. And as you got further out you got this awful smell of death. You could literally smell it. It was just a complete abomination of desolation. I wept when I came into the salient.

Private C. Miles, No. 7322, 10th Btn., Royal Fusiliers

I never had a feeling of ease the whole of the time I was in the salient. I used to notice that when the fellows came out of the line, and if they were going on into France for a rest, then as they went over the dividing line – there was the remains of a customs post on the Bailleul Road – they'd always kick the mud off their feet. Into France, leave the Belgian mud behind. You could smell a battalion coming out of the line if they were *en masse* and passed you close. A horrible smell of mud and corruption and unwashed bodies. It soaked right into you, that Ypres smell. As a runner, finding your way around in that sea of mud was the worst part. You were on your own. On a moonlight night the shell-holes full of water show up as white as silver, and you think to yourself, 'Well, I've got to go through mud, but I must be careful that I don't fall into any of these shell-holes.' It was easy to do, and even if they didn't suck you right down they were all impregnated with gas – mustard gas – and it caused terrible burns and blisters if it touched you.

The moment you set off you felt that dreadful suction. It was forever pulling you down, and you could hear the sound of your feet coming out in a kind of sucking 'plop' that seemed much louder at night when you were on your own. In a way, it was worse when the mud didn't suck you down; when it yielded under your feet you knew that it was a body you were treading on. It was terrifying. You'd tread on one on the stomach, perhaps, and it would grunt all the air out of its body. It made your hair stand on end. The smell could make you vomit. And you could always tell whether it was a dead Jerry or a dead Tommy. The Germans smelt different in death.

Major George Wade, South Staffordshire Regiment, Machine Gun Corps

Going up to the line for the first time my first indication of the horrors to come appeared as a small lump on the side of the duck-board. I glanced at it, as I went past, and I saw to my horror, that it was a human hand gripping the side of the track – no trace of the owner, just a glimpse of a muddy wrist and a piece of sleeve sticking out of the mud. After that there were bodies every few yards. Some lying face downwards in the mud; others showing by the expressions fixed on their faces the sort of effort they had made to get back on to the track. Sometimes you could actually see blood seeping up from underneath. I saw the dead wherever I looked – a dead signaller still clinging to a basket cage with two dead pigeons in it, and further on, lying just off the track, two stretcher-bearers with a dead man on a stretcher. There were the remains of a ration party that had been blown off the track. I remember seeing an arm, still holding on to a water container. When the dead men were just muddy mounds by the trackside it was not so bad – they were somehow impersonal. But what was unendurable were the bodies with upturned faces. Sometimes the eyes were gone and the faces were like skulls with the lips drawn back, as if they were looking at you with terrible amusement. Mercifully, a lot of those dreadful eyes were closed.

Private C. Davey, No. 424129, 5th Canadian Btn., 2nd Brigade, 1st Canadian Division

The duckboards were slithery with mud and many sections were slanted to one side or the other. Sometimes there were new sections where it had been destroyed and the working parties had repaired it. Sometimes there were just gaps. We came to one gap, where a shell had landed. The bodies of three Germans had been laid side by side as

a bridge in this hole. In order to avoid stepping into a sea of mud, we
had to use these bloated bodies as stepping-stones to get across.

Lieutenant J. W. Naylor, Royal Artillery

I came to hate that salient. Absolutely loathed it. I always used to
think the names were so sinister – Zonnebeke – Hill 60 – Zillebeke –
the names terrified you before you got there, they had such a sinister
ring about them. Then to end up making for Passchendaele was the
last straw. You could practically segregate the salient from the whole
of the rest of the war-zone. It wore you down. The weather, the lack
of rations, everything seemed to be against you. There didn't seem to
be anything left. You were wet through for days on end. We never
thought we'd get out alive. You couldn't see the cloud with the silver
lining. There wasn't one.

   We'd had an awful time getting the guns up the plank road on to
Westhoek Ridge – and that was before the worst of the mud. Three
weeks later we couldn't have done it at all. It was just sheets of water
coming down. It's difficult to get across that it's a sea of mud. Literally
a sea. You can drown in it. On the day I reached my lowest ebb I'd
gone down from the gun position to meet the ammunition wagon
coming up the supply road. It was my job to see that they got the
wagons unloaded at the dump and to arrange carrying parties to take
the shells and rations up to the battery. Oddly enough it was a quiet
afternoon, but they must have seen some movement on the road
because just as the wagon came up a heavy shell came over and burst
very close. There were six horses pulling that wagon and they took
fright at the explosion, veered right off the road and down they went
into the mud. We had no possible way of getting them out. In any
event they sank so fast that we had no chance even to cut them loose
from the heavy wagon. We formed a chain and stretched out our
arms and managed to get the drivers off, but the poor horses just sank
faster and faster and drowned before our eyes. The wagon and horses
disappeared in a matter of minutes. One of the drivers was absolutely
incoherent with terror. It was the thought of being drowned in that
awful stuff. It's a horrible thought. Anyone would rather be shot and
know nothing about it.

   That incident depressed me more than anything else in the war. I
just felt, 'What the hell's the use of going on? I don't care a damn who
wins this war.' Well, morale can't get much lower than that. It was a
nightmare. I have it still . . .

On 30 September young Dick Findlater was one of the happiest men in the salient. Last night, worn out by four days' heavy fighting in Polygon Wood, the dishevelled remnants of the 9th Battalion, Highland Light Infantry, had struggled exhausted out of the line and back to billets in scattered farms and barns around Dranoutre. Next morning he was hailed by McNab, the Orderly Corporal. 'Findlater! You're for leave.'

Corporal R. Findlater, D Co., 9th Btn., HLI 33rd Division

We could hardly believe it. There were eight of us to go, and we didn't hang around trying to take it in. We got our passes, drew our pay and we were off. It was eight miles to the railhead at Bailleul, but our luck was in because almost as soon as we got on to the main road we got a lift in a lorry. We were singing all the way. But when we got to Bailleul we sang another tune, for the RTO Corporal at the station told us that the leave train had left and we'd have to wait until tomorrow. We didn't think a lot of the idea. There were some open wagons being loaded on a siding, so we hung around for the rest of the day, had a sandwich at one of the canteens and kept out of the way. After dark we skirted round the station and got into one of the open trucks and lay down on the floor. A while later they shunted an engine up, coupled it to the wagons and off we went.

At five o'clock in the morning of 1 October, we got to Boulogne. We were freezing cold and as stiff as a board, and we didn't care a hoot. There were three large boats waiting to take the troops on leave. We were the first eight men on the first boat. We were the first off at Folkestone. We ran up the platform with our packs and our rifles and got into the train in the first compartment behind the engine – and we were the first off and through the barrier at Victoria. There was an air raid on when we got there and we were told to take cover. Well, we laughed at that. We weren't likely to be frightened of a Zeppelin after what we'd come out of. But the Underground was closed and there were no trains running, so we walked all the way to Euston to get the night train. We had to stand in the corridor all the way, but in the morning we were in Scotland.

Somewhere in mid-channel on his joyful journey to Blighty, Dick Findlater passed a troopship full of less high-spirited soldiers who were travelling in the opposite direction. One of them was Bert Stokes, re-freshed after Messines by a few weeks in a quieter sector of the front in France and the glorious culmination of a fortnight in Blighty. On

Monday, 1 October he was on his way back. During his absence, the New Zealand Field Artillery had moved.

Gunner B. O. Stokes No. 25038, 13th Bty., NZ Field Artillery, 3rd Brigade

Tuesday, 2 October. Back in the battery routine again, but what have we come back to? Passchendaele! The guns are in position near St Julien. The boys do not seem very keen about the prospects. Curly Cooper was wounded in the foot the first night I was back, and the same morning Jack Cantry had his foot crushed by a limber. So the battery is short-handed. To my delight I was informed that I was now to be a gunner permanently. Previous to now I have been spending a lot of time driving as well as taking my turn on the gun. Each man coming into the battery starts off driving whether he likes it or not. When I went into camp in New Zealand I said I wanted to be a gunner, so I was trained as a gunner and had nothing to do with the horses. Others wanted to be drivers and they were trained in the riding school. I arrived in France in midwinter and the first night I was billeted in a hayloft above farm animals. At six o'clock next morning the Sergeant came to me – a newcomer to the battery – and said, 'These are your two horses.' I replied, 'I'm not a driver. I'm a gunner.' To which his reply was, 'You're a bloody driver now.' So that's the way the army does it. For over six months I had two horses, and most of the time a sore bottom. I had only been on a horse a few times in my life.

3 October. Today we moved our wagon lines from Poperinghe to near Ypres. The two brigades just pulled into an open paddock, no horse lines, no bivvies, nothing. We got a few bivvy sheets and made a sort of shelter. At night it was my turn to go up with the ammunition. We filled the packs with shells from the wagons at the lines and walked all the way to the guns leading two horses. It was a long way and I thought we would never get there. We passed through Ypres, my first time in the town. It is a pitiable sight now, shell-shattered and in ruins, with the famous Cloth Hall looking stark and naked with one wall standing. The traffic on the roads was very heavy. As I passed through for the first time I marvelled and wondered at the immensity of the war and the sad state of Ypres. I am sure Webster could not have fully described the scene as I saw it tonight. Not with all the words in his huge dictionary. Fortunately we only had to do one trip. We got back to the lines at 11 pm, and, believe me, being just back

from leave, I am tired! But the weather was fine and the ground reasonably dry where we went, so it was not too bad.

It was bright moonlight, and strangely quiet on that night of 3 October. Both the British and German guns were holding back, ready to unleash a massive bombardment in the early hours – for both sides were planning to attack at dawn. The Germans had initially planned their attack for the morning of the third, and had only postponed it for twenty-four hours to give themselves time to stiffen their lines with reinforcements that would replace the heavy casualties of the last few days. It seemed to them a propitious moment to try to wrest back some of the ground they had lost, for such was the condition of the ground that they were convinced that the Allies could not possibly move their guns forward. With little artillery support, the infantry holding the front line would be easy meat.

But somehow the impossible had been achieved. The gunners and horses had toiled and strained and heaved and dragged the guns uphill through the swamp, and now they were ranged in position behind the infantry. Throughout the night of 3 October the long khaki lines of soldiers moved in single file up the infantry tracks into the damp and dripping ditches of the front line. Beyond them, long lines of grey-clad soldiers were moving down the hill into the German lines. Both armies settled down to pass the hours until zero as comfortably as they could. In the early hours of the morning, the wind changed. Clouds began to scud across the bright half-moon sky. Soon it was blotted out altogether and the men in the trenches looked up and cursed as it began to rain.

It had been decided that, for once, there would be no preliminary bombardment. Zero hour was timed for 6 am, and the British commanders were banking on the element of surprise. The Allies were going to attack along the entire front of eight miles. But the four German divisions were massed on the high ground between Becelaere, in front of Polygon Wood, and the Broodseinde Ridge in front of Zonnebeke. It was along this part of the front that the Anzacs were waiting to plunge into the assault.

The rum ration was being issued. The men were waiting, ready to pick up their loads and go over the top at six o'clock, when with a crack, at 5.30 am, the German barrage opened and shells began to rain into the closely packed ranks of the Anzacs waiting at the jumping-off positions.

W. J. Harvey, 24th Btn., Austirlian Infantry Force

They pounded our position with high explosives, including minenwerfers and eight-inch shells, and we had tremendous casualties. It was the heaviest shell-fire the battalion had ever encountered on the

jumping-off line. It was hardest on our battalion and on the 21st next
to us. We had forty killed, including two of our platoon officers, and
taking into account the wounded a third of our men were put out of
action. Everyone kept their nerve, although it was a terrible strain to
lie there under that sort of fire without being able to do a thing about
it, knowing that there was a terrible struggle ahead and that we'd be
going into it well under strength. It seemed an eternity before our
own guns opened up and we got the order to advance.

With gusts of wind from the west driving the rain into their backs,
the Aussies scrambled forward into the bogland where the waters of
Zonnebeke Lake had spilled over into the low ground in front of the
Broodseinde Ridge. It was still more than half-dark, and as they struggled
on between the two barrages smoke from the explosions covered their
advance. It wrapped them in a haze that hid them completely from the
Germans, who were packed into their front-line and assembly trenches
with no shelter from the fierce shelling which they assumed was raining
down in retaliation to their own bombardment. When the barrage lifted
and the first Aussies loomed out of the mist, the Germans were taken
completely by surprise. The Australians were no less surprised to find a
strong force of Germans waiting with fixed bayonets, ready to go over the
top and packed into their trenches in such numbers that they were unable
to deploy to defend them. Infuriated by the havoc the German shelling
had wrought in the assembly line, the Australians went savagely into the
attack, wielding bayonets to such effect that a large number of the unfortunate Germans, seeing that the Australians were in no mood to take
prisoners, shammed dead or wounded to escape the onslaught.

W. J. Harvey, 24th Btn., AIF

After we had passed on, a number of these Huns rose up and started
firing on us from the rear. That, naturally enough, made the boys see
red. Their deaths were real enough after that.★

The German forces were completely overwhelmed and by 7.30 the
troops were ready to go on to the next objective. By 9.30 the 24th Battalion had captured all its objectives and was ensconced on the Broodseinde
Ridge eating the Germans' breakfast. For, apart from over-running two

★The communiqué issued that evening read in part: *One Anzac Corps obtained all
its objectives and took 3,900 prisoners. The other Anzac Corps took all its objectives and met
the Prussian Guards whom they had met at Pozières on the Somme. This Corps took no
prisoners.*

gun positions and capturing the guns intact, they had also captured three enemy food-wagons. The hot soup was by then on the tepid side, the black bread was not particularly attractive to Australian palates, but who cared!

Just past the Broodseinde-Becelaere Road, Lieutenant Ball and a party of men rushed and captured a pillbox and found to their delight that it was a German HQ, still occupied by an Intelligence Officer and his staff. Lieutenant Ball took them prisoner and sent them back, heavily guarded, to the Allied lines; meanwhile the men took stock of their booty. It was quite a haul. By the time Ball had sent his unwilling guests on their way and returned to the pillbox the men were making merry. Every one of them, smokers and non-smokers alike, was puffing a German cigar and delightedly swigging Rheinwein – a bottle apiece. They had found two boxes of German carrier pigeons in the pillbox, and it was unanimously decided to send an appropriate message or two back to Fritz at his Divisional Headquarters.

The German Command had inevitably lost contact with its front lines and, knowing only that violent fighting was going on, some German officer must have watched with relief as the three pigeons fluttered into their homing boxes at Advanced Headquarters well beyond the Passchendaele Ridge. The content of the messages was somewhat unexpected: 'Deutschland über Alles! Ha! Ha!' and 'Hock the Kaiser – I don't think!' The third, carefully composed by Lieutenant Ball, was an unprintable request for certain information of an obscene and personal nature. It had the audacity to ask for a reply. The rest of the pigeons were plucked and stewed. They sustained the signallers and runners throughout what all of them agreed had been a satisfactory day.

But it had been a costly one. By the end of the next day the strength of the 24th Battalion alone was reduced by exactly half. They had 10 officers left of the 20 who had gone into the line and just 253 out of 500 fighting men still in action. But they were in glorious possession of the Broodseinde Ridge, and looking back over the rain-swept salient, took stock of their victory.

W. J. Harvey, 24th Btn., AIF

From the Broodseinde Ridge the whole field was under observation, and as we gazed back over the country we could see quite plainly the movements of our own units on various duties – guns, transport, men, the lot. The ridge was a prize worth having. Hundreds of German prisoners were now struggling back through our lines. By now we felt really quite sorry for them, they were in such abject

misery. You could see by the strain on their faces that they'd had a bad
time under our shell-fire. A lot of them were wounded and those
who could were hobbling along as fast as they could to get away from
the lines. There was one German officer, I remember. He was almost
running in his hurry and, when someone tried to stop him for some
reason, he said in English, 'Let me go; I'll get out all right. *Damn* the
war!' We let him go.

It was the New Zealanders who, in the adjacent sector to the left of the
Australians, had attacked over Abraham Heights and the Gravenstafel
Ridge and got a foothold on the ridge of Passchendaele. On their left the
British had made a small advance towards Poelcapelle beyond the notorious Eagle Trench. But the rain and the wind had blown up into a storm
of lashing rain and gales. After two weeks of weather that was merely
showery, the salient was once more awash. There was little chance of
counter-attacks, but nothing more could be achieved until the troops
could be relieved and the guns dragged nearer to the front. With every
hour that passed the task seemed more and more impossible. On the
confused front at Poelcapelle the troops watched and sheltered as best they
could. Sometime during the hours of darkness, separated from the rest of
the signallers, and with no chance of finding their battalion until morning,
Harold Diffey and his friend, Corporal Pugh, found a reasonably dry
stretch of trench a little way behind what they imagined to be the front
line. They were wet, exhausted, bedraggled and, not to put too fine a
point upon it, lost.

Private H. Diffey, No. 21927, 15th (London Welsh) Btn., Royal Welch
Fusiliers

Of course, it had been an old German trench. Even at this stage there
were a few stretches about that you could call by the name of
trenches. But we were suspicious as soon as we dropped into it,
because the Germans were always very careful when they retired –
they never left anything behind but empty tins and ashes of fires –
and, lo and behold, we saw this new equipment and a rifle at the
entrance to this dug-out. We immediately suspected that there were
Germans about, keeping very quiet. I still had the signal lamp with
me, so I pulled it round off my shoulder and shone a beam of light
down the concrete stairs, and there at the bottom of the steps sat a
German soldier, apparently asleep. We get down – shine the lamp –
no German to be seen. Pugh sees a candle end. We light it and then
we see a pair of boots sticking out under a lot of sacks, so we pounce

on it and haul out this German. Just a little bloke and frightened as
hell. Jabbering away in German, which we don't understand a word
of. We search him. You're supposed to search all prisoners, but what
we're after is cigarettes. We're dying for a smoke. He doesn't smoke.
No fags. But he pulls out photographs of his wife and children and
points to himself and says, 'Saxon, Saxon.' We take him to mean that
the Saxons are friends of the British. I say to Pugh that we're
supposed to escort him back to the transport lines. Pugh says, 'Well,
I'm bloody sure I'm not going back with him, with all this iron flying
about the sky!' Then he has an idea. 'Keep him here,' he says. 'If any
Jerries counter-attack, he can shout up the stairs to them. If any of
our fellows come along, *we* can shout up the stairs. We're safer here
than in London!'

We sit down on the floor and after a bit the little Jerry relaxes. We
go to sleep, all three of us huddled together for warmth.

The storm continued. In spite of gale-force winds and driving rain,
orders were issued for a fresh all-out effort. But first the guns had somehow to be dragged forward, and fresh troops, already on their way, moved
into position.

The soldiers wading thigh-deep in mud and water remarked wryly on
the presence of the Royal Naval Division, and yelled at them as they
marched into the line, 'Blimey, that's torn it. We knew they'd have to send
the Navy in.' The Navy, clinging to their rain capes and their dignity,
gave a certain familiar signal in reply.

On 6 October, with the bad weather showing no signs of abating,
Generals Gough and Plumer conferred late into the night. In the morning
they jointly proposed to Sir Douglas Haig that the campaign should be
brought to an immediate close. Courteous as ever, optimistic as ever,
elated by the advance of three days before, Haig refused to entertain the
suggestion. Plans had already been made for a fresh attack on the ninth.
Bad weather – which might clear up at any time – was not sufficient
reason for cancelling it. The men had been splendid. Haig was proud of
them. And Passchendaele was at last within their grasp. It needed one –
just one – final effort to reach it. The campaign could not be abandoned
now that the Germans must surely be at their last gasp.

Thirty-six hours later the troops were on their way, shuffling up the
long miles of sodden planks towards the tapes at the starting-point in the
valley that lay at the foot of the Passchendaele Ridge.

Chapter 17

The bleak rain-swept expanse of mud which was the rendezvous-point for the 2/5th East Lancs on the afternoon of 8 October was a far cry from the trenches in the sand-dunes at Nieuport where they had been holding the line all summer. Only a few days before, they had been brought back to the Ypres sector to miserable billets in the ramparts of the city, where they had been under almost continuous shell-fire. Admittedly at Nieuport they had been under the noses of the vigilant German guns in the next bay, and the ever-present floodwater had made life unpleasant enough. But there was fresh air to breathe and the clean ocean on their doorstep, so that Nieuport, which during their stay they had considered to be no picnic, seemed in retrospect like paradise compared to the stinking gas-soaked slough of the Ypres sector. Lieutenant Paddy King wondered how his boys of B Company were managing to keep so cheerful. They were almost all Burnley lads – 'B for Burnley' they used to quip – and Paddy himself was almost the only southerner among them. But there hadn't been a lot of quipping that day, and B Company, marching out through Ypres and into their first experience of the awful salient, had been strangely silent. Paddy King for once would have been happy to hear the strains of the long-familiar and boringly repetitive 'Burnley Mashers', with which B Company was apt to regale reluctant listeners on every possible occasion:

> We are the Burnley Mashers,
> When we go out at neet,
> The lasses all admire us
> and think we look a treat. . . .

But trudging back from the final briefing to company commanders, Paddy King thought his men presented a sorry sight, either standing in dejected groups or squatting miserably over dixies set on the smouldering tommy cookers that, given time, might just produce a lukewarm drink of tea. The four-mile march from Ypres had taken almost five hours. Now they were 'resting' in the mud at the foot of the slopes they called the

Heights of Abraham, before setting off at dusk on the long trek up the line. Many of the men were sick and shivering in the chill wind and Paddy King felt none too good himself, for there was an epidemic of feverish colds in the battalion and most of the Burnley Mashers had streaming noses and rough, sore throats. There was hardly a boy in the company whose solicitous mother would not have immediately packed him off to bed with a lemon drink and a hot-water bottle.

Their orders were to capture the lower slopes of the Passchendaele Ridge and the attack was timed to start at 5 am. The Colonel had given his company commanders a very clear idea of the conditions they would find at the front, and King now passed on the information to his NCOs. The name of the objective was printed quite clearly on the trench map. In front of it lay two closely-printed lines of the black crosses that denoted the presence of strong German defences. It was called Waterfields. The area just to the left was marked with the name 'Marshbottom'.

At 5.15, in the gathering gloom of the murky wet evening, already worn out by the morning's march and the long hours of waiting in the bone-chilling rain, the 2/5th Lancs squelched their way towards the track. Joining the line of sodden Tommies moving in single file along the slippery duckboards, they started to shuffle towards the front line. It was only possible to shuffle, for, predictably, as darkness fell, the enemy started to pound the roads and duckboards with shrapnel and high explosive. The wind rose. The rain became torrential. It was just over a mile to the front line but the winding route of the duckboards, as they corkscrewed around the craters and the floodwater, covered many times that distance. Inevitably there were accidents.

Lieutenant P. King, 2/5th Btn., East Lancashire Regiment

It was an absolute nightmare. Often we would have to stop and wait for up to half an hour, because all the time the duckboards were being blown up and men being blown off the track or simply slipping off – because we were all in full marching order with gas-masks and rifles, and some were carrying machine-guns and extra ammunition. We were all carrying equipment of some kind, and all had empty sand-bags tucked down our backs. We were loaded like Christmas trees, so of course an explosion near by or just the slightest thing would knock a man off balance and he would go off the track and right down into the muck.

Private A. T. Shaw, No. 299572, 2/4th Btn., East Lancashire Regiment

Word was passed down from the front saying, 'Every man get hold of the bayonet scabbard of the man in front. We cannot wait for any man who falls in.' This of course referred to the shell-craters brimming with stinking water on either side of the duckboards. We knew this order was not meant to be carried out, but it made you realise what could have happened if you were alone on these duckboards and staggered off. It was still raining but we were past caring.

As dawn approached I could see the faint outline of a ridge about four or five hundred yards in front, and we then left the duckboards and moved to the white tape fastened to iron stakes. It was knee-deep in slush, and then I heard the sound of a heavy gun firing and immediately our barrage started; but we had not then arrived at the jumping-off point. Heavy German shells were already falling amongst us and shrapnel was flying all over the place. There were shouts and screams and men falling all around. The attack that should have started never got off the ground.

Lieutenant P. King, 2/5th 9th., East Lancashire Regiment

It had taken us more than twelve hours to get there. The Colonel had led the battalion up the track – Colonel Whitehead, a very terse man, a very brave man. And he said to me, 'Get them into the attack.' I passed it on to the NCOs, who gave the orders: 'Fix bayonets. Deploy. Extended order. Advance!' We went over into this morass, straight into a curtain of rain and mist and shells, for we were caught between the two barrages.

Well, of course, we lost direction right away. Although the Company went into the attack in extended order it was only natural that the men got into little groups of threes and fives, and the machine-gun fire from the German positions was frightful. They were simply spraying bullets all over the place. We could hardly move because the mud was so heavy there that you were dragging your legs behind you, and with people being hit and falling and splashing down all around you, all you can do is to keep moving and look for some form of cover. The casualties were very heavy and after we'd somehow managed to get forward maybe 200 yards, I realised that the position was absolutely hopeless. I got a handful of men together and took them into a big crater, more than half full of water. We filled some of these empty sandbags that we had with slush, and put them on the edge as a base for the Lewis gun so that we could try to protect our position. And there we stayed. I sent a runner to try to report where we were to where I thought Battalion HQ was, but he never got there. I saw him blown up. So I never got in touch with Battalion HQ. We had to stop where we were – ruddy miserable. We were there for more than twenty-four hours and the rain and the shelling never stopped the whole time.

Cold and miserable, soaked and sick, and at the extreme limit of exhaustion, the 'Burnley Mashers' crouched on the bank of their muddy pool. They vacated it as darkness fell and the water rose, crawling through the mud to look for another containing marginally less water. Paddy King crawled off with his sergeant to try and find other remnants of his company. He found at most a dozen and moved them to shell-holes nearer his own. He supposed that together they formed some kind of line, but exactly where it was he didn't have the faintest idea. All he knew was that they were lying in a lake of mud in the hollow of a valley and that on their right, where the ground sloped up, was the village of Passchendaele.

The rising ground on the left was the Bellevue Ridge, and a little way beyond it, where other battalions were trying to conquer the rest of Poelcapelle, conditions were almost as bad. The Reverend Stanley Hinchliffe, who was padre to the 26th Northumberland Fusiliers, had filed up the duckboard track with his men.

Padre S. Hinchliffe, 26th Btn., Northumberland Fusiliers

It was one vast plain, interspersed by a network of small lakes and holes full of mud. Here and there, stuck amid the mud, gunners were firing on open sites. Four men had made a gallant attempt to bring up rations. All four lay dead, one with his head blown off. Legs and arms jutted out from shell-holes. There were some terrible sights, and many delays. A rifle-shot rang out in front of us, and the word went around that a man had shot his trigger-finger off. I didn't believe it. I didn't want to believe that one of my men would have done such a thing. But it was impossible to find out. One couldn't move up in the queue. The men were heavy-laden. I couldn't carry a rifle but I wanted to be as much like the men as possible, so I filled my haversack up with all sorts of things. I had a trench periscope, which was quite a big thing, so I put that in and I had a certain amount of my own equipment, but it wasn't as much as the men. They were like pack mules. They had pickaxes, and guns and rifles and sometimes a spade down their backs. So I loaded myself up as much as I could, just to save my self-respect. There was one thing I heard a padre say that always stuck in my mind. He said, 'I'm not going to see my battalion off and say, "God be with you, men, in the trenches, for I am at the transport lines."' I took that as my motto.

Of course, as a non-combatant I couldn't be in the trenches. I went with the MO, the doctor, into the advanced aid-post he'd set up. It was the best place to be, for you could comfort the wounded. Even when a man was very badly wounded and unconscious I always believed that you could penetrate right down through his consciousness. I used to whisper in his ear. Another padre gave me that tip and I always did it, just bent down and whispered, 'Put your trust in God.' Of course, if they were conscious, one had to be careful not to let them think that because the padre was bending over them they were going to die. The first thing I used to say to a wounded man was, 'Now, don't worry, we're going to get you right. You'll be all right.' Then I would have a prayer with them and say, 'Put your trust in God.' And, of course, I dished out lots of cups of tea.

Sergeant T. Berry DCM, No. 4406, 1st Btn., The Rifle Brigade

Tea was all we had that night at Poelcapelle. There was no chance of getting the rations up. We'd been in the attack, come back to support, and then we were going to attack again, because in those conditions they couldn't get reliefs up. We were just crouched in shell-holes waiting, and there was this one little chap. He made tea all night long, and kept nipping out and getting water out of flooded ground behind us and heating it up as best he could. Every half-hour he'd say, 'There you are, Tommy, a drop of tea.' It wasn't very hot, but it kept us going. The next morning when it got light he looked over the side where he'd got the water and it was a bleeding shell-hole, and there was a dead Jerry in it and blood all floating around. We'd had that and all in our tea. Well, we'd had it the night before, so we didn't worry about it today. We seemed to have no ill-effects, and we had other things to worry about.

We heard screaming coming from another crater a bit away. I went over to investigate with a couple of the lads. It was a big hole and there was a fellow of the 8th Suffolks in it up to his shoulders. So I said, 'Get your rifles, one man in the middle to stretch them out, make a chain and let him get hold of it.' But it was no use. It was too far to stretch, we couldn't get any force on it, and the more we pulled and the more he struggled the further he seemed to go down. He went down gradually. He kept begging us to shoot him. But we couldn't shoot him. Who could shoot him? We stayed with him, watching him go down in the mud. And he died. He wasn't the only one. There must have been thousands up there who died in the mud.

The morning of 10 October found Lieutenant King and the remnants of B Company stiff, cramped and chilled to the marrow – still huddled in their shell-holes with no possibility of relief until darkness fell again. King posted sentries to keep a sharp look-out for counter-attacks. None came on their immediate front, though the men watched with horror as an SOS signal went up somewhere in the waste to the right of them, where another straggle of sodden soldiers were presumably in the same situation as themselves.

The British artillery opened up promptly to thwart a supposed counter-attack. The enemy guns opened up too. In the confusion, not knowing exactly how far the advance had reached, the gunners miscalculated the range, and for almost an hour shells from both sides pounded the line while machine-guns rattled and spattered into the mud. When a shell landed dangerously close, swamping them in a tidal wave of muddy water, King, who had almost lost his voice, croaked over to the adjacent shell-hole, 'Are you all right, lads?'

'Aye, all's reet here, Paddy. We're still battin'.'

Under the circumstances Lieutenant King did not mind the lack of formality. He rather liked being called 'Paddy'.

B Company was still batting when dusk began to gather half-way through the icy afternoon. The hours had dragged interminably. Exhausted though they were, there was no question of sleep; there was no question of a smoke either, for the merest wisp rising from one of the shell-holes might attract the attention of a sharp-eyed German look-out. There was nothing at all to do but munch a hard biscuit from time to time, try to dissolve Oxo cubes in cold water, and chew over the three eternal never-resolved questions that were the constant preoccupation of conversation in the Army. Does the Army make you pay for the blanket it buries you in? Has your company been secretly chosen to be a suicide force? Will the war be over by Christmas? They also wondered whether they had been totally isolated and forgotten, for no runner, no rations, no message or signal of any kind had reached them.

Lieutenant P. King, 2/5th Btn., East Lancashire Regiment

Suddenly, to my great surprise, I heard voices behind me and I looked back and there were three very tall figures, and one was actually smoking. I could hardly speak for astonishment. I said, 'Who the hell are you? And put that cigarette out, you'll draw fire!' He just looked back at me. 'Well, come to that, who are you?' I said, 'I'm Lieutenant King of the 2/5th East Lancashire Regiment.' At which he said, 'Well, we're the Aussies, chum, and we've come to relieve you.' And they jumped down into the shell-hole.

Well, naturally, we were delighted, but of course there are certain formalities you've always got to carry out when you hand over, and I was a bit worried about that. So I explained, 'There are no trenches to hand over, no rations, no ammunition, but I *have* got a map. Do you need any map references?' He said, 'Never mind about that, chum. Just fuck off.'

They didn't seem to be a bit bothered. The last I saw of them they were squatting down, rifles over their shoulders, and they were smoking, all three of them. Just didn't care!

We struggled back. It was an awful journey and there was no sign of the battalion or any of our men, just the couple of dozen of us. Eventually we met up with another group, another officer with a few men who'd been in the same position. It took us hours to find Battalion Headquarters, but eventually a Military Policeman guide took us along, and it was in a small Nissen hut. I pushed open the door and went in. The colonel was sitting there with the adjutant and two or three other officers. The only light was from a few candles stuck into bottles and they were drinking whisky out of enamel mugs. I saluted the colonel and said, 'Lieutenant King, reporting back with the remnants of B Company.' He looked at me with a really scathing expression and said, 'At last! The bloody cotton-wool soldiers!' And he didn't even ask us to have a drink. The other bloke and myself just saluted and walked out. We thought it was a bloody fine reward, after all our efforts, to be spoken to like that.

The 66th Division's attack had resulted in a 'sag' in the line – and Colonel Whitehead was not the only one who was disappointed with the results.

The Times, 11 *October*
War Correspondents' Headquarters.

THE SAG IN THE LINE

Another day makes us better satisfied with our last success than we were inclined to be yesterday. Then, as I wrote, although we had won all our objectives on both the north and the south of the advance, there was a sag in the centre of the line, where, although we knew that bodies of troops had reached their farthest goal at various points, the general line – so far as there is any general line in this extraordinary warfare – was in places short of it.

Since the British Armies began their hammerings on this front, we have grown so spoilt by the brilliance and rapidity of successive victories that anything short of total triumph (anything less than the whole earth with a handle to carry it by) is a disappointment. But, as our new line becomes established, and communication is better across that hideous wilderness, we grow better satisfied. What robbed us of as sweeping a success as any we have seen was the weather and the indescribable condition of the ground. The German counter-attacks were few and feeble. A distinguished officer said to me this morning that it was like hitting a pudding. There was no resilience in the enemy, no reaction. But wading up to your armpits in pudding is difficult.

However astonishing the troops might have found some of the comments in the report, not one of them would have argued with the last statement, least of all the Anzacs, for they were now in it, and in it right up to their necks. The attack was to take place on the morning of the twelfth. Between them the New Zealanders on the left and the Australians on the right were to assault the Passchendaele Ridge and capture the village itself. Reaching out on either side were forests of barbed wire thirty feet deep, and behind them machine-gun posts bristled every few yards. In the flooded hollow of the valley in front, concrete strongholds dotted the marshland; and in a line of strongly fortified outposts, in conditions as miserable as those of the British a hundred yards away, garrisons of German infantry kept watch over the swamp. The Anzacs had already relieved the Tommies in the very 'front line', and just below the breast of the rise at Waterloo Farm the New Zealanders, who would carry out the assault from the left, were assembling for the attack. The day before the New Zealand artillery had moved up its guns – or, at least, it had tried.

Gunner B. O. Stokes, No. 25038, 13th Bty., New Zealand Field Artillery, 3rd Brigade

C and D guns went forward first, and didn't they have a time getting them out through the sea of mud and slush! They had to have eight horse-teams to do the job. Our team arrived at 7.30 am, and just as we were trying to get our gun out Lieutenant Chirnside told us to lay back on our SOS line, as the road was blocked by shell-fire. No sooner had he moved away than the sound of a shell coming over told us it was going to land somewhere very near. We crouched to the earth, and the shell landed only three yards away.

The next few minutes I cannot really describe. The shock was so great, the sight too awful. When the smoke had cleared away, there

lay four of our boys – dead. Then came the cries of the two wounded.
Brown had both legs shattered and Lieutenant Chirnside was simply
riddled with wounds. Brown's brother, who is also in our battery, was
terribly shaken. We carried them to the dressing-station and Brown
stayed there with his brother until he was taken away.* You can't
imagine how we felt. The shelling didn't cease for another half-hour.
Shelling. Shelling. Shelling. It was an appalling sight. The wind and
the rain lashing down. The horses screaming and rearing and plunging down into the mud as the shells exploded all around us. It seemed
as if every gun Fritz had was trained on this small area. We had to
leave the gun and shelter as best we could. Eventually, when the
shelling began to tail off, we went back and hooked the team up to
the gun.

It was five o'clock in the evening before we got to the new
position, and then we had to start getting the gun in. We only
managed to get four guns out of our six-gun battery forward – and
most of our other batteries were in the same state, or worse, which
didn't make the prospects for the morning look too good. We had to
put down a 'heavy' bombardment for our infantry going across and
the stunt was due to start at 5.25 in the morning, so as soon as we'd
dragged the gun in we looked for a place to put in for the night. We
found an empty pillbox with a foot of water in it, and none too sweet
smelling. We put some boards in it to keep us above the water. There
was no room to stretch out. We just sat on ammunition boxes and
listened to the rain and the gale outside and waited for morning.

The wind had risen to hurricane force during the evening. As he
listened to the storm lashing across battered Flanders, beating at the troops
already on the duckboard tracks for the long night's trudge towards tomorrow's battle, General Gough became more and more uneasy. He tele-
phoned General Plumer at his headquarters at Cassel and suggested that
on their own responsibility they should cancel the attack. It had, after all,
been agreed in principle that attacks should be pressed home only when
the weather was favourable. The events of 9 October, when most of the
infantry assaulting the Passchendaele Ridge had been either wiped out or,
like Paddy King and his men, isolated in hopeless positions, had shown all
too clearly the futility of attacking under such conditions that the men
were exhausted before they began. Plumer was similarly doubtful, but on
balance felt that it was a chance worth taking. In any event it was probably
too late to cancel the attack. Without General Plumer's backing, Gough

*Gunner Brown recovered from his wounds and survived.

could do nothing. The attack was on. The best that could be hoped was that German vigilance would be lulled by the violence of the storm and that the enemy would be taken unawares.

Before the war, a narrow secondary road, little more than a lane that served as an access road to the farms on either side, ran up from the Zonnebeke-Langemarck Road, over the Bellevue Ridge on the left of Passchendaele, and down into the flat plain on the other side. From a hamlet called Mosselmarkt a lane ran along the top of the ridge to the village of Passchendaele some 600 yards to the right. The hamlet, of course, had long vanished. Now the Jaegers were in residence – one of the crack German machine-gun regiments. Another, the Brandenburgers, guarded the second vital approach away on the other side of Passchendaele where the Australians would attack. In the middle, the flanks of both forces would plunge forward into the moat-like swamp that guarded the frontal approach.

The jumping-off point for the New Zealanders was the place they called Waterloo Farm. Once it *had* been a farm on a bend of the Gravenstafel Road as it rose to breast the Bellevue Ridge. On the right the road fell away to Marsh Bottom.

In the teeth of the gale the march up had been a nightmare, for the heavy shelling of the day had blown great gaps in the duckboards – too many to repair. The long files of soldiers simply dropped into the gaps, up to their waists in mud, and struggled out as best they could. They arrived soaked to the skin, exhausted and dripping with slime, many with rifles so caked with mud that they would be as useless as feathers in the coming battle.

Private W. Smith, No. 15029, 2nd New Zealand Machine Gun Co.

It was a terrible night. We dug in as best we could at the bottom of the Bellevue Ridge – but the idea of 'digging in' was ridiculous. You can't dig water! My section managed to throw up a kind of ridge of slush, but the water from the shell-holes around just poured into it. You couldn't squat down, we just stood there in the rain and wind waiting for our guns to open up with the barrage.

Gunner B. O. Stokes, No. 25038, 13th Bty., New Zealand Field Artillery, 3rd Brigade

We were stiff and cold in our flooded pillbox, but we managed to doze a bit. At 4.15 we roused ourselves to get ready for the stunt at 5.25. It was still pitch-dark, still raining with a very high wind. You had to lean against it to get out of the pillbox. Our cook, old Dick, was out before me. He was crouching in the lee of the pillbox with an oil sheet round him, trying without much success to get the billy to boil. It was a valiant effort, even though all he finally managed to produce was some lukewarm tea. At five o'clock we left for the gun 400 yards away, and what a job we had to get there through all the mud and shell-holes in the rain and dark. At 5.25 we started firing.

Private W. Smith, No. 15029, 2nd New Zealand Machine Gun Co.

Remarkable to relate, when we popped off, the excitement left me. I settled down and never turned a hair. I don't even remember thinking that I would be hit, and the Germans started spraying us with intense machine-gun fire as soon as we moved. I was next to Keith Moore, and he got it right away, a bullet through the knee. He grabbed at me as he fell and screamed at me, 'Smithy!' I kicked him. My best friend! I kicked him really viciously and knocked him away from me in my excitement. I was frothing to go and in a hurry to keep up with the main bunch on the way to Passchendaele.

We made a bad 'blue' in sticking to that main Passchendaele Road. It certainly looked the best part to get a footing on – covered with inches of mud, of course, but with a fairly firm footing underneath. I suppose Fritz had anticipated this. As we started up the road we were being caught in enfilade fire from the big pillboxes in the low ground to our right. People were dropping all the way. Then, as we turned the corner on top of the rise, we saw this great bank of wire ahead, maybe a hundred yards away. A rat couldn't have got through that. The bombardment should have cut the wire but it hadn't even dented it. Not that we could get near it anyway, for it was positively spitting fire. The hail of lead we tried to go through was simply incredible. More than half of us fell. We hadn't gone far when our oldest surviving sergeant, Jock Stewart, dropped alongside me. I just had time to see that he had fallen on his back, with a bullet-hole in his chest in the vicinity of his heart. We went a few yards more and then pulled into the side on our right for a breather. The road had been cut slightly through the ridge, and the low bank gave us the very slightest piece of shelter if we kept ourselves low down. We were down to a dozen or so men.

Young Harold Stewart was with us, Jock's young brother. He hadn't seen Jock go down. He didn't realise it until we stopped, and when he did we couldn't hold him. He crawled back on his stomach to where Jock was lying, and got hold of his body and dragged him back along the road to where we were sheltering. The machine-gun bullets were splashing up the mud all around them. Harold got right through them all. Then, just as he reached us he eased himself up slightly to pull Jock down below the road surface, and a German sniper put a rifle bullet through his throat. I practically saw the bullet that hit him. It must have got him in the jugular vein. His blood gushed out all over me.*

Gunner B. O. Stokes, No. 25038, 13th Bty., New Zealand Field Artillery, 3rd Brigade

All the morning up until about 11 am we fired according to plan, raising our range at certain intervals to coincide with the advance the boys were supposed to make. Imagine the set-back we had when we were told to lay back on our original range. We realised then that the boys hadn't really been able to move forward at all. We had bad trouble firing the gun. Every time we fired a shot the trail would dig deep into the mud, so with every shot we had to try to lift it back and re-lay the gun before we could fire again. It was a nightmare. And we knew things were bad up front. During the morning the walking wounded started to come back, and for a time our gun looked like a casualty clearing station. Some were quite badly wounded, but there wasn't much we could do except to encourage them to go on to the dressing-station.

Private W. Smith, No. 15029, 2nd New Zealand Machine Gun Co.

Now we were down to one NCO. When we had finished laying out young Stewart to die, this NCO, a Sergeant Smith, suddenly issued the order, 'Prepare to advance.' Now this was just sheer suicide. Whatever was left of the N. Zedders round about us was just a disorganised rabble, so much so that the Germans had become very cheeky. They weren't bothering to take cover, they had come out and were perched on top of their concrete forts picking off any fool who showed his nose.

I thought to myself, 'Well, Sergeant Smith, if we're going, you'll go first!' Sure enough, up he stepped. As he showed his nose the sniper

---

*Jock and Harold Stewart are commemorated on Panel 6 of the New Zealand Memorial to the Missing, directly behind the Cross of Sacrifice in Tyne Cot Cemetery.

fired. He came crashing back on top of me with his face twisted in a look I'll never forget. He was killed outright. That was the end of any advance in that direction.

Gunner B. O. Stokes, No. 25038, 13th Bty., New Zealand Field Artillery, 3rd Brigade

Our fire became even weaker, because two of our guns had got completely bogged down and simply couldn't be budged. Then, quite suddenly, when we were feeling very depressed about everything, up came our Maori Pioneer Battalion. What a sight it was to see these chaps, about forty of them on each side of the gun, up to their knees in mud as they hauled on ropes attached to the wheels, pulling the gun into position. We were told at midday that we had to get the guns into action because the push was to be renewed at 3.10 in the afternoon. This we thought was madness, but someone must have had second thoughts. Just before the time set for zero, the attack was cancelled.

Private W. Smith, No. 15029, 2nd New Zealand Machine Gun Co.

Everyone was either scattered, wounded or dead. There were only a few left in my bunch. We had no idea what to do, for we had no officers, no NCOs, no orders. Eventually Joe Hammersley and myself crawled across the road and set off crawling in the direction of Passchendaele. I have often thought since, what the hell did two of us think we could possibly do? We had gone no distance when suddenly Joe dropped with a clang. He lay quite still and I crawled on into the shelter of a shell-hole and lay low. Lo and behold, a few minutes later who should slither into the shell-hole alongside me but Joe! The bullet had hit his forehead and gone out through the top of his head, only grazing him. While we were examining the hole in his tin hat and marvelling at his miraculous escape there was a violent explosion and one of our own shells blew us right out of the hole. Poor old Joe! His arm was shattered by a splinter from the shell. When he pulled himself together he said, 'My God, Smithy, I'm getting out of here. Both lots of the blighters are after me now, ours *and* theirs!' I tried to persuade him to sit tight and wait until something turned up, but I couldn't hold him. He crawled away down the hill.* I joined two

---

* Joe Hammersley got safely back to the dressing-station and eventually back to New Zealand, where he lived to a ripe old age

other cobbers in a larger shell-hole a bit further over. We sat tight. The rain never let up and it was bitterly cold. We stayed there all night. It wasn't a picnic . . .

Nor was that night of 12 October a picnic for Bert Stokes and Brock McHerron, for they were on gun-guard, keeping alert for the SOS signals that still came occasionally from the front.

Gunner B. O. Stokes, No. 25038, 13th Bty., New Zealand Field Artillery, 3rd Brigade

We went on at 6.30 pm on the twelfth and came off at 8.30 am. All that time we sat on the seats of the gun, one on each side, and saw a night of fourteen hours out. No cover, in fact no nothing – only the oil sheets we had, which protected us but little. Brock and I have laughed since at the dejected picture we must have cut as we sat there, doing our best to keep warm, and the ground about us knee-deep in mud and slush. Anyone who had seen us with our unshaven, unwashed dials would have laughed for a week.

As darkness gave way to watery light on the morning of the thirteenth, the men who were crouched in the flooded shell-holes within sight of Passchendaele roused themselves and wondered uneasily what the day would bring. Bill Smith and his two companions were startled to see Bill Appleby appear above them and stand on the edge of the shell-hole grinning down.

Private W. Smith, No. 15029, 2nd New Zealand Machine Gun Co.

He just stood there with a broad grin on his face, and very gingerly we accepted his invitation to come up and have a look. And what an amazing sight greeted us! Between us and the concrete fort on the corner of the road was a thirty-yard belt of barbed wire right around. Up and down, near to the wire, marched a tall German in long gumboots carrying a Red Cross flag. We had no idea who had arranged this armistice. There was no officer or NCO within a coo-ee of where we were.

We took advantage of the lull to lug three or four of our wounded down to Waterloo Farm, where our part in the advance had started the morning before. We were well and truly back where we started, but what a sight the place presented now! We had only been there in the dark. Now we saw that it was a mass of shell-holes full of water, and on the parts of firm ground between the holes there were scores, even hundreds, of wounded men lying there, brought in by mates. In front were long lines of Northumberland Fusiliers and Durham Light Infantry, lying dead almost in formation where they had been mown down like wheat as they tried to go across against the machine-gun fire a few days before. They hadn't even got as far as we had.

The Maoris were there. They'd formed relays to get the wounded out. There were no stretchers. They carried them in their arms like children. We watched them go, partly envious. We had to stay in the line and there was no word of relief. There were no rations either, and I was absolutely ravenous. When I'd gone into action my haversack contained a tin of bully-beef and a pair of puttees. When I'd taken it off in the shell-hole that night before to try to get a bit of food, it was a sight for sore eyes. Both the beef and the puttees were riddled with bullets. They must have missed my back by a fraction of an inch, for the back of my tunic was in shreds. I was so hungry that I went across to the dead Durhams and rooted in a few haversacks looking for eats. But I wasn't the first. All I could find were four small pieces of shortbread. It was home-made . . .

It remained quiet all morning. On the left of the sector the 4th and 18th Divisions had been luckier in their attack of the previous day, and had finally managed to capture another bit of Poelcapelle. Tom Berry had fired his rifle-grenade to such effect that he had managed to thwart a counter-attack almost single-handed, and had earned himself the Distinguished Conduct Medal. But the fighting had been hard and bitter. The conditions had been as severe as those in front of Passchendaele. In old Flemish, 'Poelcapelle' means, literally, 'the church in the bog'. It had lived up to its name. Now the victors rested and drew breath. Over the ridge the demoralised remnants of the Anzacs wearily set about defending the line and prayed for reinforcement or relief. The wounded who had been left out in No Man's Land after the attack waited for rescue. The Germans tended their wounded and seemed glad of the brief respite, for the shell-fire was described in the evening communiqués as 'desultory'. It rained that day for fifteen hours without stopping.

The fiercest fighting took place many miles away at Plumer's head-quarters at Cassel, where there was a meeting of the staff presided over by the Commander-in-Chief himself. Now everybody had had enough. The message had travelled right up the chain of command from shaken subalterns to angry company commanders, to COs furious at the demands made on their men, to brigadiers helplessly watching their battalions being decimated, to corps commanders who were now convinced that enough was enough. Appalled by the results of yesterday's attempt, with the weather showing no signs of improvement, Generals Gough and Plumer were of the same opinion. Every officer present was unanimously agreed that no further operations should take place until conditions improved and until more guns could be got up to provide an effective bombardment. They were overruled by Sir Douglas Haig.

He was not without sympathy for their predicament. But there were stronger reasons for continuing than there were for calling a halt. The French were planning to attack in Champagne on 23 October. Until then the attention of the Germans must remain fixed on Ypres. He was now engaged in planning an alternative operation at Cambrai for which General Byng, in command of the Third Army, hoped to complete his preparations by mid-November, and he had therefore asked that the Ypres campaign should be continued as long as possible. Sir Douglas Haig was anxious to accommodate his request. It must also, he felt, be obvious that securement of the Passchendaele Ridge would not only provide a better line on which to stop for the winter, but an excellent jumping-off point for further advances in the spring.

He intended to bring in the Canadians. Vital and rested, flushed with the success of the capture of Hill 70 to the south, the Canadians would trump the German ace and succeed in capturing Passchendaele. There was such a little way to go. The men had done splendidly, although it was true that the results of the last few days had been disappointing.

Colonel Whitehead of the 2/5th East Lancashire Regiment had not recovered from his displeasure with the two companies of his battalion that had lost direction. It was just forty-eight hours after they had returned from their ordeal that they were ordered to provide men for a particularly unpleasant task. They were to go to the Frezenberg Ridge and bury the bodies of the successive waves of soldiers who had been killed there in the fighting of the two months before Borry Farm and Beck House had fallen on 20 September. The sight of the scattered dead had a depressing effect on the troops going up the line. Paddy King and the other company commander who had incurred the Colonel's displeasure were detailed to see that the job was done.

Lieutenant P. King, 2/5th Btn., East Lancashire Regiment

We were each told to take a section of men and one NCO, draw rubber gloves, sandbags, and an extra rum ration for the men, and take our sections out to the battlefield area to bury the dead. They were mostly Scottish soldiers – Argyll and Sutherland Highlanders, and Black Watch. It was an appalling job. Some had been lying there for months and the bodies were in an advanced state of decomposition; and some were so shattered that there was not much left. We did have occasions where you almost buried a man twice. In fact we must have done just that several times. There was one officer whose body we buried and then shortly after we found an arm with the same name on the back of a watch on the wrist. We had to open their tunic pockets to get out their AB64s, which we had to put separately in a sandbag. If they had any identity discs, then we marked the grave – just put the remains in a sandbag, dug a small grave and buried him. Then I had to write it on a list and give the map reference location. Where the bodies were so broken up or decomposed that we couldn't find an identity we just buried the man and put 'Unknown British Soldier' on the list. It was a terrible job. The smell was appalling and it was deeply depressing for the men.

Of course, the battle had passed well on by then, but the ground was totally destroyed. We could see nothing but these two abandoned pillboxes. There was no sign of civilisation. No cottages, no buildings, no trees. It was utter desolation. There was nothing at all except huge craters, half the size of a room. They were full of water and the corpses were floating in them. Some with no heads. Some with no legs. They were very hard to identify. We managed about four in every ten. There were Germans among them. We didn't bury them. We hadn't been told to. We did that job for two days running. And we didn't just dump them into a hole. We committed each one properly to his grave. Said a little prayer out of a book issued to us. 'Ashes to ashes, dust to dust.' The men all stood around and took their hats off for a moment, standing to attention. 'God rest his soul.' A dead soldier can't hurt you. He's a comrade. That's how we looked at it. He was some poor mother's son and that was the end of it.

Even as the 2/5th Lancs were burying the long dead of the battles of August and September, the wounded who had been left behind when the Anzacs were forced back to their starting-line the previous day were drowning in the rising water of flooded shell-holes. Or, clinging to the muddy sides of craters in the chill of the driving rain, were quietly succumbing to exposure.

But the Canadians were coming.

Chapter 18

The storm began to abate, and by 15 October the weather had improved. Now even the officers, even the commanders, even Gough himself, were beginning to be superstitious about the weather. In every attack it was the one uncontrollable factor. It seemed to the dispirited infantry that the real battle was with the elements and the terrible Flanders mud. It was almost a mockery when, after an attack, the air turned crisp and the sun shone from the hazy autumn sky, and it did little to raise their spirits. The battlefield was now so battered, so flooded, that the weak sunshine was as effective in drying the ground as a lighted match held over a bathtub full of water.

In spite of the improved conditions, General Currie, in command of the Canadian forces, refused to move. He could not disobey Haig's orders to throw the Canadian Corps into the attack; he *could* insist that the attack should take place in his own time. He would not move until sufficient guns could be concentrated to back up the infantry with a devastating bombardment. He would not move until the roads had been repaired and more had been constructed. He would not move until there were sufficient infantry tracks to allow his troops to reach the line well in advance of zero hour, so that they would be fresh and rested when the moment came for the attack. He would not move until there were enough mule tracks to supply them, and he would not even contemplate going ahead until heavy supplies had been built up in dumps very close to the line. When these preparations had been completed, and not before, the Canadians would attack. If every available man was thrown into the preliminary preparations, Currie envisaged that he would be able to mount a large-scale assault on Passchendaele on 26 October. The Canadians had come under the command of the Second Army, and General Plumer had no choice but to agree to Currie's conditions.

Everyone's attention was now focused on the fortress of the highest ridge. But it was not enough simply to capture Passchendaele. Even if the Canadians succeeded they would simply find themselves in a deep and narrow salient with both flanks in the air. Before they made that final push the shoulders of the ridge must be secured, the front must be broadened.

So, as the Second Army continued to push home attacks on the Gheluvelt plateau on the right, the Fifth Army went on battering in the area of Poelcapelle, and on *its* left the French pushed outwards into the Houthulst Forest. Once Poelcapelle had fallen, Westroosebeek would be a mere hop, step and jump away. If the troops could gain it as the Canadians advanced victorious on Passchendaele, the whole of the vital ridge, the last tier in the amphitheatre from which for so long the Germans had cocked a snook at the Allies, would be theirs.

In the south the Canucks of a dozen brigades packed up and set out on the journey north. They were to get there as quickly as possible, and every piece of rolling stock, every lorry, every rackety omnibus was pressed into service to transport them. The fighting troops could wait. What General Currie wanted was labour, and he wanted it fast.

Corporal D. R. Macfie MM and Bar, No. 6835, 1st Canadian Infantry Btn., Transport Section

I was in charge of mules and men for four battalions. A whole brigade. I was called to Divisional Headquarters and was paraded up to this big bunch of staff, all red braid and all that, and they started asking me questions about pack trains. How many trips I could make over so many miles, and how much of this could be carried on so many mules. They told me to get a brigade pack-train organised, and they wanted the stuff so bad that the pack-trains would have to keep going night and day. Our base lines were at St Julien. There was an engineers' dump there with everything – munitions, sandbags, shovels, water-cans, the lot. I'd get a list of what we had to load up. So many shovels, so many sandbags, so many water-cans, so much small arms ammunition. Then we'd get these mules, about twenty of them, and get them loaded up and their load balanced and then start off. It was a plank road. I went up to the end of the plank road and then it was a trail – just bricks out of buildings, thrown into the mud. In one part of it we had to go over a man's back. He had been killed and just fallen into where they made the track. The clothes were all worn off his back with the mules tramping over him.

We were shelled all the time, because with their observation balloons they could see the whole area. We could see the balloons sitting up there looking right at us. The most nerve-racking would be the searching. You never knew when the shells were coming, or where they were coming. You just got kind of stupefied and went on with your work and never noticed anything. I came home one night and went out to clean my horse, and I noticed a little blood on his side. So I picked around, got my jack-knife and picked out a shrapnel-ball between his ribs. Then I looked at my saddle and it had gone through the pigskin flap – just where my leg would have been if it had been in the stirrup. Boy, I sure wished it had been!

The Germans were edgy. Once before they had been caught off guard, thinking that it was too late in the season and that the weather was too stormy for the Allies to continue the attack. Now, with the fighting on the flanks continuing undiminished, they were well aware that another major assault was more than likely. Short of themselves attacking, their only means of thwarting it was to pound the line, to pound every road and track, every gun-site, to saturate the salient and its back areas with shells and bombs as fast as they could be fed into the guns and loaded on the aeroplanes. The Germans were well aware that troops were arriving in greater concentrations than ever.

Corporal R. G. Pinneo, 10th Canadian Infantry Brigade

Our arrival at Passchendaele was on a train that took us up through Vlamertinghe to the outskirts of Ypres. There we got off. The first thing I saw as I got out of the train and looked to the east towards the German line were five German observation balloons in the sky. I said to myself, 'It won't be long now.' And it wasn't. While we were still unloading our equipment the Germans started to shell the train. The confusion was murderous. We were dodging here and there, trying to shelter. Trying to unload at the same time. We were lucky. We only came in for the first of it and we managed to form up and start off through Ypres. The company behind us got it hard – they had sixteen men killed and forty wounded. We were shelled all the way as we marched through Ypres to the Menin Gate and out the Gravenstafel Road. We called it the Grab-and-Stumble Road.

We stopped at this cemetery and we thought at first they were pulling our legs when they said this was our billet. It was a terrible place, there was no cover, no place to go, no dug-outs or anything. The graves and tombstones had all been knocked to hell by gunfire, and even the crypts and coffins had been blasted open. You could see the sheeted dead. We bivouacked as best we could. All night long a British battery of fifteen-inch howitzers just at the back of us was blasting away and the Germans were answering. There was a direct hit on the runners' bivouac of the 44th Canadian Infantry Battalion – and that was the end of them. Ypres was a terrible place.

I was there three times and I never heard the name without a shiver of apprehension.

Acting Captain E. Mockler-Ferryman MC, Royal Artillery

Our troubles on the Steenbeek began on about the thirteenth. To our horror a sixty-pounder battery arrived and dumped itself down on the road, five yards in front of our pillbox. A sixty-pounder makes more noise firing and has a bigger flash than any other gun. The Boche hates them like poison and always does his utmost to destroy them. To make matters worse, ammunition was scattered in heaps all round our dug-out, so that we were in a continual state of wondering when we might be blown to bits by an explosion. As a result of the three days' rest after the battle of 12 October, the Boche guns had begun to settle down comfortably in their positions and to annoy us considerably. He shelled us all day and all night and added to our joys by coming low over us in broad daylight, dropping bombs on the roads and battery positions. Three or four of the sixty-pounder dumps went up from time to time, though luckily they were only charges and not shells. We lived in hourly dread of an eight-inch concentration, which we knew was bound to come sooner or later.

On 18 October, in the Second Army sector in front of Passchendaele, the first of the Canadians went into the line to relieve some of the hard-pressed Tommies and Anzacs. Even for those who had been in the salient before, it was a revelation.

Gunner J. J. Brown, No. 41217, Canadian Field Artillery

We had been behind St Julien in the gas attack in 1915. Now I wouldn't have recognised the place. The whole area was utterly devastated, just a few bits of foundations left. There was no trace of the farms or barns that were there in 1915, nothing but this ocean of mud and dumps and a few battered pillboxes. We were sent in to relieve a New Zealand gun battery and we had to go a long way to get to it, up a plank supply road. Having just come from billets we were all spruced up in nice clean khaki suits, and we hadn't gone far when we saw some infantry coming down from the line, all tattered and dishevelled and covered in mud. When they spotted us they started waving and yelling, 'Turn back, boys! You'd better not go any further. There's a war going on up there!'

For the first time the relieving artillery brigades were not hauling their guns forward; they simply took over the guns where they stood embedded in the swamp. Still the Canadians poured in.

Nurse C. Macfie, No. 11 Casualty Clearing Station at Godwaersveldt

We used to see the trains going past at Godwaersveldt, for the railway line ran past the casualty clearing station. And we would wave and the boys would be hanging out of the train waving back. They used to shout, 'Keep a bed for us, Sister. We'll be back in a few days. Keep us a bed.' And we knew that very likely they would be back the next week, as patients, for we had terrible casualties in October even when the stunts weren't on. The shelling was terrible. We never had a bed empty and we never stopped. We were under fire ourselves a lot of the time; they'd started using these long-range shells, and night after night we were bombed, because there was the railway line and a big RE dump just opposite us. We had to douse the lights and lie flat. I remember the night of 20 October because it was the worst of all. The bombs rained down. We thought we'd been hit. But it wasn't us, it was the CCS just up the road. Oh, what a shambles it was! A terrible sight.

There was no warning that night and Sister Madeleine Kemp was just going on night duty. Holding a hurricane lamp in her hand, she had squelched across the duckboard pathway to the big marquee of the post-operative ward when an orderly ducked out through its canvas flap. She stopped to speak to him just as the first of the bombs fell. Sister Kemp and the orderly were killed outright. So were five of the soldiers in the marquee. A hundred more severely wounded men were wounded yet again by shrapnel and flying splinters.

As soon as the graves could be dug, the long funeral cortège wound its way past the tents, along the road, past the station and up the lane to the left, where row upon row of white wooden crosses marked the cemetery on the slope of the hill. It was a big cemetery, for with three casualty clearing stations at Godwaersveldt there were many deaths and many burials. There were eighteen coffins in the cortège, and the engineers from the dump near by who had supplied them had also supplied a party of men to carry them on the 300-yard journey to the graveyard. The nurses followed, as many as could be spared from the wards, and as the cortège passed No. 11 CCS other nurses joined them – Catherine Macfie, Sister Lyle, Sister King, the Matron.

A train chugged past, bound for the front. It was packed with Canadians hanging out from the doorways of the open trucks, on the look-out for pretty nurses. It passed in silence. As the train cleared the level-crossing over the lane that led down to Godwaersveldt, it revealed a group of local people waiting to join the procession. The villagers of Godwaersveldt knew the nurses well. Most of the nurses had found a family who would sell them a few eggs or who, for a small sum, would do the personal washing which none of them cared to entrust to the far-from-tender mercies of the Army Laundry. In return the nurses were always willing to smile, to have a chat, to bandage a grazed knee, to admire the photograph of a *poilu* son or husband. Now the people of Godwaersveldt had come to pay their last respects to 'Soeur Madeleine'.

There were more than a hundred mourners in the cemetery. It was a perfect autumn morning, with bright sunshine and a hard frost and a low ground-mist drifting over the clustered white crosses and the eighteen open graves. After the padre had finished the service and the coffins had been lowered, the nurses filed past, each sprinkling a handful of muddy earth on to Sister Kemp's coffin. As the engineers began to fill in the grave another sound rose above the steady crump of guns at the front. It was the first of the day's convoys of soldiers who had been wounded in working parties during the night. As the ambulances trundled into sight the nurses pulled their capes closer about them and hurried along the road, back to work.

In the days before the 'stunt' of 26 October, the casualties sustained by the working parties surpassed those of the infantry.

Private P. H. Longstaffe, No. 922046, 107 Canadian Pioneer Btn., 1st Division

21 October. Up at 2.30 am. Very dark. Breakfast. Started at 3.15. Long walk past transports and ammunition column. Arrive at Dump at 4.30. Work on plank road. Huge guns all round. Mud awful. Dead men and horses all round. Thousands of men working. Rush job on road through swamp. Ammunition, mules and horses passing in continuous stream. Fritz shelling both sides.

22 October. Up at 2.30. Drizzle of rain. Fritz overhead. Dressed and ate in darkness in shell-hole and lost tea. Same walk as 21 Oct. Arrive 4.15. Terrific bombardment opens up. Hundreds of guns all around us flashing and banging away. Impressive sight. Guns being hurried up. Exciting scenes as mules and horses flounder in mud. Wrecked tanks and pillboxes all round. Worked on road, sandbags and carrying planks. Shells dropping quite close. Up to our knees in mud. Shell on road, three killed, five injured. Horrible sights. Quit at 11 am.

That same night, as the working parties toiled around the clock, the first of the Canadian infantry who were to attack Passchendaele on the twenty-sixth were moving up the line. But in order to delude the Germans the bombardment was thundering down across the entire front of the salient; while, on the left, the Fifth Army and, beyond them, the French mounted a vigorous attack between Poelcapelle and the forest of Houthulst. It was here more than anywhere that the front was confused. It straggled so haphazardly among shell-holes and pillboxes in the swamp that mistakes inevitably were made. During the hours of darkness, a ration party of the 10th Essex was only just prevented by a French patrol from delivering its load to a pillbox which was still occupied by the enemy; while some British officers in an advanced dug-out were surprised when the sacking hanging over its entrance was pulled back with the unfamiliar enquiry, 'Herr Hauptmann?' On discovering his mistake the unfortunate German sergeant dissolved into loud and noisy tears. His distress was due neither to weakness nor fear. He pulled a paper from his pocket and between sobs waved it in disconsolate explanation. It was a leave pass to Hanover, effective next morning, and he had been taking it to his captain to be signed. It took some considerable time and several shots of whisky to pacify him sufficiently and send him, under escort, down the line. It was left to the corporal signaller to sum up the feelings of his captors. 'Poor old Jerry. I'd have let him go,' he remarked, to no one in particular.

Two hours later the 10th Essex went into the attack with the Norfolks, and, having lost more than a third of their fighting force, succeeded in capturing Meunier House and in distracting the attention of the enemy from General Currie's dispositions and intentions in front of Passchendaele.

Major Sansom of the 16th Canadian Machine Gun Company had marched his group of machine-gunners all the way from Lens to Ypres. On the evening of 23 October they eventually arrived. No billets had been arranged for them. The officers – Sansom, Taylor, Stinson and Gauvereau – managed to beg shelter in a dug-out in the ramparts. The men had to fend for themselves.

Private R. Le Brun, No. 790913, 16th Canadian Machine Gun Company, Canadian Machine Gun Corps, 4th Canadian Division

The only space we could find was alongside the heap of rubble that had once been the cathedral. There was nothing much left of the road. We laid our groundsheets in a circle and made camp. We had a limber that carried our rations, the guns for our section, ammunition and the officers' kits. The driver of the limber put up a tripod to hang the large stewpot from, while we lay back on our groundsheets watching the fire. Suddenly there was a tremendous explosion and we were all thrown backwards. The fire *and* the stewpot had exploded into the air. It turned out that the cook had made his fire directly over a layer of five-inch shells which had been left by an artillery unit before us and had sunk into the mud. The cook, who had been bending over the pot, was badly wounded. The stretcher-bearers took him away to the dressing-station but he didn't have much of a chance. We were very depressed. We felt heartbroken. We lay down again on our groundsheets. It was bitterly cold and none of us slept much that night. Next day we were on our way on our terrible journey up the line.

We went on a main plank road, which was a mistake because the Jerry planes were buzzing about, and we were bombed incessantly. It raised havoc with the horses and mules, the trucks and the limbers – we lost a lot of them and most of the day we spent trying to get reorganised. As we neared the front the officers mapped out their headquarters in an old German pillbox, and then they picked out another spot nearer the front for a delivery point for ammunition, water and rations. This was as far as the mules were allowed to venture. There had been a lot of casualties among the mules and they were trying to conserve them, but it seemed to us that their attitude was that one mule was worth twenty good men. We had to take a careful note of this dump, because they were putting us into the line, and every morning two or three of us had to get down there and carry our supplies to our shell-holes and dug-outs at the front.

I had that duty the very first morning we were there. It was only a quarter of a mile or so from the front, and the whole way was nothing but shell-holes with bodies floating in them. It always seemed worse when you didn't see the whole body, maybe just legs and boots sticking out from the sides. The shelling never let up. The very first trip back on the morning of the twenty-fifth, the day before the first attack, I heard someone near by calling for help. I dodged round a shell-hole and over a few hummocks before I saw him. It was one of our infantrymen and he was sitting on the ground, propped up on his elbow with his tunic open. I nearly vomited. His insides were spilling out of his stomach and he was holding himself and trying to push all this awful stuff back in. When he saw me he said, 'Finish it for me, mate. Put a bullet in me. Go on. I want you to. Finish it!' He had no gun himself. When I did nothing, he started to swear. He cursed and swore at me and kept on shouting even after I turned and ran. I didn't have my revolver. All my life I've never stopped wondering what I would have done if I had.

The infantry attacked early in the morning of 26 October. We had been ordered to fire 500 rounds every twenty minutes throughout the previous night at targets in front. We were right out in front of the line, and the mud was so deep in our shell-holes that we had to put at least six boxes of ammunition underneath us – 303 ammo with 1,000 rounds to a box – just to stand on to get out of the mud. We had to keep on filling up our belts with ammo. Whenever we did that, we put our groundsheets across to cover the shell-holes while we loaded up. At dawn the infantry went on past us, and we elevated our sights to cover them.

Once agains the weather had broken. During the night before the dawn attack, the wind blew up and the rain poured down. In spite of it, the Canadians did well. On the left of the curving ridges that enclosed Passchendaele village, it had been the lethal fire from pillboxes on the Bellevue Ridge and a complex lower down at Laamkeek that had massacred first the Tommies then the Anzacs struggling in a frontal attack through the morass, long before they even got within range of the defences of the village itself. Before anything could be done, these pillboxes had to be knocked out, and it was a tall order.

Sergeant C. F. McLellan, No. 111371, 5th Canadian Mounted Rifles

Our company commander was one of the very finest men I ever knew, and certainly the best officer we had. He called in his platoon commanders and worked out a plan to deal with the forts. We had to take them by stealth – get our men together, work our way in sections behind the pillboxes, and start bombing. Of course, by doing it this way, in sections and not altogether, we blinded the enemy. He had no real target to destroy. There was terrible fighting and we had many, many casualties, but we did achieve something.

Working with the 52nd Manitoba Battalion, they succeeded in silencing a dozen strategically-placed pillboxes and gained a determined toehold on the ridge. There was still a long way to go, but in the light of the disasters earlier in the month, it was a magnificent beginning. They achieved the objectives they had been given and jubilantly dug in.

Thanks to the knocking out of the deadly enfilade machine-gun fire, the infantry lower down were able to make a little headway through the swamp. Across the valley on the other side, the 46th and 47th Battalions were also making progress. Their objectives were a shattered wood named Decline Copse, which lay on the edge of their sector just where the Canadian line met that of the Australians; and Crest Farm, one of the strongpoints guarding the outskirts of Passchendaele village. They didn't quite make it to Crest Farm. It was Decline Copse that caused the trouble and no little confusion, for both the Canadians and the Australians were attacking it.

The 46th Battalion moves forward and captures Decline Copse. About noon they are counter-attacked and have to retreat, and Decline Copse is reoccupied by the enemy. All through the afternoon conflicting orders are received from Brigade HQ. The whole forward area is apparently disorganised. Hours crawl slowly by till about midnight, when a runner from the 47th slides through the narrow door of the HQ pillbox with a message that Decline Copse had been retaken. Enthusiasm reigns. A runner speeds to Brigade. The news flashes to Division and across to the Anzacs on the right. Curiously, no one thinks of checking on the report. Some two hours later a stalwart Anzac officer bursts into the little dug-out, boiling with indignation, and explodes shrilly, 'I'm lookin' for the bloke as climes 'e took Decline Copse just now.' All eyes swivel to the CO of the 47th, who stands his ground valiantly. For a full minute the two stare at each other like a pair of bantam roosters. The tension is broken by the CO of the 47th, who suggests that it is the proper time for a drink. The newcomer explains that he is scout officer of the Anzac unit on the right and, on receipt of the report, he crashes over into Decline Copse with four scouts and runs slap into what he describes as 'the 'ole blinkin' German Army'. For the first time in his entire military service he has been forced to 'crawl awy like a bloody snike'. Fortified by a few more libations, the Australian strides out into the night, leaving a very chastened group of 10th Brigade officers to think over the situation anew.

During the hours of darkness the scene on the battlefield up in front is awful beyond description. Stretcher-parties work doggedly in the almost hopeless task of caring for the countless wounded who mingle with the dead in advanced positions.*

*From the Battalion history, '6,000 Men'.

*Private F. Hodgson, No. 536066, 11th Canadian Field Ambulance,
Canadian Army Medical Corps*

I was at a place called Tyne Cot. We had two pillboxes there. It was a
group of pillboxes. The doctor and his helpers were in one and we
stretcher-bearers were in another about a hundred feet away. It was
half under the ground and the entrance was so low that you had to
wriggle through on your stomach.*

The battalion bearers brought the wounded in from the line,
which was about a thousand yards away or less. They had the worst
job. The doctor dealt with those he could and then we took them
down the line. There were three squads of us. Three squads of eight –
because it took six of us at a time to get one stretcher out through the
mud. That day we drew lots to see who should go first. My squad
drew the last carry. This was night-time by now, because it was that
late before they could get the seriously wounded out, although the
walking wounded had been coming in all day. It was a terrible job
carrying in the dark – almost impossible. The first call came at about
two o'clock in the morning. We wished them good luck, and off they
went. They were a long time away. They hadn't come back when No.
2 Squad were called out. After a long, long time they returned. Next,
No. 3 Squad went out. We were glad that it was daylight by then.
Away we went with our wounded man, struggling down the track.
After a few hundred yards we were caught in a barrage. We put the
stretcher-case in a depression in the ground. He was very frightened,
the wounded boy. He said to me, 'Am I going to die, mate?' I said,
'Don't be stupid, fella. You're going to be all right. As soon as Heinie
stops this shelling we'll have you out of here, and they'll fix you up
OK. You'll be back across the ocean before you know it.' The
shelling eased off and we picked him up and set off again. He died
before we got him to the dressing-station. On the way back we
passed the remains of our No. 1 Squad. There were nothing but limbs
all over the place. We lost ten of our stretcher-bearers that day. Hell
was never like that . . .

That night, 27 October, the Canadians attacked again. A night attack
was almost unheard of, but this time it paid off.

*The two pillboxes referred to have been preserved and can still be seen in Tyne
Cot Cemetery. Ivy grows over them and the entrances have been sealed up. The
one which was the stretcher-bearers' HQ is on the left of the entrance and central
pathway. The pillbox on the right was the doctor's aid post.

Private R. Le Brun, No. 790913, 16th Canadian Machine Gun Co.,
Canadian Machine Gun Corps, 4th Canadian Division

As the companies advanced, there was terrific machine-gun fire. It came from the front and the flanks and it swept right over them. We replied until our guns were burning hot. We had to support the attack wearing gas-masks. Not that the Heinies were firing gas. The Vickers guns we were using were water-cooled. The steam from the gun was forced through a tube into a can of water. The condensed steam flowed through the air, producing a fog – so we wouldn't have been able to spot a gas attack if it had come. Therefore, safety dictated the constant wearing of gas-masks. That made you twice as tired in half the time.

By daylight Decline Copse was firmly in Canadian hands, and on both sides of Passchendaele their feet were gloriously planted on the slightly higher, slightly drier ground. To no one's surprise, the day after the attack the weather changed for the better. It was Private Longstaffe's twenty-seventh birthday.

Private P. H. Longstaffe, No. 922046, 107 Canadian Pioneer Btn., 1st
Division

27 October. Birthday. Up 8 am. Built fireplace in billet. Working party at 2.30. Fine day. Carried planks up the Menin Road. Long walk. Worked until 8 pm. Home. No rum ration. Miller sick. Sergeant Webb and W. B. Smith missing. Smoke and bed. Heard 43rd badly cut up.

On the whole he had known better birthdays, and as his brother, Vic, was in the 43rd Battalion, he went uneasily to bed.★

In spite of some urging from GHQ, General Sir Arthur Currie refused to move again until the thirtieth. The basis of his strategy was to allow sufficient time for the troops to be relieved, and to give the new men time to rest and accustom themselves to the situation before the assault. An interval of three days was the minimum time in which this could be accomplished. In view of the Canadians' moderate success, nobody argued. The only people who felt like arguing were Reg Le Brun and his fellow machine-gunners. There was no relief for them, for machine-gunners were in short supply. They had to stay where they were for the

---

★Vic had been wounded but was evacuated and recovered.

next attack. Reg and his team were only slightly mollified when a daring
Canadian photographer braved the hazards of the support line and
snapped them for the delectation of the Canadian public as they wound
their way among the shell-holes. They managed to summon up a smile.★

   In the three days' fighting of 26–28 October, the Canadian Corps had
suffered 2,481 casualties. During the three days' interval while the reliefs
were taking place and fresh troops made their way into the line, the
stretcher-bearers, under continuous shelling, plodded up and down the
duckboards taking the wounded out.

*Private L. Williams, 60th Canadian Battalion and 11th LTMB (Stokes
gun)*

I was a Stokes gunner. As the Stokes mortar could only fire up to half
a mile, our place was up front and not exactly bomb-proof. Our one
advantage was rapid fire. Pull pins and drop the shell into the gun,
putting half a dozen ten-pound shells into the air before the first one
landed, then scoot for cover – for Fritz didn't love us. Obviously we
were useless as gunners in the conditions prevailing at Passchendaele,
so they made us stretcher-bearers instead. We were under fire all the
time.

   The whole place looked like something out of hell. We just
slugged along carrying the stretchers, hoping for the best. One of the
lads from our battery caught up with us and walked along with us a
way. I knew him. We called him Zippo. In a lull in the shelling as we
waded through all this muck and mire, he said to me, 'What's your
home town?' 'Ottawa,' I replied. He said, 'Same here.' Then he
looked around at the mess everywhere and, after a pause, said, 'Believe it or not, I was manager of the fuckin' Theatre.' It was almost a
blood-tie. 'Anyway,' he said, 'I'm off. Got to get on and find billets
for you guys. You'll be relieved in a couple of days.' We were sure
glad to hear it. He waved us goodbye and pushed on ahead. A couple
of minutes later some shells exploded near the road. Zippo got a bad
head-wound. We carried him to the ambulance, but he died in
hospital a couple of days later.

   Zero hour for the next attack was 5.50 am, 30 October, and for once it
looked as if the weather was going to be on the side of the Allies. After
heavy rain the twenty-ninth was cold and windy, but it was bright moonlight and there seemed to be no sign of storms. The attack started with

★The picture is reproduced in this book.

the Canadians making straight for Passchendaele and its enclosing ridges, with the Australians on their right and the Royal Naval Division just over the Bellevue Ridge on their left.

A large proportion of the Canadians were very recent Canadians. Although they were citizens and qualified to serve in the Canadian Army, many of them had emigrated in the years preceding the war. Reg Le Brun had been born in Jersey. Jim Pickard was a native of Selkirk. But if, at first, the war had seemed to present an opportunity for a free trip back home, the new Canucks were quickly disillusioned. In spite of leave in Blighty and reunions with relations, Canada had never seemed more attractive. Jim Pickard went over the top that morning as one of a group of signallers.

Private J. Pickard MM, No. 624781, 78th Btn., Winnipeg Grenadiers

No previous unit had been able to maintain any communication by telephone with Battalion Headquarters, but our CO decided that that was no reason not to try again. His name was Colonel Jimmy Kircaldy and he was a great soldier and a dour Scot who had served some time in the Black Watch before emigrating to Canada. He picked seven signallers, including myself, to go over with the first wave under the command of Sergeant Nicholson. We collected our equipment of two reels of wire – thin wire, no thicker than darning wool – and two D Mark 3 buzzers and a Fullerphone.

The bombardment was murderous – ours and the Germans' – and they weren't only flinging over shells, they were simply belting machine-gun fire for all they were worth. But it was a case of 'Over the top with the best of luck.' So off we went with the first wave of infantry and started stringing out the wire. We hadn't gone many yards before the Sergeant and Private Houlihan were 'napooed'. We kept on going, but it was utterly useless. We could see that the wire we were stringing was being chopped to pieces as fast as we laid it. By the time we'd gone a few more yards the other three signallers were knocked out, and only Corporal Sims and myself were left. There was no choice but to go forward, for we knew full well that Colonel Kircaldy wouldn't welcome us back. It was difficult to see what was happening. The shells were falling thick and fast and by some sort of capillary action the holes they made filled up with water as you looked at them – or as you lay in them, for the only way we could move was to dodge from one hole to another, hoping that lightning really didn't strike twice in the same place. Sims and I were separated.

I splashed and wallowed through the mud, hoping I was going in the right direction, but none too sure.

Then I saw something extraordinary. It was a small willow-bush growing out of the side of a shell-hole. It must have been the only growing thing in the whole of the hellish salient, for I had never seen so much as a blade of grass. It seemed like an invitation almost. So I dropped into this shell-hole and lit up a cigarette while I took time to decide what to do. It was an Oro cigarette we used to reckon that stood for 'Other ranks only.' Maybe it did. But I'd just got it going nicely when I heard this shell coming straight for me like a freight train. I threw myself down, not bothering about the water in the hole – then there was a thud, then silence. When I looked up again, there was the shell stuck into the root of the willow-bush. It was a dud. 'Well,' I thought to myself, 'if Jerry had my number on that one it was the wrong number.' But I got out of there like a bat out of hell and made for where the boys were digging in, linking up a row of wet shell-holes to make a new front-line. They'd done well. They'd got far ahead. I reported to a major and explained what had happened to the communications department. He greeted me with open arms, for his runner had just been wounded and he had a report to send back to Battalion HQ. Would I volunteer to get it back? Would I! The Germans were massing for a counter-attack and the shelling and machine-gun fire was wicked. I would have volunteered to walk across the floors of Hell barefooted to get out of that, so I started back to HQ. It was in a pillbox that we called Hamburg House.

It started to rain in the afternoon, but it went well that day. I was back and forward to the line as acting-runner, and every time we'd got a bit nearer Passchendaele. They stopped eventually at the foot of a lane leading into the village. You could tell it had been a lane by the ruined cottages on either side, and you could see the church just beyond them. It was a place they called Crest Farm. They had to fight hard to get it and the place was thick with bodies. But we took it, and we held the line. Two days later we were relieved.

Pickard and the 78th went out. Baker and the 28th went in. The unfortunate Le Brun and the other machine-gunners stayed where they were to support the next attack.

The 78th Winnipeg Grenadiers had actually thrown some forward patrols into Passchendaele itself and excitedly reported back, perhaps optimistically, that the Germans were evacuating. But the German artillery and machine-gun fire showed no signs of diminishing, and the patrols were pulled back to strengthen the line. To capture Passchendaele itself without knocking out the fortifications that lay below it on the swamp and on the flanks would be asking for trouble. The final assault could only succeed if fresh troops undertook it, and so General Sir Arthur Currie turned a blank face to the urging of GHQ. He would mount the next attack in his own good time. He decided on the 6 November.

For once it was not raining. Even though zero hour came just before dawn, Pastor van Walleghem was up and about.

> 6 November. On my way to morning mass at 6 am, I suddenly saw a very bright light over Ypres and a few seconds later hundreds and hundreds of flashes, interspersed with shrapnel and many red and white rockets. I had an open view of the whole Ypres salient, and the fireworks in the semi-dark over the whole of the front from Wytschaete right up to Vrijbosch was really awe-inspiring. Several thousand cannons spewed their murderous fire over the fighting troops. All the same I heard little noise, as the wind was in the wrong direction, and had I not seen that hellish fire would hardly have believed that an attack was under way. It is now several months since I last witnessed an artillery attack so openly. I had already experienced some nearer ones with thunderous noise, but never had I seen one over such a wide front with so many fire-monsters.

By the time the pastor had returned from mass and was sitting over his bowl of coffee in the presbytery at Dickebusch, fifteen miles away the first of the Canadians had penetrated the German defences and were entering Passchendaele village.

From the jumping-off line of 31 July it was rather less than five miles to Passchendaele. It had taken the troops exactly ninety-nine days and three hours to get there.

Corporal H. C. Baker, 28th North-West Battalion, Canadian Expeditionary Force

The buildings had been pounded and mixed with the earth, and the shell-exploded bodies were so thickly strewn that a fellow couldn't step without stepping on corruption. Our opponents were fighting a rearguard action which resulted in a massacre for both sides. Our boys were falling like ninepins, but it was even worse for them. If they stood up to surrender they were mown down by their own machine-gun fire aimed from their rear at us; if they leapfrogged back they were caught in our barrage.

Fritzy opened up with his heavies and gave us a pretty good idea that there would shortly be a counter-attack. I got down into a shell-hole with my friend Tom, and Corporal Reid came crawling over and yelled at us, 'We've got to keep spread out. Five fellows over there got bunched up in a cellar and Fritzy made a direct hit and killed the works. So spread out, or we'll all get nappooed too!' Since he made no move to spread out, and I was the boy of the bunch of three, I knew who was meant to do the spreading. I had just crawled away when a shell dropped behind me. Bits of Tom's body came showering down on top of me.

They started to counter-attack. Our SOS flared up: our artillery thundered and sent a screening barrage over our heads; machine-guns and rifles blazed; the earth and the air quivered. Hades was let loose all over again. The bullets of a brigade machine-gun stationed directly behind us and twenty yards further down the slope were whistling so close to my ears that I couldn't help ducking every time the line of fire came over my head. I could only fire my rifle in the interval before the gunner swung it back again. Our machine-gun fire was particularly vicious because not only did we have Lewis guns and brigade guns, but quite a few captured German ones.

Private R. Le Brun, No. 790913, 16th Canadian Machine Gun Co., Canadian Machine Gun Corps, 4th Canadian Division

The bodies of our men were piled up all over the place, including the body of Lieutenant Gauvereau, who had been killed by a shell the day before while he was on his way from another gun emplacement to ours. We'd buried him and I stuck a salvaged rifle on his grave, but his body had been blown up again and what was left of it was lying a few feet away. We were taking terrible casualties. By mid-day we had lost two machine-guns out of our section of four. By half-way through the afternoon we had lost two men of our own team of five.

Corporal H. C. Baker, 28th North-West Battalion, Canadian Expeditionary Force

In dropped a corporal. 'We've got to try to get the wounded out. Baker, you're detailed for stretcher-bearer – follow me pronto.' I was glad to go. I'd never experienced anything like the savagery of that assault. I was burning. My eyes, my nostrils, my throat, even deep in my lungs seemed to be on fire and, no matter what I did, I couldn't stop shaking. Three stretchers were brought up and we loaded the wounded and set off, three carriers to a stretcher and each party twenty yards apart. We were getting along fairly well; then, just as we were passing a shallow ravine which led down to the swamp, an enemy battery opened up on us. The first shell made a direct hit on one stretcher. Few of us were left whole. We had four men killed out of twelve and two of the stretcher-bearers were now stretcher cases. That left me with a 200-pound Yankee, who'd been on one of the stretchers. The bones in his right foot had been smashed by machine-gun fire, but miraculously he had come to no further harm during the shelling.

We started off again, this time with his arm round my neck. This time we made it to a captured German trench with 'funk-holes' dug into the side. Our wounded had been packed into them to protect them from the shelling and the shrapnel flying all around. They started waving as we passed, calling to me to get them out and back to the aid post. I lowered my Yankee friend and went over and explained that I was on my own and couldn't help. There was almost a chorus, and it was piteous. 'For God's sake, give us water then.' One of my water bottles was empty. I unslung the other and poured a swig down the throats of one after the other. They were all in a bad way, and there was no chance of getting them out, for they were on the Passchendaele side of the morass and the shelling was too heavy for many stretcher-parties to get through.

The Germans had been pushed out of the village, but they were pouring shells into it. Eventually I got my Yank to the dressing-station. What a station! What a sight! It was a captured concrete pillbox and outside it a doctor's orderly was crouching among the wounded. There were twenty or more men lying there, badly wounded, groaning and waiting to be carried in for attention. Some were already dead.

The orderly got up and said, 'Get the hell out of here. No walking cases, only stretcher-cases here.' He wasn't impressed when I explained that the Yank *had* been a stretcher-case until he had been blown off the stretcher. 'Look,' he said, 'it's no good. We've got more than we can handle.' He pointed at the wounded lying around, 'Most of these men have been put out here to die. Get your bloke to the supply dump. They'll get him out from there. But move!' We moved. The shells were beginning to fall too close for comfort. We got to the dump and, as I handed him over, the Yank said, 'Thanks, comrade.' I wished him the best of luck. I don't know which of us was the most grateful to be rid of the other.

I made my way back over the shattered slope to the firing line. As I passed the aid-post I saw that a heavy shell had dropped where the wounded had been lying. There was only a huge hole and a few fragments of bodies to be seen. Then I crossed the sea of water and slime, dodging the explosions as best I could, and climbed up to Passchendaele.

Private R. Le Brun, No. 790913, 16th Canadian Machine Gun Co., Canadian Machine Gun Corps, 4th Canadian Division

They pushed the machine-guns right out in front. There was nothing between us and the Germans across the swamp. Three times during the night they shelled us heavily, and we had to keep on spraying bullets into the darkness to keep them from advancing. The night was alive with bullets. By morning, of our team of six, only my buddy Tombes and I were left. Then came the burst that got Tombes. It got him right in the head. His blood and his brains, pieces of skull and lumps of hair, spattered all over the front of my greatcoat and gas-mask. I stood there trying to wipe the bits off. It was a terrible feeling to be the only one left.

Corporal H. C. Baker, 28th North-West Battalion, Canadian Expeditionary Force

We were relieved at nightfall on the seventh. We were told to pick up a wounded man, deliver him to the dump and proceed to Ypres. The mud had sucked me almost lifeless. When we got back to the support trench I tried to find a fresh man to help us back as far as the dump. I went up to the trench and called down, 'Hi there.' There was no answer, but I could make out blurred figures below, so I slithered down in, thinking they were sleeping. I shall never forget what I found. Down that stretch of trench the boys were sitting in grotesque positions, and every one was dead. The trench was only shell-holes joined up, and it was open to overhead shrapnel fire from both sides.

We took a brief rest and hurried on as best we could to the dump. Our wounded man was too near the Beyond even to know that we were handing him over. Then we set out across the mud and corruption for Ypres. By heading in a general direction, sometimes by blasted roadway, sometimes by duckwalk, sometimes through mud and swamp, we reached the precincts of Ypres. A sentry directed us to a covered-in stall, and here a comrade was ladling out hot soup. I will never forget that bowl of soup. When I've forgotten every sumptuous meal I've ever had, I'll still remember that bowl of good hot soup after seventy-two hours' sleepless battle.

They guided us to bivouacs in the cemetery. At daybreak I took stock of my surroundings. I was looking for a not-too-rotten pool in which I could wash my face and hands and get some water for a shave. I found myself in what had been No Man's Land in the First Battle of Ypres. Two years later all those churned-up remains were still lying there. Unless you walked blindfolded, you couldn't have avoided seeing them. They were French and Belgians. They must have been élite corps, for pretty well all that was left of them were high-topped boots and bits of gold-braided uniforms and broken fancy-dress helmets.

A time was set for parade and roll-call. There weren't too many of us left to answer our names. If there was no response when a name was called, the sergeant would shout out, 'Anybody know anything about him?' Sometimes someone replied. More often there was silence.

My impression was that we had won the ridge and lost the battalion. . . .

They hadn't quite won the ridge. But, with the help of the Anzacs on their right and the Royal Naval Division on their left, they had pushed well on to it. What mattered was that at last Passchendaele had been taken.

Another attack on 10 November secured the ridge itself and 156 days after the curtain-raiser of Messines, the survivors of the men who had fought their way up the salient were able to turn their backs from the terrible slough of the battlefield and look out across open land to the green fields of Belgium beyond.

Part 6

The Aftermath

Chapter 19

The Third Battle of Ypres was officially over. Five divisions had already been transferred to the Italian front; several more were on their way south to take part in the Battle of Cambrai. The interest of the strategists had been transferred elsewhere.

Since 1914 the defence of the salient had cost 430,000 British and Allied casualties, killed, wounded and missing – a quarter of a million in the last three months alone. 90,000 men were reported 'missing', and although rather more than half must be buried as 'Unknown Soldiers', 42,000 bodies were never recovered at all. Many were simply blown to pieces. Many still lie where they sank into the mud. As many Germans probably lie there with them, for their casualties at Ypres were roughly similar. It has never been possible to calculate the precise number of men who were killed during the Third Battle of Ypres. After the war the official estimates ranged from as few as 36,000 to as many as 150,000. The truth probably lies somewhere between the two. On both sides it had been one of the most costly campaigns in history, and although it had ended officially on 10 November, the toll of casualties, British and German, went on mounting: for the troops held the salient throughout the bitterly cold winter, and although there were no more major attacks, the fighting and shelling never really abated.

When the German Army summoned up the last of its strength and pushed forward on its great offensive in the spring of 1918, it was no longer possible to continue to hold the ridges. There was a strategic withdrawal. Passchendaele was given up. The troops fell back and the salient was reduced to a tight little circle which consisted of little but Ypres and its outskirts. It was smaller than ever before. It was precisely the size to which General Sir Horace Smith-Dorrien had proposed to reduce it in 1915. He had been sacked for his pains. But no one remembered that. By 1918 that was a lifetime and some 200,000 lives ago.

Bibliography
Author's Note
Index

Bibliography

The Supreme Command, 1914–1918, Lord Hankey (George Allen & Unwin Ltd., 1961)

The Fifth Army, General Sir Hubert Gough GC, MC, KCB, KCVO (Hodder & Stoughton Ltd., 1931)

Haig, Duff Cooper (Faber & Faber Ltd., 1935)

Field-Marshal Earl Haig, Brigadier-General John Charteris CMG, DSO, MP (Cassell & Co. Ltd., 1929)

Goughie; Anthony Farrar-Hockley (Hart-Davis, MacGibbon, 1975)

Four Years on the Western Front, Aubrey M. Bowes-Smith MM (Odhams Press Ltd., 1922)

De Oorlog Te Dickebusch En Omstreken 1914–1918, Pastor A. van Walleghem (Genootschap voor Geschiedenis, Société d'émulation, 1964)

The Golden Horseshoe by Men of the 37th Division BEF (Cassell & Co. Ltd., 1919)

The Ypres Times, Volumes 1–6

The Unreturning Army, Huntly Gordon (Dent, 1967)

The Slaves of the War Lords, Henry Russell (Hutchinson, 1928)

History of the First World War, Liddell Hart (Pan Books Ltd., 1972)

The Fifteenth (Scottish) Division, 1914–1919, Lieutenant-Colonel J. Stewart DSO and John Buchan (William Blackwood & Sons, 1926)

The Twenty-Third Division 1914–1919, Lieutenant-Colonel H. R. Sandilands (William Blackwood & Sons, 1925)

Military Operations in France – Belgium, 1917, Volume 2, Brigadier-General Sir James E. Edmonds (HMSO, 1948)

The History of the 36th Ulster Division, Cyril Falls (McCaw, Stevenson & Orr Ltd., 1922)

The 8th Division in War, 1914–18, Lieutenant-Colonel J. H. Boreston and Captain Cyril E. O. Bax (Medici Society, 1926)

War History 1st/4th Battalion, The Loyal North Lancashire Regiment, 1914–18, Battalion Records (Battalion History Committee, 1921)

Australian Imperial Force in France and Belgium, 1917, C. E. W. Bean (Angus & Robertson, Sydney, 1943)

History of the 9th (Scottish) Division, J. Ewing MC (John Murray, 1921)

History of the 47th (London) Division, 1914–19, edited by A. H. Maude (Amalgamated Press Ltd., 1922)

History of the Queen's Royal West Surrey Regiment, Volume 7, compiled by Colonel H. C. Wylly CB (Gale & Polden Ltd., 1923)

Record of the Battles and Engagements of the British Armies in France and Flanders 1914–18, Captain A. E. James (Gale & Polden Ltd., 1924)

Cap of Honour – The Story of the Gloucestershire Regiment, D. S. Daniels (Harrap, 1953)

History of the Guards Division in the Great War, C. Headlam DSO (John Murray, 1924)

The Manchester Regiment, 16th, 17th, 18th and 19th Battalions – A Record, 1914–18, The Manchester Regimental Committee (Sherratt & Hughes, 1922)

History of the Rifle Brigade in the War of 1914–18, William W. Seymour (The Rifle Brigade Club, 1936)

The 42nd Lancashire Division, 1914–18, F. P. Gibbon (Country Life Library, 1920)

Per Mare Per Terram – A History of the Royal Marines, P. C. Smith (Balfour Books, 1974)

A Short History of the 48th Division (TA), 1914–18 (HQ 48th Division TA, 1962)

The Story of the 5th (Cinque Ports) Battalion, Royal Sussex Regiment, Colonel E. A. C. Fazan (Royal Sussex Regt. Association, 1971)

War Underground, 1914–18, Alexander Barrie (House Journals Ltd., 1962)

Canada in Flanders, Volumes 1 and 2, Sir Max Aitken, MP (Hodder & Stoughton, 1916)

The Tank Corps Book of Honour, edited by Major R. F. G. Maurice (Spottiswoode, Ballantyne & Co. Ltd., 1919)

The Rifle Brigade Chronicle for 1920, Colonel Willoughby Verner (John Bale, Sons and Danielson Ltd., 1921)

A Frenchman in Khaki, Paul Maze DCM, MM with Bar, C de G (William Heinemann Ltd., 1934)

Twenty Years After, edited by Major-General Sir Ernest Swinton KBE, CB (George Newnes Ltd., 1938)

The Battle Book of Ypres, Beatrix Brice (John Murray, 1927)

The Pilgrim's Guide to the Ypres Salient, issued by Talbot House (Herbert Reiach Ltd., 1920)

The Immortal Salient, Lieutenant-General Sir William Putteney KCB, KCMG, KCVO and Beatrix Brice (John Murray, 1925)

The Home Fronts, 1914–18, John Williams (Constable, 1972)

Unknown Warriors – Extracts from the Letters of K. E. Luard RRC (Chatto & Windus, 1930)

In Flanders Fields, Leon Wolff (Longmans, Green & Co., 1960)

The Wipers Times and After (Herbert Jenkins Ltd., 1918)

A Passionate Prodigality, Guy Chapman OBE, MC (Ivor Nicholson & Watson Ltd., 1933)

For the Duration, D. H. Rowlands (Simpkin Marshall Ltd., 1932)

Vain Glory, Guy Chapman OBE, MC (Cassell and Co. Ltd., 1937)

With the BEF in France, Adjutant Mary Booth (The Salvation Army, 1916)

The Artists and the SAS, B. A. Young (21st Special Air Service Regiment (Artists), TA, 1960)

The Balloonatics, Alan Morris (Jarrolds, 1970)

With the 10th Essex in France, Lieutenant-Colonel T. M. Banks DSO, MC and Captain R. A. Chell DSO, MC (Gay & Hancock Ltd., 1924)

From BC to Baisieux (102nd Canadian Infantry Battalion History), L. McLeod Gould MSM (Thos. R. Cusack Presses, 1919)

As From Kemmel Hill, Arthur Behrend (Eyre & Spottiswoode, 1963)

From a Surgeon's Journal, Harvey Cushing (Constable & Co. Ltd., 1936)

Contemporary Europe, H. Stuart Hughes (Prentice-Hall Inc., 1961)

The Pillboxes of Flanders, Colonel E. G. L. Thurlow DSO (Ivor Nicholson & Watson Ltd., 1933)

The Ypres Salient, John Giles (Leo Cooper Ltd., 1970)

Unpublished Works

An Artillery Officer in the First World War, Colonel R. Macleod DSO, MC

Great Battles Fought during the First World War, 1914–1918 and Flanders 1917, translated from German Official History and General von Kuhl's Account by Colonel R. Macleod DSO, MC

Saturday Afternoon Soldiers, H. G. R. Williams

Historical Records of the British Infantry Regiments, The Great War 1914/18, compiled by Brigadier E. A. James OBE, TD

Author's Note

I wish to acknowledge my debt to all of the
following, without whose valuable assistance this book
could never have been written.

Gunner J. L. Addy, 4th
Battalion, Tank Corps.

Captain H. C. Allen MC, 317
Northumbrian Brigade,
Royal Field Artillery.

Lieutenant A. J. Angel,
24th London Battalion,
Royal Fusiliers.

Lieutenant J. B. Annan, 9th
Battalion, Royal Scots
Fusiliers

Lieutenant R. G. Appleby
MM, 1st Battalion, London
Irish Rifles.

Sergeant C. W. Archer, 402nd
Battery, Royal Field
Artillery.

Gunner F. Backhouse MM,
4th West Lancs. Battalion,
Royal Field Artillery.

Private W. Bagley, 1st
Battalion, Royal
Warwickshire Regiment.

Corporal H. W. Bainbridge,
87th Battalion, Canadian
Grenadier Guards.

L/Sergeant A. Baker DCM,
1st Battalion, Hertfordshire
Regiment.

Lieutenant F. A. Baker, Royal
Scots Fusiliers.

Corporal H. C. Baker, 28th
Canadian North-West
Battalion.

Lieut.-Col. L. J. Baker MC,
2nd Battalion, Suffolk
Regiment (A/Captain).

Private L. M. Baldwin MM,
8th Battalion, East Surrey
Regiment.

Corporal C. R. Bampton MM,
13th Battalion, RHC.

Private F. W. Barber, Seaforth
Highlanders.

Rifleman W. Barnard, The
Rifle Brigade.

Private H. J. Barnett, 19th
(Pioneer) Battalion, Welch
Regiment.

Private R. Bartram, 1st London
Welch (Royal Welch
Fusiliers).

Private W. G. Bell MM, Army
Cyclist Corps.

Corporal A. B. Belyea, 1st
Canadian Divisional
Ammunition Column.

Private F. R. Berridge DSO,
MC, 3 bars, 7th Battalion,
Northamptonshire
Regiment (Lieut.).

Sergeant T. Berry DCM, 1st
Battalion, The Rifle
Brigade.

A/Corporal W. J. Billington,
163 Brigade, NZ Field
Artillery.

Private J. W. Binns, 2/4th
Battalion, East Lancashire
Regiment.

Major H. L. Birks, Tank Corps
(Lieut.).

Private H. C. Bloor, 11th
Battalion, East Lancashire
Regiment.

Bombardier B. Bloye,
116 Heavy Battery,
Royal Garrison
Artillery.

Lieutenant W. L. Blythe
CMG, 152 Brigade, Royal
Field Artillery.

Captain T. S. Bond, 11th
Battalion, The Rifle
Brigade.

Sergeant W. T. Booth, 11th
Battalion, Royal Sussex
Regiment.

Private J. H. Bovey, Royal
Army Medical Corps.

A/CSM Bray, 2/4th Battalion,
Lincolnshire Regiment.

Sergeant T. A. H. Breaden, 17th
Battalion, AIF.

Lieut.-Col. G. A. Brett DSO,
OBE, MC (all subsequent
to Ypres), 23rd Battalion,
London Regiment
(Captain).

Private A. Briggs, 2nd
Battalion,
Northamptonshire
Regiment.

Lieutenant G. H. Brooks, 6th
Battalion, Tank Corps.

Captain F. N. Broome MC,
173rd Brigade, Royal Field
Artillery.

Private A. A. Brown, 9th
Battalion, Norfolk
Regiment.

Lieut.-Col. A. T. A. Brown
MM, TD, 28th Battalion,
Royal Fusiliers (L/Cpl.).

Signaller G. W. Brown MBE
(1962), 1st Battalion,
Honourable Artillery
Company.

Gunner J. J. Brown, Canadian
Field Artillery.

Private F. Buckingham, 1st
Battalion, Honourable
Artillery Company.

Private R. Buckley MM, 9th
Battalion, Royal Irish
Fusiliers.

Sapper G. A. Bundy, 211
Infantry Battalion, CEF.

Driver E. G. V. Burton, Royal
Regiment of Artillery.

Driver L. G. Burton,
Ammunition Column, MT,
ASC.

A/Sergeant H. W. Calcraft,
16th (S) Battalion, The Rifle
Brigade.

Sister J. Calder, Territorial
Force Nursing Service.

Rifleman T. E. Cantlon, 21st & 18th Battalions, King's Royal Rifles.

Sergeant J. Carmichael V C, 9th Battalion, North Staffordshire Regiment.

Sapper A. W. Cave, Royal Engineers.

Sergeant S. F. Chalk, 172 Company, Machine-Gun Corps.

Captain R. A. Chell DSO, MC 10th (S) Battalion, Essex Regiment.

Private G. Chew, 2/5th Battalion, Royal Warwickshire Regiment.

Captain C. J. D. Church, 2nd Battalion. The King's Own Scottish Borderers.

Corporal P. J. Clarke MM 13th (S) Battalion, The Rifle Brigade.

Driver J. Clery, Royal Engineers.

Rifleman F. H. Cobb, 13th (S) Battalion, The Rifle Brigade.

Sergeant W. J. Collins, Royal Army Medical Corps.

Captain P. R. Coltman, 11th (S) Battalion, The Rifle Brigade.

Private/Sergeant (Forewoman) Comrie, RAOC.

Captain M. Concannon DSO, MC, TD, Royal Field Artillery.

Gunner R. Cooper, 24th Battery, 8th Army Brigade (Canadian).

Corporal L. O. Cottam MM, Liverpool Scottish Regiment.

Private M. Cousins MM, Royal Army Medical Corps.

Rifleman C. R. Cox, London Rifle Brigade.

Riffleman H. W. Cozens MM, 1st Battalion, Queen's Westminster Rifles.

Private E. G. Creveld, The Buffs, attached 2/2nd Battalion, Royal Fusiliers.

Signaller A. J. Cridland, 10th Battalion, Royal Fusiliers.

Corporal A. Critchley MM, 1/7th Battalion, King's Liverpool Regiment.

Rifleman A. J. Croak, 11th Battalion, The Rifle Brigade.

Corporal W. H. Crocker, 2nd Division, Canadian Ammunition Column.

Private J. Crouch, 8th Battalion, Devonshire Regiment.

Corporal F. J. Cubitt, 4th & 7th Battalions, Norfolk Regiment.

Rifleman S. J. W. Cuckson, 13th Battalion, The Rifle Brigade.

Signaller J. Currie, Royal Field Artillery.

Private C. Davey, 5th Canadian Battalion, 1st Canadian Division.

Private S. Davies, 2/7th Battalion, Manchester Regiment.

Private R. Dawson, Royal Army Medical Corps.

Private W. Derbyshire, 19th Canadian Infantry Battalion.

L/Corporal A. F. T. Diamond, Special Gas Brigade, Royal Engineers.

Lieutenant L. G. Dickinson, Lincolnshire Regiment.

Captain B. T. Dickson (Croix de Guerre), 4th Battalion, South Lancashire Regiment.

Corporal H. Diffey, 15th Battalion, Royal Welch Fusiliers.

Major W. G. Dipper, 2nd Battalion, Northamptonshire Regiment (Lieut.).

Major D. O. Dixon, Machine Gun Corps.

Private W. E. Dixon, King's Own Yorkshire Light Infantry.

L/Corporal E. H. Dormand MM, 1/18th Battalion, London Irish Rifles.

Sir Sholto Courtenay Mackenzie Douglas Bt., MC, 6th Battalion, Seaforth Highlanders (Lieut.).

Private C. E. Dowsing MM & Bar, 2nd Auckland Battalion, New Zealand Division.

Corporal W.M. Draycott, Princess Patricia's Canadian Light Infantry.

A/Sergeant A. W. Dunbar, 236 Brigade, Royal Field Artillery.

A/Captain F. E. Dunsmuir MC, 17th Battalion, Highland Light Infantry.

Private T. Easton, 2nd Battalion, Tyneside Scottish Regiment.

Driver A. A. Elderkin, 2nd Brigade, 1st Canadian Division.

Lieut.-Col. D. B. Eliot, Lincolnshire Regiment (Lieut.).

L/Corporal W. Ellett, Leicestershire Regiment.

Signaller J. C. Ellis, 250th Siege Battery, Royal Garrison Artillery.

Major General H. Essame CBE, DSO, MC, Northamptonshire Regiment (Lieut.).

Private V. E. Fagence, 11th Battalion, Queen's Royal West Surrey Regiment.

Private A. W. Fenn, 2nd Battalion, Suffolk Regiment.

L/Corporal J. B. Fenner, 3/5th Battalion, Lancashire Fusiliers.

Private J. Fenton, Gordon Highlanders.

Lieutenant C. C. Ferrie, 72nd Battalion, Seaforth Highlanders of Canada.

Driver J. J. Field, 1st East Anglian Brigade Territorials, Royal Field Artillery.

Corporal R. Findlater, 9th Battalion, Highland Light Infantry.

Major C. H. K. Fisher MC, Honourable Artillery Company (Lieut.).

Sergeant G. W. Fisher, 1st Battalion, Hertforshire Regiment.

Corporal O. W. Flowers RASC (MT).

Captain H. A. Foley MC, 7th (S) Battalion, Somerset Light Infantry.

Rifleman A. Foreman, The Rifle Brigade.

Lieutenant E. C. Foulsham, 1st Battalion, Suffolk Regiment.

Rifleman F. W. Froud, 1st Battalion, 18th London Irish Regiment.

Private P. H. J. Fry, 11th Battalion, Queen's Royal West Surrey Regiment.

Brigadier R. E. Fryer OBE, 62 Field Company, Royal Engineers (Captain).

Private J. Gadsby, 6th Battalion, Sherwood Foresters.

Bombardier J. W. Gale MM, 6th Brigade, 1st AIF.

CQMS S. A. Garman, 11th (S) Battalion, Queen's Royal West Surrey Regiment.

Corporal J. Garner, 5th Battalion, Border Regiment.

Driver C. W. Garrard, B 89th & D 87th Brigade, Royal Field Artillery.

Lieutenant P. H. Gates, 2nd Battalion, Lincolnshire Regiment.

Private H. J. Gee, 6th Battalion, Somerset Light Infantry.

Gunner L. S. Gifford, 14th Brigade, RHA.

Private G. J. Giggins, 62 Company, Machine Gun Corps.

Private A. R. J. Glazier, 5th Battalion, Royal Sussex Regiment.

Corporal E. J. Gooch, 2nd Battalion, Suffolk Regiment.

Private W. Good, The Royal Highlanders.

Private P. J. Goodland, 188th Battalion, CEF.

Lieutenant H. Gordon MBE, Royal Field Artillery.

Captain A. L. Goring MC, 6th Battalion, The Yorkshire Regiment (Lieut.).

Private M. Gosden MM, 168 Machine Gun Corps.

Gunner W. Graham, New Zealand Artillery.

Private F. S. Green, 2nd Battalion, Royal Warwickshire Regiment.

Captain M. Greener, 175 Tunnelling Company, Royal Engineers.

Corporal Greenwood, 12th Battalion, The Rifle Brigade.

Driver A. K. Greves MBE, New Zealand Artillery.

Major D. A. Ross Haddon MC, 9th Battalion, Royal Scots Fusiliers.

Sergeant C. W. Haines MM, 13th Battalion, Gloucester Regiment.

Lieut.-Col. B. M. Hall, 1/2nd Battalion, Northamptonshire Regiment (Lieut.).

Rifleman F. Hancock, 2nd Battalion, London Rifle Brigade.

Sergeant J. Hancox, 6th Battalion, Dorsetshire Regiment.

Lieut.-Col. P. W. Hargreaves MC, 3rd Battalion, Worcestershire Regiment (A/Captain).

Corporal A. Harris, Royal Marines.

Captain T. A. Harris, Royal Field Artillery (Bombardier).

Drummer B. H. Hart, 7th Battalion, Royal West Kent Regiment.

Private A. Hartland, 2/6th Battalion, South Staffordshire Regiment.

Private W. J. Hartley, North Lancashire Regiment.

Rifleman J. G. Harvey, 2nd Battalion, Scottish Rifles.

Captain J. G. Hassell, 8th Battalion, Tank Corps.

Captain A. W. Hawes MC, Honourable Artillery Company.

Brigadier T. W. R. Haycraft, Royal Engineers (Lieut.).

Lieutenant C. W. Healey MC, TD, MD, Manchester Regiment.

Private E. W. Heath, 15th Battalion, Hampshire Regiment.

Brigadier T. E. H. Helby, 59th Siege Battery, Royal Garrison Artillery (Captain).

Private O. Hewitt, 2nd CMR (Canadian).

Rifleman A. W. Hill, 2/9th Battalion, London Regiment.

Private F. A. Hill, 6th Battalion, Gloucester Regiment.

Padre S. Hinchcliffe, 26th Battalion, Northumberland Fusiliers.

Private A. L. Hodges, 12th Battalion. The Rifle Brigade.

Signaller A. B. Hodgson, 9th Siege Battery, RGA.

Private F. Hodgson, 11th Canadian Field Ambulance.

Gunner C. Hodson, G Battalion, Tank Corps.

Lieutenant G. P. Hoole MC, Royal Garrison Artillery.

Brigadier H. E. Hopthrow CBE, Royal Engineers (Sapper).

Sergeant H. A. Horne, Lincolnshire Regiment.

Major G. D. Horridge TD, 1/5th Battalion, Lancashire Fusiliers (Captain).

A/Corporal J. Howard, 2nd Battalion, The Rifle Brigade.

Corporal F. E. Hudson, D/58 Brigade, Royal Field Artillery.

Lieutenant W. R. Hudson, 11th Battalion, The Rifle Brigade.

Gunner W. Hughes, 226th Siege Battery, Royal Garrison Artillery.

Private B. Hussey, 3rd Battalion, East Surrey Regiment.

Rifleman H. S. Hyman, 11th Battalion, The Rifle Brigade.

Corporal S. V. James, Machine Gun Corps.

Private H. Jefferson, 5th Battalion, Yorkshire Regiment.

Private B. Johnson, 8th Battalion, Norfolk Regiment.

Corporal F. F. Johnson, A/70 Brigade, Royal Field Artillery.

Bugler H. Johnson, 2nd Battalion, Lancashire Fusiliers.

Private R. W. Johnston, 15th Battalion, Highland Light Infantry.

Lieutenant A. R. Jones, Princess Patricia's Canadian Light Infantry.

Lieut.-Col. W. D. Joynt VC, 8th Australian Battalion, AIF (Lieut.).

Sergeant W. J. Kemp DCM, Royal Garrison Artillery.

Private C. C. King, 44th Canadian Battalion.

Captain P. T. King, East Lancashire Regiment.

Corporal J. E. Kingsley, 102 Battalion, CEF.

Private N. Kinivig, 3rd New Zealand Field Ambulance

Captain J. Kirkwood, Seaforth Highlanders.

A/Corporal R. Knott, 21st Field Ambulance.

Captain W. Lambert, Tank Corps.

Sapper C. Lancaster, 1st London Field Company, Royal Engineers.

Private E. W. S. Lang, 1st Battalion, Artists Rifles.

Sergeant R. Lawseth, 88th Battalion AIF drafted to 2nd Tunnelling Company.

L/Bdr. L. L. Lawson, 'A' Battery, London Field Brigade, RATA.

Private R. Le Brun, 16th Canadian Machine Gun Company.

Corporal A. E. Lee MM, 'A' Battalion, Tank Corps.

Corporal C. A. Lee, 3rd Battalion, Rifle Brigade.

Major F. L. Lee MC, Royal Artillery.

Bugler N. Legge, 13th Battalion, Royal Irish Rifles.

Sergeant W. E. H. Levy MM, 4th Battalion, Machine Gun Corps.

Rifleman H. E. Lister MM, 12th Battalion, The Rifle Brigade.

Private E. Lloyd, 1st Battalion, Worcestershire Regiment.

Private W. Lockey, 1st Battalion, Sherwood Foresters.

Private O. H. Longstaffe, 107 Canadian Pioneer Battalion.

Bombardier J. Lowe, B. 149 Brigade, Royal Artillery.

Gunner W. Lugg MM, 83rd Brigade, Royal Field Artillery.

Canon W. M. Lummis MC,

2nd Battalion, Suffolk Regiment (Lieut.).

Colonel C. E. Lyne, Royal Field Artillery (Lieut.).

L/Corporal J. G. Mackie, Military Mounted Police (NZ).

Signaller N. F. Maltby MM, 291st Brigade, Royal Field Artillery.

Corporal J. H. Marks, 1/1st Battalion, Warwickshire Battery, RHA.

Private H. Marshall, 1/5th Battalion, King's Own Yorkshire Light Infantry.

Lieutenant S. C. Martel-Page, 330th and 331st Brigades, Royal Field Artillery.

Captain D. Martin, South Staffordshire Regiment.

Corporal P. Mason, 9th Battalion, West Yorkshire Regiment.

Sapper W. Mathieson, 20th Light Division, Royal Engineers.

Sergeant G. W. Maxwell, 2nd Battalion, Northamptonshire Regiment.

Rifleman J. E. Maxwell, 11th (S) Battalion, The Rifle Brigade.

Corporal C. Miles, 10th Battalion, Royal Fusiliers.

Lieutenant L. J. Miles, 1st Battalion, Essex Regiment.

Sergeant J. Miller, 46th Brigade, Royal Field Artillery.

Private W. Minds, 2nd Battalion, East Lancashire Regiment.

Sergeant J. H. Mitchell, 'A' Battery, 1st Canadian Motor Machine Gun Brigade.

Brigadier E. Mockler-Ferryman MC, Royal Artillery (A/Captain).

Lieutenant H. Moore MC, 2nd Battalion, Essex Regiment.

Private G. E. F. Morgan, Honourable Artillery Company.

Private W. Morgan, 10/11th Battalion, Highland Light Infantry.

Private W. M. Morriss, Canterbury Regiment, NZEF.

Private J. G. Mortimer MM, The York and Lancaster Regiment.

Corporal E. Moss, 3rd Battalion, Grenadier Guards.

Driver R. H. Mumford, 2 (A) Battery, Honourable Artillery Company.

Private D. Macdonald, Royal Army Medical Corps.

Private W. Macdonald, 9th Battalion, Gordon Highlanders.

Bombardier J. A. MacDougall, Royal Horse Artillery TF.

Miss Catherine Macfie, Territorial Force Nursing Service.

Corporal D. R. Macfie MM and Bar, 1st Canadian Infantry Battalion

Sergeant C. F. MacLellan, 5th Canadian Mounted Rifles.

Colonel R. Macleod DSO, MC, Royal Field Artillery (Major).

Mrs McCall, Territorial Force Nursing Service.

Driver J. McPherson, 9th Lowland Division, RA.

Sergeant N. M. McRae DCM, 43rd Canadian Infantry Battalion.

Lieut.-Col. J. W. Naylor, Royal Field Artillery (Lieut.).

Major-General Sir R. Neville KCMG, CBE, Royal Marines (Captain).

Corporal T. Newell, 171 Tunnelling Company, Royal Engineers.

Brigadier A. L. W. Newth CBE, DSO, MC, DL, 4th Battalion, Gloucestershire Regiment, (A/Major).

Private H. J. Nicholls, 58th Battalion, AIF.

Private R. J. Noble, 1st Auckland Infantry Battalion, NZEF.

Captain J. H. Noake MSM, Royal Engineers (Sergeant).

Private W. T. Norris, 1/16th Battalion, London Regiment.

Private F. G. North, 1st Battalion, Lincolnshire Regiment.

Private A. J. Notley, 4th Battalion, East Lancashire Regiment.

Sergeant J. E. Odlin, 1/5th Battalion, Lincolnshire Regiment.

Private A. M. Ogston, 7/8th Battalion, King's Own Scottish Borderers.

Sergeant R. E. Owens, 1st Battalion, Royal Welch Fusiliers.

Brigadier E. K. Page MC, 130 Battery, Royal Field Artillery (Lieut.).

Private T. V. Palfreyman, 2/6th Battalion, Manchester Regiment.

Lieutenant E. W. Parker MC, 2nd Battalion, Royal Fusiliers.

Sergeant I. Pearce MBE, 5th Battalion, 19th Lancashire Fusiliers.

Lieut.-Col. G. R. Pearkes VC, DSO, MC, 116th Battalion, CEF.

Sergeant G. Peck MM, 5th Battalion, Yorkshire Regiment.

Guardsman S. L. Perry, 3rd Battalion, Grenadier Guards.

Corporal J. Pickard MM, 78th Winnipeg Grenadiers, CEF.

Rifleman J. A. Pincombe, 1st Battalion, Queen's Westminster Rifles.

Corporal P. G. Pinneo, 10th Canadian Infantry Brigade.

Corporal J. Pleasant, Royal Army Medical Corps.

Corporal H. Pocock, Royal Army Medical Corps.

Private F. R. Pope, 1/4th Gloucestershire Regiment.

Private W. H. Pryor, Machine Gun Corps.

L/Corporal F. V. Rand, 21st Battalion, KRRC.

Gunner J. B. Ranley, Royal Field Artillery.

Private C. F. Reddie, The Rifle Brigade.

Corporal C. H. Rellie, Tank Corps.

Corporal H. E. Rickman, 15th Battalion, London Regiment, Civil Service Rifles.

Captain A. W. M. Rissik, The Rifle Brigade.

Private J. Ritchie, 6th Battalion, Gordon Highlanders.

Lieut.-Col. Sir T. L. H. Roberts Bt., CBE, DL, Royal Field Artillery (Lieut.).

Major C. A. A. Robertson, 1st Battalion, Scots Guards (Lieut.).

Private R. S. K. Rolfe, 26th Battalion, Royal Fusiliers.

Lieut.-Col. A. J. Ross DL, Royal Field Artillery (Lieut.).

Corporal S. T. H. Ross, Signal Company, Royal Engineers.

Corporal E. T. Rossiter MM and Bar, 7th Canadian Infantry Battalion.

Gunner J. W. Rowe, 5th Battery, Royal Field Artillery.

A/L/Corporal H. Russell, 10th Battalion, Worcestershire Regiment.

Major-General Sir G. Salisbury-Jones MC and Bar, GCVO, CMG, CBE, Guards Division (Lieut.).

Private S. Sanders, 61st Field Ambulance, Royal Army Medical Corps.

Rifleman A. T. Sears, 11th (S) Battalion, The Rifle Brigade.

Lieut.-Col. G. R. Seton OBE, MM, ERD, ED, Siege Battery, Honourable Artillery Coy. (Lieut.).

Wing-Commander W. H. N. Shakespeare OBE, MC, AFC, Royal Flying Corps (Captain).

Lieut.-Col. B. D. Shaw, 2/4th Battalion, South Staffordshire Regiment.

C. Shea, CEF.

Sergeant W. G. Sheath DCM, MM, IWM, Machine Gun Corps.

Private W. Shields MM, 9th Battalion, Royal Irish Fusiliers.

Lieutenant C. M. Slack MC and Bar, 1/4th Battalion, East Yorkshire Regiment.

Lieutenant A. E. Slater, Machine Gun Corps.

Lieutenant J. E. Smart MC, Croix de Guerre, 8th Battalion, Manchester Regiment.

Major R. Smart MC, TD, 1st Battalion, Worcestershire Regiment (Lieut.).

Lieut.-General Sir A. Smith DSO, MC, Croix de Guerre, Coldstream Guards.

Captain A. E. Smith MC, MM, Royal Artillery.

Private H. F. Smith, 3rd Canadian Infantry Battalion, CEF.

Corporal J. Smith, Royal Inniskilling Fusiliers.

Lieutenant J. E. T. Smith, Royal Field Artillery.

Private J. S. Smith, Northern Cyclist Corps.

W/O S. A. Smith, 11th (S) Battalion, The Rifle Brigade.

Private W. Smith, 2nd New Zealand Machine Gun Company.

Corporal W. T. Smith, 11th Battalion, The Rifle Brigade.

Private G. T. Snelgrove DCM, MM, The King's Own Royal Lancaster Regiment.

Signaller J. W. Spencer, Royal Garrison Artillery.

Sergeant Spinks, Worcestershire Regiment.

Sergeant H. J. Staff, Essex Regiment.

Signaller C. A. Starr, 25th Canadian Battalion.

Private F. Stephens, 1st Battalion, Border Regiment.

Sergeant J. A. Stevens, 58th Battalion, 5th Australian Division.

Private J. A. Stewart, 2nd Brigade, 1st Canterbury Regiment (NZ).

Private F. Stockton, 8th Battalion, Yorkshire Regiment.

Bombardier B. O. Stokes, 3rd Brigade, New Zealand Field Artillery.

Sapper C. A. Strachan MBE, 9th Brigade, 3rd Australian Division.

CQMS J. Summerfield BEM, MSM, 7/8th Battalion, Manchester Regiment.

Sapper A. E. Sutton, 1st Canadian Engineers.

Private R. E. Sutton, The Rifle Brigade.

Sergeant J. W. Swales MM, 5th Battalion, Green Howards.

Private J. L. Swallow, 'G' Battalion, Tank Corps.

A/Captain W. A. Tackley, 144th & 49th Siege Battery, Royal Garrison Artillery.

Chaplain E. V. Tanner MC and Bar, 2nd Battalion, Worcestershire Regiment.

Guardsman W. Tate, 4th Battalion, Coldstream Guards.

Private F. Taylor, 8th Battalion, Argyll & Sutherland Highlanders.

Driver G. Taylor, Royal Artillery.

Private S. E. Taylor MT, ASC.

Lieutenant J. J. Taylor-Rose, No. 6 Squad., Royal Flying Corps.

Lieutenant C. Thomas OBE, 23rd Battalion, Middlesex Regiment.

Lieutenant F. W. C. Thomas, 2nd Battalion, Suffolk Regiment.

Lieutenant L. C. Thomas, 9th Battalion, East Surrey Regiment.

Private W. R. Thomas, 1st Battalion, Royal Welch Fusiliers.

Corporal R. E. Thompson, 13th Battalion, The Rifle Brigade.

Rifleman A. E. Thorne MBE, 13th Battalion, The Rifle Brigade.

Colonel W. Tickler MC and Bar, 10th Cheshires, 2nd Garrison Battalion, Cheshire Regiment, 5th Lancs. Fusiliers, 5th Manchester Regiment (Captain).

Lieutenant J. D. Todd, 11th Battalion, Prince of Wales' Own West Yorkshire Regiment.

L/Corporal C. Tomlinson, King's Liverpool Regiment.

Corporal F. C. Toogood, 3rd Wellington Battalion, 4th Brigade (NZ).

Corporal J. Turnbull, 8th Battalion, King's Own Yorkshire Light Infantry.

Rifleman W. B. Turnbull, 12th Battalion, The Rifle Brigade.

Sergeant E. E. Turner MM, 1st Battalion, Queen's Royal West Surrey Regiment.

Private J. E. Tyam, 3rd Battalion, King's Own Royal Lancaster Regiment.

Corporal E. C. Vickery, 13th Battalion, Gloucestershire Regiment.

Colonel E. Wade MC and Bar, South Staffordshire Regiment/Machine Gun Corps (Major).

ABHQ J. A. Wade, 63 Royal Naval Division.

L/Corporal A. Waites, Yorkshire Regiment.

Sapper F. R. Waldron, 30th Div. Signals, Royal Engineers.

Sergeant R. Walker MM, 126 Co., Machine Gun Corps.

Sergeant A. B. Walsh, Royal Engineers.

Private J. A. Walton, 5th Battalion, Green Howards, Yorkshire Regt.

Lieut.-Col. S. W. Warwick GM, TD, DL, 8th Battalion, York & Lancaster Regiment (Corporal).

Private W. H. Watkins, Royal Canadian Regiment.

Sapper A. S. Watts, 13 Field Company, Engineers, 4th Div. (Australia).

Sergeant W. Weaver, 1st Battery, 1st Brigade, CFA.

Private W. Webster, 20th Battalion, Manchester Regiment.

Private A. E. West, Middlesex Regiment.

Sergeant F. Wheatcroft, Machine Gun Corps.

F. White, King's Royal Rifle Corps.

Corporal H. C. White, Sherwood Foresters.

Bombardier J. T. Whitehouse, 32nd Battery, CFA.

A/Corporal W. L. Whitney-Griffiths MM, 29th Battalion (Canadian).

Corporal D. Whittaker, 1st Battalion, Kings Royal Rifle Corps.

Sergeant F. W. Whittle, 104 Siege Battery, Royal Garrison Artillery.

Gunner A. E. M. Williams, Royal Field Artillery.

Corporal E. Williams, Royal Welch Fusiliers.

Signaller G. A. Williams MM and Bar, Royal Field Artillery.

L/Corporal H. G. Williams, 1st Battalion, London Rifle Brigade.

Private L. Williams, 60th Canadian Battalion.

Guardsman C. A. Wilson MM, 1st Battalion, Grenadier Guards.

Private G. W. Wilson, Northumberland Hussars.

L/Corporal J. Wilson, Durham Light Infantry.

Major General D. Wimberley CB, DSO, MC, DL, Lld., Queen's Own Cameron Highlanders (Captain).

L/Sergeant G. E. Winterbourne, 1st Battalion, Queen's Westminster Rifles.

Lieutenant T. H. Witherow, 8th Battalion, Royal Irish Rifles.

Sergeant A. Wolfman, Tank Corps.

Private A. H. Woodman, 6th Battalion, Royal Berkshire Regiment.

Guardsman J. H. Worker, 1st Battalion, Scots Guards.

Sergeant W. J. Worrell, 12th Battalion, The Rifle Brigade.

L/Corporal G. Worth, 6th Battalion, North Staffordshire Regiment.

L/Corporal F. Wright, Royal Warwickshire Regiment.

Sergeant G. S. W. Yarnall, 1st Battalion, London Scottish Regiment.

Captain H. J. Young TD, 1st Battalion, Essex Regiment.

T/Sergeant R. Zealley, Gas Company, 37th Division, Royal Engineers.

Index

Visit Penguin on the Internet
and browse at your leisure

- ◆ preview sample extracts of our forthcoming books
- ◆ read about your favourite authors
- ◆ investigate over 10,000 titles
- ◆ enter one of our literary quizzes
- ◆ win some fantastic prizes in our competitions
- ◆ e-mail us with your comments and book reviews
- ◆ instantly order any Penguin book

and masses more!

'To be recommended without reservation ... a rich and rewarding on-line experience' – Internet Magazine

www.penguin.co.uk

READ MORE IN PENGUIN

In every corner of the world, on every subject under the sun, Penguin represents quality and variety – the very best in publishing today.

For complete information about books available from Penguin – including Puffins, Penguin Classics and Arkana – and how to order them, write to us at the appropriate address below. Please note that for copyright reasons the selection of books varies from country to country.

In the United Kingdom: Please write to *Dept. EP, Penguin Books Ltd, Bath Road, Harmondsworth, West Drayton, Middlesex UB7 ODA*

In the United States: Please write to *Consumer Sales, Penguin Putnam Inc., P.O. Box 999, Dept. 17109, Bergenfield, New Jersey 07621-0120.* VISA and MasterCard holders call 1-800-253-6476 to order Penguin titles

In Canada: Please write to *Penguin Books Canada Ltd, 10 Alcorn Avenue, Suite 300, Toronto, Ontario M4V 3B2*

In Australia: Please write to *Penguin Books Australia Ltd, P.O. Box 257, Ringwood, Victoria 3134*

In New Zealand: Please write to *Penguin Books (NZ) Ltd, Private Bag 102902, North Shore Mail Centre, Auckland 10*

In India: Please write to *Penguin Books India Pvt Ltd, 210 Chiranjiv Tower, 43 Nehru Place, New Delhi 110 019*

In the Netherlands: Please write to *Penguin Books Netherlands bv, Postbus 3507, NL-1001 AH Amsterdam*

In Germany: Please write to *Penguin Books Deutschland GmbH, Metzlerstrasse 26, 60594 Frankfurt am Main*

In Spain: Please write to *Penguin Books S. A., Bravo Murillo 19, 1° B, 28015 Madrid*

In Italy: Please write to *Penguin Italia s.r.l., Via Benedetto Croce 2, 20094 Corsico, Milano*

In France: Please write to *Penguin France, Le Carré Wilson, 62 rue Benjamin Baillaud, 31500 Toulouse*

In Japan: Please write to *Penguin Books Japan Ltd, Kaneko Building, 2-3-25 Koraku, Bunkyo-Ku, Tokyo 112*

In South Africa: Please write to *Penguin Books South Africa (Pty) Ltd, Private Bag X14, Parkview, 2122 Johannesburg*

READ MORE IN PENGUIN

HISTORY

A History of Twentieth-Century Russia   Robert Service

'A remarkable work of scholarship and synthesis . . . [it] demands to be read' *Spectator*. 'A fine book . . . It is a dizzying tale and Service tells it well; he has none of the ideological baggage that has so often bedevilled Western histories of Russia . . . A balanced, dispassionate and painstaking account' *Sunday Times*

A Monarchy Transformed: Britain 1603–1714   Mark Kishlansky

'Kishlansky's century saw one king executed, another exiled, the House of Lords abolished, and the Church of England reconstructed along Presbyterian lines . . . A masterly narrative, shot through with the shrewdness that comes from profound scholarship' *Spectator*

American Frontiers   Gregory H. Nobles

'At last someone has written a narrative of America's frontier experience with sensitivity and insight. This is a book which will appeal to both the specialist and the novice' James M. McPherson, Princeton University

The Pleasures of the Past   David Cannadine

'This is almost everything you ever wanted to know about the past but were too scared to ask . . . A fascinating book and one to strike up arguments in the pub' *Daily Mail*. 'He is erudite and rigorous, yet always fun. I can imagine no better introduction to historical study than this collection' *Observer*

Prague in Black and Gold   Peter Demetz

'A dramatic and compelling history of a city Demetz admits to loving and hating . . . He embraces myth, economics, sociology, linguistics and cultural history . . . His reflections on visiting Prague after almost a half-century are a moving elegy on a world lost through revolutions, velvet or otherwise' *Literary Review*

READ MORE IN PENGUIN

HISTORY

The Vikings Else Roesdahl

Far from being just 'wild, barbaric, axe-wielding pirates', the Vikings created complex social institutions, oversaw the coming of Christianity to Scandinavia and made a major impact on European history through trade, travel and far-flung colonization. This study is a rich and compelling picture of an extraordinary civilization.

A Short History of Byzantium John Julius Norwich

In this abridgement of his celebrated trilogy, John Julius Norwich has created a definitive overview of 'the strange, savage, yet endlessly fascinating world of Byzantium'. 'A real life epic of love and war, accessible to anyone' *Independent on Sunday*

The Eastern Front 1914–1917 Norman Stone

'Without question one of the classics of post-war historical scholarship' Niall Ferguson. 'Fills an enormous gap in our knowledge and understanding of the Great War' *Sunday Telegraph*

The Idea of India Sunil Khilnani

'Many books about India will be published this year; I doubt if any will be wiser and more illuminating about its modern condition than this' *Observer*. 'Sunil Khilnani's meditation on India since Independence is a *tour de force*' *Sunday Telegraph*

The Penguin History of Europe J. M. Roberts

'J. M. Roberts has managed to tell the rich and remarkable tale of European history in fewer than 700 fascinating, well-written pages . . . few would ever be able to match this achievement' *The New York Times Book Review*. 'The best single-volume history of Europe' *The Times Literary Supplement*

READ MORE IN PENGUIN

HISTORY

Hope and Glory: Britain 1900–1990 Peter Clarke

'Splendid ... If you want a text book for the century, this is it' *Independent*. 'Clarke has written one of the classic works of modern history. His erudition is encyclopaedic, yet lightly and wittily borne. He writes memorably, with an eye for the telling detail, an ear for aphorism, and an instinct for irony' *Sunday Telegraph*

Instruments of Darkness: Witchcraft in England 1550–1750
James Sharpe

'Learned and enthralling ... Time and again, as I read this scrupulously balanced work of scholarship, I was reminded of contemporary parallels' Jan Morris, *Independent*

A Social History of England Asa Briggs

Asa Briggs's magnificent exploration of English society has been totally revised and brought right up to the present day. 'A treasure house of scholarly knowledge ... beautifully written, and full of the author's love of his country, its people and its landscape' *Sunday Times*

Hatchepsut: The Female Pharaoh Joyce Tyldesley

Queen – or, as she would prefer to be remembered king – Hatchepsut was an astonishing woman. Defying tradition, she became the female embodiment of a male role, dressing in men's clothes and even wearing a false beard. Joyce Tyldesley's dazzling piece of detection strips away the myths and restores the female pharaoh to her rightful place.

Fifty Years of Europe: An Album Jan Morris

'A highly insightful kaleidoscopic encyclopedia of European life ... Jan Morris writes beautifully ... Like a good vintage wine [*Fifty Years*] has to be sipped and savoured rather than gulped. Then it will keep warming your soul for many years to come' *Observer*

READ MORE IN PENGUIN

A CHOICE OF NON-FICTION

Jane Austen: A Life   Claire Tomalin

'I cannot think that a better life of Jane Austen than Claire Tomalin's will be written for many years ... a truly marvellous book' *Mail on Sunday*. 'As near perfect a Life of Austen as we are likely to get ... Tomalin presents Austen as remarkably clever; sensitive, but unsentimental' *Daily Telegraph*

A Wavering Grace   Gavin Young

'By far ... the most moving account of Vietnam to be written in recent years' Norman Lewis. 'This delicate, terrible and enchanting book ... brings the atmosphere of Vietnam so near that you can almost taste and smell it' *The Times*

Clone   Gina Kolata

On July 5 1996 Dolly, the most famous lamb in history, was born. It was an event of enormous significance, for Dolly was a clone, produced from the genetic material of a six-year-old ewe. Suddenly, the idea that human beings could be replicated had become a reality. 'Superb' J. G. Ballard, *Sunday Times*

Huxley   Adrian Desmond

T. H. Huxley (1825–95), often referred to as 'Darwin's Bulldog', became the major champion of the theory of evolution and was crucial to the making of our modern Darwinian world. 'Nobody writes scientific biography like Adrian Desmond, and this account of Huxley's progress ... is his best so far' *The Times Literary Supplement*

Cleared for Take-Off   Dirk Bogarde

'It begins with his experiences in the Second World War as an interpreter of reconnaissance photographs ... his awareness of the horrors as well as the dottiness of war is essential to the tone of this affecting and strangely beautiful book' *Daily Telegraph*

READ MORE IN PENGUIN

A CHOICE OF NON-FICTION

Time Out Film Guide Edited by John Pym

The definitive, up-to-the-minute directory of every aspect of world cinema from classics and silent epics to reissues and the latest releases.

Four-Iron in the Soul Lawrence Donegan

'A joy to read. Not since Bill Bryson plotted a random route through small-town America has such a breezy idea for a book had a happier (or funnier) result' *The Times*. 'Funny, beautifully observed and it tells you things about sport in general and golf in particular that nobody else thought to pass on' *Mail on Sunday*

Nelson Mandela: A Biography Martin Meredith

Nelson Mandela's role in delivering South Africa from racial division stands as one of the great triumphs of the twentieth century. In this brilliant account, Martin Meredith gives a vivid portrayal of the life and times of this towering figure. 'The best biography so far of Nelson Mandela' Raymond Whitaker, *Independent on Sunday*

In Search of Nature Edward O. Wilson

'*In Search of Nature* makes such stimulating reading that Edward O. Wilson might be regarded as a one-man recruitment bureau for tomorrow's biologists . . . His essays on ants tend to leave one gasping for breath, literally speaking . . . Yet he is equally enchanting in his accounts of sharks and snakes and New Guinea's birds of paradise' *The Times Higher Education Supplement*

Reflections on a Quiet Rebel Cal McCrystal

This extraordinary book is both a vivid memoir of Cal McCrystal's Irish Catholic childhood and a loving portrait of his father Charles, a 'quiet rebel' and unique man. 'A haunting book, lovely and loving. It explains more about one blighted corner of Ireland than a dozen dogged histories' *Scotsman*

BY THE SAME AUTHOR

1914
The Dawn of Hope

'A mammoth, vivid compendium of the first months of the war ...
What Lyn Macdonald captures is the extraordinary resilience of the
British regulars faced with the brutal shattering of their expectations'
Campbell Ferguson, *Daily Mail*

'Lyn Macdonald's research has been vast, and in result is triumphant'
Raleigh Trevelyan, *Tablet*

The Roses of No Man's Land

'On the face of it', writes Lyn Macdonald, 'no one could have been less
equipped for the job than these gently nurtured girls who walked
straight out of Edwardian drawing rooms into the manifest horrors of
the First World War ... '

'The tale is allowed to tell itself without any frontal assault on the
emotions, and is all the more stirring thereby' *Observer*

1915: The Death of Innocence

Drawing on extensive interviews, letters and diaries, this book
brilliantly evokes the soldiers' dogged heroism, sardonic humour and
terrible loss of innocence through 'a year of cobbling together, of
frustration, of indecision'.

'She is the recording angel of the common soldier ... Her identification
with her witnesses is total' Kate Saunders, *Sunday Times*

Somme

The year 1916 was one of the great turning points in British history, as
the youthful hopes of the generation were crushed in a desperate
struggle to survive, and traditional attitudes to authority were
destroyed for ever.

'A worthy addition to the literature of the Great War' *Daily Mail*

also published:

1914–1918
Voices and Images of the Great War